MW00593501

ESOTERIC
ASTROLOGY

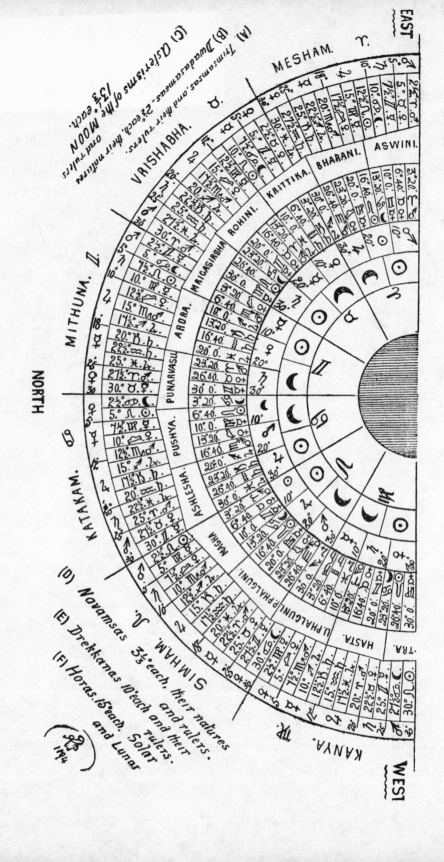

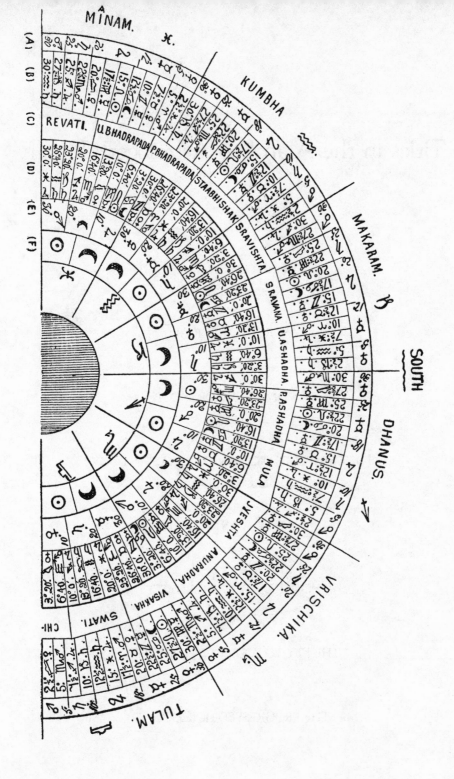

Titles in the Alan Leo Astrologer's Library

Esoteric Astrology

by

ALAN LEO

DESTINY BOOKS
Rochester, Vermont

Destiny Books
One Park Street
Rochester, Vermont 05767

First U.S. Edition 1983
This edition reprinted in 1989 by Destiny Books

Library of Congress Cataloging-in-Publication Data

Leo, Alan.
    Esoteric astrology : a study in human nature / by Alan Leo.
        p.   cm. — (Alan Leo astrologer's library)
    ISBN 0-89281-181-1 :
    1. Astrology. 2. Horoscopes.   I. Title.   II. Series: Leo, Alan.
Alan Leo astrologer's library.
BF1711.L46   1989
133.5 — dc20
                                                              89-16888
                                                              CIP

Printed and bound in the United States

10 9 8 7 6 5 4 3 2 1

Destiny Books is a division of Inner Traditions International, Ltd.

Distributed to the book trade in the United States by Harper and Row
Publishers, Inc.

Distributed to the book trade in Canada by Book Center, Inc., Montreal, Quebec

PREFACE

IT was not until I had made a second visit to India that I was able to obtain the clue to the central idea that could unify all my numerous thoughts upon the subject of Esoteric Astrology. In one of the Holy Places, I met a sage whose mind and my own were in complete harmony. I had only to express a few ideas to this marvellous Pundit, and he would run through the whole sequence of my thought and in a few words link those ideas into a consecutive whole to achieve which I had laboured many years. At one of our meetings he spoke but a few words, but with them he conveyed to my mind ideas which illuminated my thoughts to such an extent that I instantly saw light to which I had been formerly blind. On one occasion we rode many miles in an old gharry to visit an ancient Temple, and while he chanted his sacred hymns continuously, my mind was filled with beautiful thoughts suggesting the very questions a sage alone could answer.

In collecting the ideas that have filled my mind for many years, and even—so I have been given to understand—for many lives, and in setting them forth in this volume, I am actuated by the primary motive of expressing what I believe to be the true Astrology for the new Era that is now dawning upon the world. I have no wish to force these ideas upon the exoteric school of astrologers, they may accept them or reject them as they wish; but I can at least point to a large body of students, and some sincere colleagues, who are attracted more by this than by any other form of Astrology.

To many, the ideas put forth in this book will come as a revelation concerning the laws which guide the evolution of the world; infallible laws which work incessantly for the ultimate good of humanity. The theories expressed are not imaginary, they are capable of demonstration to all who apply themselves thoughtfully to the methods required to obtain first-hand knowledge.

The experiences are unique that led up to my association with this subject, which I have studied continuously for a quarter of a century, and they have resulted in investigations made quite independently of the opinions or influence of others.

Born of Puritan parents, strict in moral and religious principles, and brought up to believe that if not chosen for eternal bliss the only alternative was everlasting torment, it was natural that the problems of a life that seemed so complex to a youthful mind should engage my deep and earnest attention. Many years of anxious striving to understand why I had been born into this world without apparently having asked to come, and many visits to religious teachers of all types, brought the conviction that either the religious teachings regarding heaven and hell were false, or that the God I had heard about was unjust; and as I could not believe that which I did not understand or know to be true, I concluded that I must be one of the lost souls. My dear good mother, a devout Christian, converted at the age of 11, who had made it the habit of her life to pray for two hours each morning on waking, besought God that I might be saved; but her prayers did not succeed in commending to me her peculiar way of thinking and believing; and years afterwards, in the darkest hours of my life, the light of Wisdom came through Astrology.

At 9 years of age, while standing upon the heights of Edinburgh Castle and looking over Carlton Hill, I had an internal vision which liberated my soul from a bondage that had hitherto held it. At 17 I was present at a discussion between my mother and a gentleman of the same religion who had just returned from India, in which the theory of reincarnation was mentioned. I told my mother that it was the most reasonable hypothesis I had yet heard; and after thinking about it I formed the opinion that our souls were connected with the stars.

Until the age of 25 I worked in the slums of London, and there found myself face to face with some of the deepest problems of human life; my experiences at that time amongst the poorest and most degraded of human creatures would supply sufficiently interesting facts to fill the pages of this book. The sights that I daily witnessed, together with the realisation of the hopelessness of the condition and environment into which thousands of my fellow-creatures were being born, set me thinking continually on the terrible inequalities of the human race, together with other problems of life, and I sought for the solution in every possible way. At that time I suffered greatly, for with the faculty of benevolence largely developed, together with ideality, the utter want of refinement, combined with the sufferings of those about me, made life a hideous nightmare.   At last I discovered that in the science of Astrology light could be thrown upon these problems, but not without blending it with the theory of Reincarnation, for hitherto Astrology had lacked this complete explanation of the inequalities of human life.   From 17 to 25 Astrology seemed to satisfy my disturbed mind, and from 25 to 28 Astrology and Reincarnation together were splendid working hypotheses ; but in the midst of a great upheaval of my social life, for which Astrology and Reincarnation alone did not account, I was introduced to a body of teachings concerning the law of Karma.

I then began an exhaustive examination of the horoscopes of all persons whose times of birth I could rely upon, mainly children, and without mentioning the results to anyone, collected sufficient facts to establish beyond all question the permanent value of Esoteric Astrology ; which may be said to be the study of natural Astrology, or *astrologia sana*, plus the eastern teachings concerning Reincarnation and Karma.

For many years after the publication of *The Astrologer's Magazine,* now *Modern Astrology,* my investigations were silently continued, and these ideas embodied in my books, writings and practice ; with the result that on my recent visit to India I was enabled finally to learn from unquestionable sources that these teachings were part of the ancient mysteries of Astrology.   To-day my whole belief in the science of the stars stands or falls with Karma and Reincarnation, and I have no hesi-tation in saying that without these ancient teachings, Natal Astrology has no permanent value.   The law which gives to one soul a nativity of good environment in which refinement, opportunity, and sound moral training are uppermost ; and to another poverty, disease, and immoral training, is manifestly unjust, to say the least, apart from its being without any apparent purpose.

It is of course true that Astrology may be studied in any of its branches without entertaining the ideas of Reincarnation or Karma, just as the physical body of a man may be studied without regard to his soul or spirit ; but the deeper students of human nature know that physiology acquires a profounder meaning by the addition of psychology.

TABLE OF CONTENTS.

FIRST PART.

CONTENTS

CHAPTER VII

SECOND PART

EXPLANATORY DIAGRAMS AND ILLUSTRATIVE HOROSCOPES

CONTENTS

THIRD PART

CHAPTER XX

CHAPTER XXI

CHAPTER XXII

CHAPTER XXIII

CHAPTER XXIV

CONTENTS

CHAPTER XXV: CONCLUSION

LIST OF DIAGRAMS, ETC.

HOROSCOPES

INTRODUCTION

IT will hereafter be proved, I know not when or where, that the human soul stands even in this life in indissoluble connection with all immaterial natures in the spirit world, that it reciprocally acts upon these and receives impressions from them. KANT, *Träume eines Geistersehers.*

To everything existing there are two sides, the spiritual and the material, the essential and the formal. We are living in a world of duality through which something subtle and undefinable is continually passing and flowing, as an essence or principle behind all things that have this dual manifestation.

This may be fittingly illustrated by the contrast of Day and Night, sub-divided again by Sunrise and Sunset, Noon and Midnight, when the conditions of the earth are completely changed and reversed. The only external factor here is the rotation of the earth upon her own axis before the face of the Sun. But what is it that causes the rotation, and the changing influence of Sunrise and Sunset?

Spring, Summer, Autumn and Winter, are four distinct seasons of one year, produced by the annual revolution of the earth round the Sun. Infancy, youth, maturity, and old age are correspondences resulting from birth, growth, decay and death. But *why* the Birth and the Death?

A million exoteric facts will not suffice to answer these questions, for they are concerned with our esoteric enquiry into that subtle, indefinable *something* which is the essence and cause of all manifestation. There is always a higher and a lower, a finer and coarser aspect of the same substance, an abstract and a concrete, a past cause and a future effect of everything in nature; and there are two corresponding points of view by which it may be studied and known.

With these ideas before us we may safely assume Astrology to have its dual expression, or what may be termed its esoteric and exoteric points of view.

Esoteric Astrology deals with the abstract cause, the philosophy and the inner or more subtle point of view; whilst Exoteric Astrology is content with the effect, the practice, and the concrete or outer expres-

xiii

sion, preferring the more tangible and evident to the speculative and theoretical.

To those who hold extreme views on this subject, the esoteric side on the one hand, or the exoteric on the other, is the only side worthy of attention; but to those who are broad-minded and free from bias, both sides are of *equal* value. It is merely a question of temperament as to which has the preference, and the wise know that one side of a story is always good until the other is told.

We may define Esoteric Astrology as that side of the subject which views all stellar phenomena from the standpoint of unity; whilst Exoteric Astrology begins its study from the side of diversity and separateness, The Esoteric Astrologer looks upon the whole expression of life as proceeding from one central and primal source, and therefore seeks to understand the subject from the point of view of the One flowing forth into the many. In the solar system the Sun is the centre of all and the starting point of his philosophy, for to him all things come forth from the Sun; and it is the solar life in which all things live and move and have their being. Coming forth from this centre are the life currents which pass through the material organisms of every living thing on earth. This life descends and ascends, through each of the seven planets, and is transformed in the process for the *use* of evolving entities, and adapted to the stage they have reached in the scale of evolution; the seven planets being either directly or indirectly connected with the seven principal substances in the human body.

Man, as we know him, is composed of the great elements Fire, Air, Water, Earth and Ether. At the head of each of these is a living conscious entity of which the vital force and consciousness flowing through the element is an emanation.

In the course of these Chapters we shall deal with these forces and substances from an esoteric standpoint by elaborating and extending the ideas that are associated with them in exoteric studies; for although these elements have been known to astrologers for many centuries, their esoteric meaning has never been fully revealed, and yet it is upon the seven primary divisions of the zodiac into Fire, Air, Earth, Water, Cardinal, Mutable and Fixed signs, that the real meaning of every horoscope is fundamentally based. We shall take up these signs and the planets, but before doing so, an endeavour must be made to get a deeper insight into

First Principles

When we attempt to explore the noumenal worlds that underlie the outer realms of phenomena as the spiritual underlies, or rather precedes, the material, we have no choice but to use the language and terms of the physical world. Every writer who has sought to do this has realised the limitations and drawbacks that beset the subject; for there is always difficulty and even danger in trying to express in every-day language thoughts and ideas that in themselves transcend the material and commonplace. The life of the subtler realms becomes disguised and misunderstood when embodied in concrete forms, and the writer or speaker on these subjects often realises, with something of a shock, that he has managed to convey quite an erroneous idea to the enquirer. For this result neither the one nor the other is wholly to blame, nor does it avail to complain of the inadequacy of the language. When we deal with great and far-reaching ideas or with very abstract thoughts and feelings, there always seems to be something that refuses to the last to be expressed completely in any language at our disposal, and that can only be learned and realised by actual personal experience.

The emotion of love in a perfect friendship cannot be fully explained by the most eloquent words or completely expressed by the most perfectly proportioned features and actions, even though these are mutually reciprocal and moved by a spontaneous and harmonious impulsion. No matter how perfect it may be, something indefinable is lost in the expression.

"For words, like nature, half reveal
And half conceal the soul within."

as Tennyson truly wrote of the expression of grief at the loss of a loved one.

We realise the thoughts and feelings of another only to the extent that we have had similar experiences ourselves, and if these are in any way lacking, our realisation and appreciation of the subject will also be lacking in an equal degree. We understand only in so far as we have experienced, even when the matter refers only to this physical world; and still more is this the case when the reference is to inner planes of being that do not appeal to any of the five senses.

Bearing these facts in mind, the sages of all times have stated that it is unwise to speculate upon the unknowable ; for to know THAT would mean our becoming one with It, and then our silence would be complete.

In the deeper philosophy, and in the majority of religions, there has always been postulated the ONE absolute and supreme First Cause, arising out of that unknowable *suchness* which is the rootless root from which all things have arisen.

This One and Supreme cause of all is the God of very God, the unnameable Being and substance from which all the mighty Intelligences of the whole universe have come forth. Living and moving in the vast ocean of Being and substance, of which The Absolute is both centre and circumference, are millions of universes, and solar systems. These are units having a Sun, or Solar Logos, at the centre ; the Sun being the physical and outward glory of the Spiritual Intelligence, or supreme consciousness, whose whole Being is the Solar system with its planets and mighty centres of consciousness seen and unseen by physical sight.

To aid our thought let us think of the Sun or Solar Logos as the visible expression of the God of our Universe, and the planetary bodies as the vehicles or mansions of His ministering Angels, each world or globe living and moving in His life and vast sphere of influence.

Our globe, the Earth, is also a unit, having its place in the great universe of life, and also having its ruling Spirit, known to some as the Spirit of the Earth, and to others as the Lord of the world. Around the earth is the great sea of Ether, a subtle substance in which are floating myriads of finer particles of matter, forming a vast sphere of which the earth is the centre. This substance is the earth's aura, and in it is reflected everything concerning the earth and its evolution.

This aura and the signs of the zodiac are very closely related, and out of it come the various modes of motion, known to the Hindu Astrologer as the *tattvas*.

From the point of view of one who studies the star lore of Astrology on its inner or esoteric side, the zodiac as a limiting circle of the Earth's aura is the field and storehouse of all that was, is, and is to be. It is the battlefield of Arjuna, the playground of the Logos, and the stage upon which the great drama of life is enacted ; and those who would penetrate into its mysteries must lift the veil of Isis.

The planets are the principal actors or players whose movements upon the vast stage determine the theme of the orchestra, the changing colours of the robes, and the ordered march of those cast to play their allotted parts.

There is but one Author of the play and His mighty will and thought breathe life into the persons of the drama who are grouped and moved by His imperial imagination; while the purpose of the whole and the end of the play are known beforehand to none save those who have regained that cosmic consciousness which the rest have lost.

To produce the divine comedy of universal life, God sends forth from Himself certain spiritual embodiments of power, love and wisdom. The planetary Spirits or Intelligences who carry out His will are manifestations of His consciousness, and their glorious life and activity transcend even the expanded consciousness of super-man.

These limitations or centres in the cosmic life produce certain vibratory energies known as planetary influence, each vibration vitalising and animating one definite department and kingdom in nature over which the planetary Spirit presides; but each also having a *sub*-influence in the other departments and kingdoms.

THE GUNAS

There is but One material substance in the universe, primordial or root matter. Into this the One Life, pulsating in three waves, sends forth its three fundamental modes of motion, Stability, Flexibility and Harmony; and these are manifested to our senses as rotary, translatory and vibratory motion. The *extremes* or excessive action in our bodies of stability or resistance, and flexibility or non-resistance, produce pain, but their balance or harmony causes pleasure.

These three great modifications of matter known for ages to the Hindu philosophers as the three Gunas, Tamas, Rajas and Sattva, are equivalent to the three qualities of zodiacal signs Fixed, Cardinal and Mutable. By combination these three are again modified so as to produce seven kinds of energy, seven modes of motion or vibration which express themselves in the matter or form side of the universe.

From the point of view of Astrology these are the seven primary abstract divisions of the signs of the zodiac which we know as the three quadruplicities of Cardinal, Fixed and Mutable, and the four triplicities of Fire, Earth, Air and Water.

THE TATTVAS

The Hindu astrologers of ancient times synthesised these four triplicities into a fifth which comprised the essence both of the four and the three. This represents the highest Ether, the most rarified form of matter, known as the Akasha tattva. It is potentially triple, and therefore includes the quadruplicities as well as the triplicities. The other four tattvas corresponding to the four triplicities are Agni, Prithivi, Vayu and Apas respectively; and according to the ancient astrologers and sages:—"The Universe proceeds from the tattvas; it goes into the tattvas; it vanishes into the tattvas."[1]

Over each of these "tattvas," which we may consider as either modes of motion or modifications of matter or qualities of certain signs of the zodiac, a Lord is presiding who is directly connected with the planetary sphere of influence. They give the measure of consciousness and the type and direction of the vibration in matter, known as the "tanmatra."

THE SIGNS OF THE ZODIAC

Thus each sign of the zodiac represents firstly a particular state of matter, secondly a characteristic mode of motion, and thirdly a co-ordinated type of consciousness or Self. These three, the matter, the motion and the consciousness, correspond and agree. They are correlated with the fundamental classification of Self, Not-Self, and the Relation between them. The creative life proceeds from the Self and runs through the other two, and upon this fact all the laws of Astrology are based; the Planetary Spirits or Intelligences, through their numerous angels or agents showing the various states of consciousness, and the signs in their many combinations exhibiting the forms of matter in motion in which consciousness is working.

It therefore follows from this that a change in consciousness produces a change in form, and *vice versa*.

Over the whole zodiac, or the Akasha, Indra is Lord. He is the King of all the Devas or Shining Ones. These beings shape the combinations of elements, and guide the vibrations that play through the various conditions of matter corresponding to the divisions of the zodiac into minute portions such as degrees and fractions of a degree.

---

[1] Shivagama.

Over the Airy triplicity of signs Vayu stands as Lord of Air. Agni, Lord of Fire, rules over the Fiery triplicity. Varuna is Lord of Water and the Watery triplicity ; and finally Kshiti or Kubera is Lord of Earth. The hosts of the lower devas, angels, and elementals were anciently known as Sylphs, Salamanders, Undines and Gnomes ; the knowledge of these spirits of nature has faded out in our time, however, and with it the deeper wisdom connected with Astrology.

Now in the study of Esoteric Astrology which it is proposed to unfold in the following chapters, we shall deal with the matters mentioned in this introduction with a view to making the teachings on the subject more clearly understood, and to this end the following three principal ideas should always be borne in mind :

1.   There is but One Life within the Universe—The Supreme Life of God, streaming through the Sun.

2.   This life is expressed in various ideal states of consciousness, through the planetary spheres of influence, and :—

3.   The force and matter of the universe are expressed in innumerable modifications through the various groups and divisions of the signs of the zodiac, which represent the Ether, or inner planes of matter, and are reflected downward into our material universe.

To impress these ideas on the minds of students they will be repeated in various forms in the following chapters, which, although each is more or less complete in itself and may be read apart from the rest of the book, have as far as possible been arranged so as to follow in a definite sequence.

ESOTERIC ASTROLOGY

First Part

CHAPTER I.

ASTROLOGICAL SYMBOLOGY

MAN is a spiritual Intelligence, who has taken flesh with the object of gaining experience in worlds below the spiritual, in order that he may be able to master and to rule them, and in later ages take his place in the creative and directing Hierarchies of the universe.   *The Riddle of Life.*

ESOTERIC ASTROLOGY is chiefly concerned with the science of human nature, and seeks to explain, through its unique symbolism, the realities or fundamental principles governing humanity under the rule of the heavenly bodies.

The ordinary symbols used to describe the signs of the zodiac, the planets, and their relationships, have served to preserve this inner meaning safely through the dark ages of materialism out of which the human race is just emerging. So far as the planets are concerned, these symbols are built up of the circle, the semi-circle, and the cross, either alone or in various modes of combination.

The circle, taken quite alone, signifies the incomprehensible unity that underlies all manifestation. If applied to the whole vast universe, it stands for the Absolute, God unmanifested, the source of all, equally present in all things, in matter as much as in spirit, in so-called evil as well as in good. If applied to our solar system, it stands for the One Life which underlies and includes all forms of manifestation within the system, which existed before the first atom of the solar system was formed, and which will continue to exist after all things have disappeared. Because it is absolute unity, without distinction of parts, neither self nor not-self, it transcends our comprehension, and cannot be classed in terms of any form of consciousness familiar to us. It has no limits either in space or time, and enters into no relations ; and because of this, the One Life cannot be said, logically, to have any symbol ; for even the empty circle suggests limitation, because of its circumference, and is therefore strictly speaking inappropriate. The human mind however always demands symbols in which to sum up and express great conceptions by one convenient synthesis, and, in the symbolism of geometrical form, the circle is less open to objection than any other. In terms of the symbolism of numbers, this will be number Nought ; in that of light and colour, it will be Darkness ; and in that of sound and music, it will be Silence. As a factor in astrological symbology, the circle is taken to represent Spirit in general, abstract and unindividualised, which gains self-consciousness through limitation and combination.

When a point is placed in the centre of the circle, something is coming into existence out of the depths of the incomprehensible No-thing ; Light is beginning to shine forth out of the darkness ; Sound is arising within the silence ; Being is coming forth from Non-being ; number One, the relative unity of all things manifested, is making its appearance. As applied to the total universe, this stands for God manifest, or with attributes, universal in manifestation but comprehensible to those who can unite their consciousness with His. As applied to our solar system, it signifies the Solar Logos, the one supreme God of the system. There is no form of life within the whole Solar system that is not His life, and no form of consciousness that is not an aspect of His consciousness ; He created the whole system from His own being in the beginning, and he will destroy it in the end by reabsorbing it into Himself. The solar system, taken as one whole, may be considered as His body, and the planets as definite centres or organs within that body, each utilising and manifesting a different type of vitality and of consciousness, of which the Sun is the heart and—*for those who dwell on this globe*—the earth is the head. Although omnipresent, His life and power are more especially manifested through the Sun, which great luminary this symbol represents astrologically. Cosmic vital force comes down to the Sun from higher planes of being, the so-called fourth dimension of space, and is sent forth thence to every globe within the system, flowing through the ether like blood through the human body, or like prāṇa along the nerves, keeping every globe in touch with every other and with the Sun.

When the circle is divided into two halves by a diameter, it signifies that abstract spirit is manifesting the two polarities of spirit-matter, not separated into two extremes of spirit on the one hand, and matter on the other, but held together in one, a duality with unity underlying it. In terms of consciousness, it may be described as Self-Not-self, giving the

possibilities both of consciousness, or the world within, and matter, or
the world without.   It signifies therefore, a state of duality, a mean
between two extremes, combining two states and not belonging exclusively to either; and in this way it is employed as the symbol
of the Soul, regarded as intermediate between Spirit above and
Body below.   When written in this form, a circle divided by a
diameter in the same way as in the Greek letter *Theta*, the symbol in
Astrology represents the horizon; but taken in the form of the semi-
circle, it signifies the Moon in its dual phases of light and dark, waxing
and waning; the representative of the personal soul with its varying
moods, which can rise up to and become one with the spiritual consciousness above, or can descend and be bound to body below.   New Moon,
the conjunction of Moon and Sun, symbolises the union of soul and
spirit, personality and individuality, whether taking place after death in
the spiritual world, or during life in the trance of the body.   Full Moon,
the opposition of the two luminaries, represents the personality illuminated
by the Sun, or spirit, and throwing its borrowed light upon the earth,
physical consciousness.

When the second diameter divides the first at right angles, the cross
is formed within the circle.   This is a familiar symbol of very wide
application both in Astrology and elsewhere.   It gives the ground plan of
the ordinary horoscope, showing the horizontal line of the horizon, running from the ascendant on the east to the descendant on the west, and
the vertical line of the meridian from zenith to nadir.   It implies
complete manifestation and incessant activity; for it cannot be formed
until Self and Not-self have each become polarised, active and passive,
positive and negative, each acting upon the other, and each reacted upon
by the other.   This action and reaction between the two has various
consequences and implications.   Firstly, it sub-divides the two halves
into four quarters; secondly, it implies unceasing activity, for if the
action and reaction were to stop, the quadrants would disappear and
nothing would be left but the two semi-circles of the previous symbol;
the quadrants only existing so long as activity continues.   Thirdly, it
implies a current of influence passing round the circle, following the
direction of the action and reaction, and setting the circle itself spinning
round on its axis just as does the earth.

This is usually represented by the familiar symbol of the Svastika,
a cross that is supposed to be whirling round rapidly and leaving a trail

behind from the end of each of the four arms.   These small end-pieces
are usually drawn as short straight lines at right angles to the arms ; but
this is obviously incorrect, for if the cross were really set spinning it
would describe a circle, and the trail would be circular, the end pieces
being small arcs of a circle, not straight lines.   In fact, this symbol is
the same as the last, the cross within the circle, but portions of the
circumference of the circle have been omitted.   Its application is very
extensive.   It may signify the whirling motion of atoms, both as vortices
in ether and as spiral currents round a central axis ; and, on a greater
scale, it represents the axial rotation of the earth, closely analogous to that
of an atom.   It indicates the spiral movement of electricity round a
magnetic axis ; the serpentine motion of the fiery electric life power,
called Kundalini ; and the whirling of the chakrams or force-centres in
the etheric counterpart of the physical body.   It stands for one of these
centres in particular which is described as follows :

" The first centre, at the base of the spine, so arranges its undulations as
to give the effect of its being divided into quadrants, with hollows between them.
This makes it seem as though marked with the sign of the cross, and for that
reason the cross is often used to symbolise this centre, and sometimes a flaming
cross is used to indicate the serpent-fire which resides in it."

Theosophist, Vol. XXXI., page 1077

When a wheel, while turning round, advances in the line of its axis
it describes not a circle but a spiral.   In all these cases the Svastika
indicates some sort of spirally moving force working in matter, moulding
matter and setting it in motion, from the globe down to the atom.   In
man, this cross stands for Body, as distinguished from the circle, Spirit,
and the semi-circle, Soul.

Astronomically the cross within the circle is used as the symbol of the
earth, for which it is obviously very appropriate.   When the circle is
omitted, and nothing but the equal-armed cross is left, the spiritual origin
of the symbol is, in a sense, forgotten or left unexpressed, and only force
working in matter is suggested.

When the Svastika is depicted as rotating from right to left, it stands
for the direction of revolution of the earth in its orbit round the Sun,
and also for its direction of axial rotation.   When represented as turning
from left to right, it indicates the apparent direction of motion of the Sun,
Moon, and planets in their rising and setting, as seen from the earth.

The Symbols of the Planets

From these three glyphs of circle, semi-circle, and cross the symbols of the astrological planets may be derived as follows.

⊙ SUN. Unity. Life or Consciousness. The individual self. *Spirit.*

☽ MOON. Duality, relationship. The formative principle. The personal self. *Soul.*

⊕ EARTH. Differentiation. Activity in matter. The material self. *Body.*

♀ VENUS. The spiritual self or individuality, risen above matter.

♂ MARS. Matter dominating spirit. Spirit working through material activities.

♃ JUPITER. The soul expanding beyond matter, but retaining the material form.

♄ SATURN. The concrete soul, limited by material conditions.

☿ MERCURY. The cross below signifies astral consciousness, desire ; the circle in the middle, mental consciousness ; the semi-circle above indicates that evolution has been pushed beyond the mental and is reflecting downwards light received from a still higher plane, the buddhic, which dominates all. This symbol may also be interpreted as the caduceus of Hermes, two serpents intertwined round a central rod, referring to the fiery power, kundalini, full control of which makes the practical magician.

♅ URANUS. Individualised self-consciousness.

♆ NEPTUNE. Personal self-consciousness.

Esoteric Astrology, however, is not only a symbolical interpretation of human nature, it is also a philosophy, by which the inner laws of nature are clearly explained, and the system in which we live is brought nearer to one's understanding.

The Sun is more than a symbol of spirit, it is the actual focus or centre of the life of our Solar system, the heart of the Solar Logos, and the planets are the vehicles, or bodies, of His spiritual messengers, each the centre of a great spiritual Hierarchy. Every department of nature is ruled or governed by one of the great planetary spirits, Saturn having rule over the mineral kingdom, Jupiter and the Moon over the vegetable world, and Mars over the animal and animal-man, each carrying out the Will of the supreme intelligence.

These planetary spirits are Rays from the one Great Light, and stand at the head of their own department in the universe and govern the main principles as well as the minutest details of life. Every race and sub-race, every nation and colony of that nation as well as every religion, with its sub-divisions, is influenced by one of these mighty Intelligences. They know the Will of God and seek to co-operate with that Will in guiding the destinies of the world.

Esoteric Astrology teaches the Immanence of God, and seeks to discover through the positions of the heavenly bodies the changes in Nature we know as the laws of God. It recognises the important part these divine Intelligences must play in the destiny of Man, for they are his celestial prototypes, and therefore the nearer he approaches to a union with his Father in Heaven (his real star), the nearer is he to salvation or individualised consciousness; and the farther he recedes from it, the more dangerously fateful and inharmonious his life becomes. Herein lies the main difference between Esoteric and Exoteric Astrology, the former is concerned with man's actions *within* and with the power to harmonise himself with nature's laws, and the latter with man's impulses prompted by the attractions that are *without;* for Esoteric Astrology shows the possibilities, latent within all mankind, of unification with the divine will, or as stated by the ancient astrologers " The wise man rules his stars, the fool obeys them."

The author of the *Secret Doctrine* has expressed these ideas in beautiful language when she says :

"Yes, 'our destiny is written in the stars': Only the closer the union between the mortal reflection Man and his celestial *Prototype*, the less dangerous his external conditions and subsequent reincarnations. There are *external* and *internal* conditions which affect the determination of our Will upon our actions, and though man cannot escape his ruling Destiny, he has choice of two paths, and it is in his power to follow either. Those who believe in Karma have to believe in *destiny*, which from birth to death man is weaving round himself as a spider weaves his web; and this destiny is guided either by the heavenly voice of the invisible prototype, or by our intimate *astral* or inner man who is but too often our evil genius."

In this work a serious attempt will be made to convey some ideas of the influence of the Planetary Spirits, and Zodiacal Signs upon mankind, and an effort will be made to show how closely related all manifested things are to the Sun, Moon, and planets through their connecting link, the signs of the zodiac.   It must however be clearly understood at the beginning that it is not the physical planets themselves that affect mankind, but the supreme Intelligences who use the planetary bodies as their physical vehicles so to speak.

Each planetary body has a sphere of influence peculiarly its own, and each commingles its special influence with that of all the others. In colour language this is best expressed by saying that the white light of the Sun is changed on passing through the planetary sphere into the colour of that particular planet, the indigo, violet, and blue of Venus, Moon, and Jupiter, having their reflection in the yellow, orange, and red of Mercury, Sun, and Mars, balanced by the green of Saturn, the middle note and colour.   Man's body, soul, and spirit, absorb these colours by a mental process which changes the pure and original colour which he inherits by physical, psychic, and spiritual heredity, into a coarser or lighter shade according to his choice of thoughts, feelings and actions.   All of which we hope to explain in succeeding chapters.

CHAPTER II

Occult Astronomy

THE whole essence of truth cannot be described by any pen, not even that of the recording angel, unless man finds its response in the sanctuary of his own heart, in the innermost depths of his divine intuition. *Secret Doctrine.*

ASTROLOGERS speak of planetary influence with a degree of confidence that is rather trying at times to those who do not approach the subject along mystical or occult lines of study, but who are more familiar with the methods of concrete science on the one hand or those of ordinary practical utility on the other. Ultimately, when our knowledge of the subject is complete, all these methods of regarding Astrology will be found to blend in one. The man of action will find it of practical value to him in every-day life ; the student will realise that it is a science as definite as any other, and one that forms a chapter in a very grand and far-reaching scheme of philosophy ; while the mystic will discover that its religious value is transcendent and sublime, for it belongs to one of the seven methods of approach towards spiritual things.

At the present day, however, we are only at the alphabet of the science, so many are the chapters yet to be learned ; and it is not always easy to explain the undiscovered in terms of the familiar, to map out heaven as if it were a London suburb.

The " wireless telegraphy " by means of which the heavenly bodies influence man may be regarded from various points of view : as a system of vibrations, each of its kind and each conveying some peculiar type of energy capable of producing its effect upon us ; as a method whereby the specialised vitality of one planet is radiated forth to all the others, to be utilised by them and by their inhabitants according to their ability to receive it ; and as a scheme by which the type of consciousness evolving in connection with each heavenly body sends forth to all the others within the solar system its will-power, its thought, and its feeling to be utilised by all, in return for that which it receives from them.

Whichever view be taken, any influence that reaches us and our earth does so only through the zodiac, which modifies and adapts all that

8

passes through it.   The primary and unmodified form of planetary
energy we never experience, but only that blended and compounded kind
which results from its adaptation to the special conditions of the zodiacal
signs and the earth's aura.   For instance, we never receive the influence
of, say, Jupiter alone, for it is always intermixed with that of the zodiacal
sign in which it is placed in any given horoscope.   In fact, the complexity
is greater even than this, because, as every astrologer knows, aspects
from other planets exert a powerful modifying effect upon any heavenly
body.   Jupiter in opposition to Saturn is by no means the same as Jupiter
in trine to Mars ; the events that it causes and the type of character it
reveals are quite different in the two cases ; and seeing that a planet is
often in aspect with half a dozen others in a horoscope, and that each one
of them is modified by the sign through which its influence is transmitted
to the earth, the resulting complexity is greater than is generally realised
or than some students would be willing to admit.   The nearest approach
to simplicity is when the planet is free from aspects, which is rarely the
case ; and yet even here complete simplicity or what may be called
atomic isolation is not achieved.

The results of these blendings of influences seem to be more analogous
to chemical compounds than to simple mixtures.   Water is formed of the
chemical combination of Hydrogen and Oxygen gases, but water
possesses properties that are not shown by either of its constituents when
taken alone.   Or, again, we may use the analogy of musical harmony.
When two notes, C and G, are sounded together, we hear something more
than the sound of C added to the sound of G ; we hear also that special
kind of harmony characteristic of the musical interval called a fifth ; and
it is easy to see that if a man had never heard musical notes except in
combination, his estimate of the value of any single note taken alone
might be very inaccurate.

This, however, is the position occupied by every astrologer; he
never experiences the influence of a planet except in combination with
that of a sign.   This is certainly the cause of many of the mistakes
that have been made in the attribution of powers and characteristics to
signs and to planets.   Each student approaches the subject from the
point of view primarily of his own horoscope with its special intricacies
and complexities, and secondarily from that of a few horoscopes of persons
whom he knows well ; and thus we have the spectacle of investigators
holding quite different opinions on some subjects.   One will take Neptune

as a malefic, another as a benefic.   One regards Saturn as the type of the
priest, and another as that of the statesman.[1]   One finds Libra to be a sign
of isolation and independence, and another that it implies union and mutual
dependence.   These and other divergent opinions are actually held and
expressed at the present day.

In much the same way a person who is beginning to see clairvoyantly
perceives the auric colours of others only through the modifying hues
of his own, and is liable to attribute characteristics to them that really
belong to himself or that have been altered by being seen through the
special colours surrounding himself.

In practice the astrologer tries to overcome the difficulty by
extending his experience and taking an average of a large number of
observations.   It is true that Mars rising in Aries will not give the same
type of personality as Mars rising in Taurus, and both these will differ
somewhat from the same planet rising in Gemini ; but at any rate
Mars enters into each of these combinations, and if it is possible to
abstract him from the influence of the successive signs, the type due to
the planet will remain and will be the same in each case.   The
clairvoyant occultist tells us that illusions existing on one plane cannot
be perfectly overcome until the consciousness can rise to a higher plane
and view the lower from there ; that the endless complexities and
intricacies of the astral plane, for instance, can only be seen in their true
proportions by means of vision pertaining to the next plane beyond ; and
that the truth about the personality, its formation, dissolution, and career
in the various worlds to which it belongs, cannot be understood completely
until consciousness can rise above personality altogether.   Similarly, the
influence of Jupiter can never be perceived clearly by an astrologer who
is subject to the disturbing and distorting conditions inevitable to one
who lives on this earth.   Even the earth itself is not seen in the right
relation to its companion globes until the limitations of earth and what
may be called the earth's personality are transcended.   The zodiac
cannot be understood until a degree of consciousness has been evolved
that enables the circle of necessity to be explored from above and beyond
it.   The chain of globes in connection with which we evolve, and of
which our earth is one, are not seen truly until a degree of evolution is
attained sufficient to carry the soul beyond that plane to which the

---

[1] A knowledge of human nature is wanted for both.   A true priest has the qualities
of the statesman.

highest of them belongs, when they will be viewed in their right relations and the real function of each understood.

It may be taken as a broad general principle that any higher plane or world represents a relative unity when compared with that which is next below it, which is a relative multiplicity. To understand is to gather together scattered fragments of sense or relatively isolated ideas and to discover that which they have in common, the unity underlying them all. The unity represents the higher plane or world or point of view and the multiplicity the lower. The last word of the mysteries of our solar system, whether from the point of view of the astrologer or of any other, cannot be understood until the final unity of the system is reached in consciousness; and that is the reason for the insistence on the mystical view of things and on metaphysics as the means of supplementing and unifying what would otherwise be scattered and uncoördinated laws and experiences. Science is its own justification for existence and needs no defence, but it cannot reach completion until the soul has learned how to step across the threshold of the outer phenomenal world into the inner world that transcends it.

One consciousness, one life, one energy permeates the whole solar system, namely that of the great Being who formed it in the beginning and who still sustains it, the Solar Logos. Every form of energy flowing through the matter of the various planes of the system is derived directly from Him; His vitality radiated forth from the Sun animates the bodies of all living beings; and every mode of consciousness, whether human or otherwise, originates in Him. He is the underlying unity that transcends and synthesises the vast multiplicity of the whole system, whether in terms of consciousness, of force, or of matter.

Any unit, whether material or spiritual, during manifestation as a separate existence, must necessarily exhibit three aspects. Firstly, it acts upon its surroundings, is positive to them, effects changes within them; secondly, it is acted upon by them, is negative to them, becomes responsive to them in terms of stimuli received from without; and thirdly, it co-ordinates and balances these two aspects in a neutral mean between the two extremes. Similarly the Solar Logos during manifestation shows the three aspects or " Persons " of the divine Trinity, called the three Logoi. Coming forth into manifestation from out of the unknown darkness beyond, He is a transcendent unity, but exhibits three aspects during the life of the Solar system. The Third Logos moulds the

matter of the future system, shapes it into atoms, of which there
are seven types fitted to act as vehicles for seven different kinds of
consciousness, and arranged in seven great planes of which the physical
is the lowest. The keynote here is separation or creation. The Second
Logos evolves vehicles, bodies, of various grades animated by life and
moved by consciousness ; and the keynote here is harmony, balance, the
drawing together of scattered atoms and separated lives. Finally, the
First Logos evolves the Self within the vehicles, bestows that kind of
self-consciousness which, beginning in separation and isolation within its
own vehicles, ends by realising the actual unity of all. The three quadruplicities of zodiacal signs illustrate by a very far off analogy these three
sublime modes in which He manifests everywhere; the Movable or
Rajasic signs corresponding to the Third Logos, the Common or Sattvic
to the Second Logos, and the Fixed or Tamasic to the First Logos.

We must not make the mistake of supposing that these signs really
are the three Logoi, for this cannot be said either of signs or of planets ;
but because the divine energy, life and consciousness are universally
diffused through matter on every plane, it is legitimate to look for the
underlying reality amid the superficial diversity.

The Solar System

The solar system as a whole may be looked upon as a body of the
Logos. Every plane of it, from the lowest physical to the highest
spiritual, is energised and animated by this life and consciousness, just
as is the human body by the human life and consciousness. The properties of matter on every plane are planned and evolved by Him in
His aspect of the Third Logos; the life of every plane and Kingdom,
including the invisible elemental life, is derived directly from Him as
Second Logos; and every form of self-consciousness originates in Him
as First Logos.

From Him as the one Father of all are sent forth Seven great
Beings, called Archangels or Planetary Logoi, inferior only to Himself,
but superior to all other beings within the solar system. Each presides
over one-seventh part of the whole system, and is the supreme head of
one of the seven schemes of evolution. These seven Beings are the *real*
"Seven Rulers," and not the globes that are often referred to on the
physical plane. They are mighty spiritual intelligences who derive their
energy, life and consciousness from the great central One Life of all, the

Solar Logos, each manifesting a different mode of it according to the kind of work they have to do, the type of evolution over which they have to preside.

Each of the seven planetary Logoi has within his charge thousands of millions of souls at all stages of development, some still in the elemental, mineral, vegetable, or animal stage; some human such as ourselves; and others far beyond the human. They are the primary source, under the Solar Logos, of the seven Principles of man, working through the lesser twelve Creative Orders represented by the spiritual (as distinct from the physical) signs of the zodiac; and collectively they represent the septenary Word. They are the real Creators of the septenary universe, and they work in accordance with the design outlined by the wisdom of the tri-une Solar Logos, whose seven creative rays, powers, or centres they really are; and to one or other of the seven every soul on earth belongs, spiritually.

Existing themselves in high spiritual regions, they superintend the formation and evolution of every globe visible and invisible within the solar system. Within each of their seven domains are multitudes of lesser Intelligences, obeying their will, building up planes, globes, and the various kingdoms of nature, supplying the intelligence that underlies the so-called Laws of Nature, and guiding the streams of influence passing from every planet to every other. Various names have been given to these subordinate hosts who work in the administration of nature's laws; they have been termed gods, angels, and elementals or nature spirits, according to their stage of evolution and the plane or state in which they are working. At one time, when the gods walked with men, they were known and their function in nature fully understood; but now they are no longer recognised and they are forgotten for the most part save by the few who know the part they play in the workings of nature.

The Planetary Chains

Each Planetary Logos presides over a distinct scheme of evolution, which is carried on upon seven different globes existing upon the three lower planes of the solar system, as in the accompanying illustration. (DIAGRAM I., overleaf.)

Such a group of seven globes is called a Chain, and there are seven such chains within the solar system, to one or other of which every visible planet belongs. In the case of our earth, globes A and G exist on the

THE CHAIN OF GLOBES

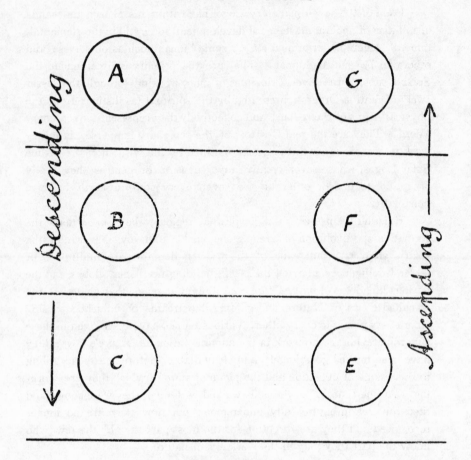

DIAGRAM I.

Mental plane, and globes B and F on the Astral Plane ; and these four are therefore invisible to ordinary physical sight. But globe C is the planet Mars, globe D is our earth, and globe F is the planet Mercury; so that three out of the seven are visible physical planets, and the other four are invisible.[1]

There is only one other septenary Chain that also has three physical planets, namely the Neptune Chain; for there are two physical planets existing beyond Neptune that belong to his Chain. And this fact shows that the evolutions represented by the earth and Neptune are, spiritually, both at the same stage of evolution, namely the fourth stage or manvan· tara, because only at this stage are there three physical planets in one Chain. The first and seventh incarnations of any Chain have no planet lower than the mental; in the second and sixth the lowest planet of the Chain is astral; in the third and fifth one is physical; in the fourth three are physical.

The seven planetary Logoi are represented on the physical plane by the planets Vulcan, Venus, the Earth, Jupiter, Saturn, Uranus, and Neptune. Each of these is globe D in a septenary Chain; so that although the Earth and Neptune are at the same evolutionary stage, they belong to quite different types. The Sun, the eighth, is the great Father of the seven Fathers; for each of these seven Planetary Logoi is the "Father in Heaven" of those souls who belong to His type of spiritual evolution.

Our Solar System is one organic living conscious Whole, and there are millions of such systems, some smaller, some enormously larger, within the total universe. It receives one particular type of life and consciousness through the Solar Logos, who is in conscious union with the vaster universe beyond, receiving life from it and returning life to it, just as each planet sends forth and takes back within the system. This life received from outside may be compared to a ray of white light, one and uniform in itself but immediately decomposed into three fundamental bases of colour corresponding to the three aspects or Persons of the Solar Logos, and then analysed into the seven colours of the spectrum, corresponding to the seven Planetary Logoi, each of whom receives from the Solar Logos a different type of life and of consciousness resulting from this decomposition and analysis.

---

[1] For full details about the planetary chains, rounds, etc., the *Secret Doctrine* should be consulted, but a useful outline will be found in the sixpenny manual on "Theosophy" in Messrs. T. C. and E. C. Jack's series of *The People's Books*.

The Seven Planes

Starting afresh at this stage, we see in imagination each Planetary Logos receiving a special type of life and consciousness, and utilising it for the purposes of the kind of evolution carried on upon the Chain of globes over which he presides.   For instance, the Planetary Logos of our earth Chain has his own special "colouring"; and the ray which he receives is again split into seven sub-rays, one of which belongs to each of the seven globes in the Chain.   At our present stage of knowledge it would seem that each such globe is itself animated by a Being called the Spirit of the globe, whose body the globe appears to be, and who receives and adapts to the type of evolution carried on there the sub-ray which is transmitted to him through the Planetary Logos.[1]   Just as the Solar Logos sends forth seven sub-rays to the seven Planetary Spirits of his Chain, so there is a general correspondence between rays and sub-rays according to the septenary scale.   What the seven globes are to the Chain as a whole, that the seven Chains are to the Solar system as a whole ; but what is the precise order of correspondence we have not yet sufficient information to enable us to decide.

The solar system is one organic whole, and in a subordinate sense each Chain of seven globes is also an organic whole.   Each whole is composed of parts, but these are mutually interdependent.   In the case of a Chain, a circulation of physical and other forces and of vitality is constantly going on between the seven globes, although the point of greatest activity is centred sometimes upon one globe and sometimes upon another, according to the stage of evolution reached.   So that the seven globes of a Chain are more closely associated with each other, more dependent upon each other for the interchange of vital and conscious influences, than are the various physical planets.   This is a department of occult astrology of which practically nothing is known as yet; but in some mysterious way the position and conditions of the seven physical planets previously mentioned are a clue to the conditions and influences of the seven Chains.

With regard to the seven planes of which the solar system is composed, a similar sub-division and correspondence is found.   The Physical plane is the lowest, the Astral plane is the next, the Mental

---

[1] In the view of later knowledge this idea has been modified but the information obtained cannot as yet be clearly expressed.

follows the astral, then comes the intuitional plane, then the Atmic or spiritual, then the Anupadaka and the Adi, or super-spiritual planes ; each higher plane being more ethereal, subtler, and greater in extent than the one below it. Upon the lower three planes, as we have previously seen, all the seven globes of the earth Chain are situated. Each plane is divided into seven sub-planes, which are to the plane as a whole what the seven planes are to the solar system as a whole, and the sub-planes of any plane correspond in order to the seven planes. In what follows it is necessary carefully to distinguish between statements applying to planes and those applying to sub-planes.

On the physical plane, the lowest four sub-divisions are solids, liquids, gases, and ethers ; which answer to what are called earth, water, fire, and air. These four enter into the composition of each physical planet, and are specialised in some way in doing so, for atoms are said to vary their combining proportions on every planet. The three higher sub-planes of the physical, which are sometimes referred to as the higher ethers, but which also bear the names of super-etheric, sub-atomic, and atomic, the latter being the highest, are not specialised in this way but are common to the whole solar system and are the channels through which various forms of energy and vitality are transmitted from one planet to another, including astrological influence in so far as this is physical.

The types of life and consciousness that characterise the seven planes of the solar system are summed up in seven great Intelligences, the Rulers of the planes, who correspond to and are aspects of the seven Planetary Logoi. Two of these planes, the highest two, are altogether beyond our comprehension at our present stage of development, and do not enter into our evolutionary activity ; so that only five may be considered as actual for us at present. These are the Lords of—the Physical plane, earth, Kshiti or Kubera ; the Astral plane, water, Varuna ; the Mental plane, fire, Agni ; the Buddhic or intuitional plane, air, Vayu ; and the Atmic or spiritual plane, æther or akasha.

These are also connected with the Tattvas, modes of motion in matter, which determine the shape and properties of the ultimate atoms on each plane, which correspond to the five platonic solids, and which appeal to us through our five active senses as follows, Earth, smell ; Water, taste ; Fire, sight ; Air, touch ; Akasha, sound.

The four states or planes are universally permeated by the Fifth, æther or akasha, which is itself triple, in a sense, because it includes the higher two that lie beyond it, to which we are not yet separately responsive. Upon this akasha is imprinted the memory of all that takes place in nature, every thought, word, and deed, on each of the other planes. The five planes have certain qualities exceedingly difficult to describe, resulting naturally from the structure of the matter of the plane as expressed in the ultimate atoms and tattvas, and capable of expression either in terms of matter or of consciousness. Earth, contraction and cohesion, action ; Water, the balance of expansion and contraction, feeling ; Fire, expansion, separation, individualisation, self-consciousness; Air, interpenetration, relation, wisdom ; Akasha, space, unity, will.

Each of the five states or elements is polarised, being positive and negative, out-breathing and in-breathing, descending and ascending, making ten in all ; and these, with the two that lie beyond, make twelve, corresponding to the signs of the zodiac.

PLANES AND SUB-PLANES

It will be seen that such a term as " earth," as used for a state of matter, is applied sometimes to the physical plane as a whole and some- times to the lowest sub-division of it ; and similarly that " water " sometimes signifies the astral plane and sometimes the second or liquid sub-division of the physical. This is because planes and sub-planes correspond exactly to each other ; in fact, in a sense, the " water " of the physical plane may be said to result from the influence of the astral plane being thrown down upon the physical ; so that the sub-division of the lower plane is in direct touch with the higher plane as a whole, and it is possible to pass from the one to the other.

The septenary classification is the clue to the solar system whether in terms of consciousness or of matter. It results from the three aspects of all manifested things, and it gives rise to the twelve-fold classification familiar in the zodiac. It has been pointed out that the four lower sub- divisions of the physical plane enter into the composition of the physical globes, and that the three higher are common to the whole system. The influence of the three higher acting upon the four lower gives the three varieties of each of these four; twelve in all; and the same principle may be applied in a more extended manner to include the planes of the solar system and the bodies of man. Judged by the number of globes, the influence of the duodenary prevails at present on the physical plane

for the number of actual physical planets is eleven, including Vulcan and
the two outside Neptune, and then the Sun makes up the twelve.   This
number, however, apparently varies at different periods in the vast history
of the whole system, and changes occur in enormously long rhythms to
which science has as yet no clue.   Our earth Chain has three of its globes
on the physical plane, and the same is true of the Neptune Chain; but
this was not the case in the far past, nor will it always be so in the long
distant future.

CHAPTER III

"SPHERES OF INFLUENCE"

Planets and Principles

THE THREE GREAT TRUTHS :—
    THE Soul of man is immortal.
    The principle which gives life dwells in us and without us, is undying and
        eternally beneficent.
    Each man is his own absolute lawgiver.

The Idyll of the White Lotus.

AT our present stage of astrological research, we have very little first hand knowledge of the functions of the angelic host who rule over the planetary spheres of influence. Some valuable occult information has been passed on to the author by students of occultism who are working along another line of activity than that of the Astrological Ray, and for the most part the finer vibrations of each planet have been discovered by practical experience ; so that by fitting the two together we have a system which gives a very fair representation of the planetary relationship to the principles of man.

If we could obtain more information concerning the Seven Rays, the seven sub-divisions of each, and their connection with the Seven planets, we should know considerably more concerning Esoteric Astrology. This information, however, is decidedly fragmentary. The little that has so far been given out by our primary teachers, has been so guardedly expressed, and they have been so remarkably reticent, that it seems clear that a knowledge of the Rays must be concerned with the inner mysteries.

So far as can be known by those who are not initiated into these mysteries, it would appear probable that only one of the great Rays affects our Solar System; for as the second Stanza of the *Secret Doctrine* tells us, "Her heart had not yet opened for the One Ray to enter, thence to fall, as three into four, into the lap of Illusion." And in Stanza III., we read, " Darkness radiates Light and Light drops—-one Solitary Ray."

This one Ray is the Logos of our Solar System, symbolised for us in Astrology by the Sun. Its seven sub-divisions, and the other seven

Creative Rays, are the Planetary Logoi or Builders. "Space and Time are one." "Space and Time are nameless, for they are the incognizable THAT, which can be sensed *only through its seven rays*—which are the *seven creations*, the *seven worlds*, and the *seven laws*," etc., etc.

The Rays from this *one* immaculate Ray are unnumberable, from It the one becomes the many. Astrologically we are now concerned with the seven sub-rays of this *one* great Solar Ray, each of which has its own seven sub-divisions, making in all forty-nine primary rays directly connected with the planets. These rays are always distinct in the forms and vehicles through which they pass, and all mankind belong to one or other of them.

To illustrate this idea from an astrological standpoint, we may take the spirit of Mars as the head of the Animal Kingdom. All animals as a class are under the dominant ray of Mars, but it is obvious that different animals may be ranged under various sub-rays. For instance, the elephant is under a Saturnine sub-ray of Mars, and the horse under the Jupiterian sub-ray; so that it is clear that the impulse of the universal life which is now animating an elephant or a horse will continue to manifest through the same species until differentiation into the human evolution takes place. This may be illustrated by taking the ruling planet in any horoscope as the personal ray. If Venus is the ruler and is placed in the sign Aries, we have then a Venus ray with a sub-influence of Mars. This may also be applied to races and sub-races, religions and sects, politics and parties; in fact to every department of nature in all their main and sub-issues.

In order that the subject may be made more clear, we may consider the seven Rays as divided into three classes. The first Ray forms the first class, Will; the second Ray forms the second class, Wisdom; and the other five Rays form the third class, Activity. The third is the astrological Ray and includes the whole of the four below it; standing at the head of a group of five Rays. The first and highest two are exceptional and govern states above the human; for humanity as a whole is now working along a five-fold evolution; the other two, making the seven, being above and beyond the normal man at present.

We may now arrange these seven rays, represented by the planets, in a horizontal line, with seven sub-divisions of each in a vertical line beneath. Each planet thus stands at the head of a Ray having seven sub-divisions, as is shown in the following diagram. (DIAGRAM II.)

THE SUN

Life ☉ Prana

THE PLANETS AND PRINCIPLES

SYMBOLICAL CORRESPONDENCE	♅	☿	♀	♄	☽	♂	♃	CORRESPONDENCE SYMBOLICAL
Spirit	♅							AQUARIUS The Man Ray of Will
Spiritual Soul		☿						GEMINI The Twins Ray of Wisdom
Human Soul			♀					LIBRA The Balanced Soul. Manas
Critical State				♄				The Bridge between the Higher and Lower
Personal Mind					☽			Lower Manas The Brain Mental Moods
Personal Feelings						♂		Kâma The Animal Soul
Physical Conditions							♃	The Body Etheric and Physical

DIAGRAM II.

The Sun here stands for the One solitary Ray, signifying the One Life which permeates all things. It symbolises cosmic life or consciousness which afterwards becomes the separated life of body, soul and spirit. It stands beyond and above the form side of manifestation, functioning through matter of the finest and most rarefied degree, being the Light, Life and Consciousness of the worlds.

In the same way that the airy signs of the zodiac synthesise the other triplicities, so does the Sun synthesise the influence of the planets in their relationship to these triplicities.

From the standpoint of the form, or vehicles of consciousness alone, Jupiter is the great synthesiser. For instance, when the physical body is dropped at death, all that is latent in the earthy signs is preserved in the influence of the planet Jupiter and carried upward to the next vehicle of manifestation, so that on the astral plane we have the influence of its own triplicity plus that of Jupiter ; Jupiter being the seed planet of the physical plane.

From the standpoint of the life, or states of consciousness, Uranus is the synthetic planet and represents the "houseless wanderer," the fully individualised and self-conscious being. Between these two powerful planets Saturn is placed as the individualising planet.

It will now be seen why in Exoteric Astrology the Sun has always been used as a symbol for the individuality and also why it is said to be a substitute for another mystic planet ; which we now know to be Uranus, the planet representing the true Will. For the majority of evolving souls the Sun will continue to represent the strongest or centre position in the horoscope, because it gives light and expression to the sign it illumines each month, and brings out of latency into active manifestation those signs and planets within range of the Sun's most potent aspects ; but it is not the planet of individuality in the true sense of the word. It is purely a question of understanding the difference between the terms life and consciousness. "Consciousness turned *inward* is life, and life turned *outward* is known by the name of consciousness."

In Esoteric Astrology the Monad is represented by the triple aspect of Uranus, Mercury and Venus. Any of these may be placed at the apex of the triangle according to the line of development, and all below the sphere of their influence must first receive the individualising qualities of Saturn before the Ego or individuality can be strong enough to respond to their subtle vibrations.

In the very highly evolved individual, Uranus shines forth as genius and originality; Mercury as adaptability and the perfection of the humane principles; and Venus as refinement and beauty, as expressed in the creative arts.   Put as plainly as possible, the mediocre individual does not touch any of these principles, he constantly vibrates below the belt of Saturn, so to speak.   To touch the higher vibrations of Saturn even, one must have evolved beyond the average, or commonplace.   At our present stage of evolution, the real influence of Uranus, Mercury and Venus may be considered more or less latent; for complete Manasic consciousness, free from Kama or desire, is only manifested on the physical plane by highly evolved individuals, who are able to conquer and control matter to such an extent as to use their bodies and vehicles self-consciously, not allowing themselves to be used by them; and as such they display wisdom and skill in all their actions.

For the most part these three planets affect the etheric body and not the physical; and their influences being etheric are dependent upon a sensitive body for clear and favourable expression.   They act mainly through the sub-conscious mind, and with regard to Uranus this may be said to be wholly the case, for its vibrations are too subtle to be felt in the physical body, except through a highly organised nervous system.

In the abstract, Uranus represents the Will aspect of the spirit, its motives and purpose in life; and while not actually connected with any sign of the zodiac, Aquarius and the airy signs, with the fixed signs as sub-influence, are for this planet the signs of least resistance and those with which it has the most affinity.   If Uranus is not angular, or in an airy sign at birth, it is open to serious question whether its influence can be particularly felt; it should also be in aspect with the luminaries or at least with Mercury and Venus.

Uranus is said to be the astrologer's planet, because it is connected with Will and magic, or occultism.

Mercury is also a planet whose influence is felt more etherically than physically, for its vibrations are far too fine and subtle to be distinguished by those who are not very refined and sensitive, and it is only by way of the nervous system that its influence can act freely.   Its physical effects are, more often than not, experienced through its relation with other planets or their aspects.

Mercury governs Pure Reason or what is known as Abstract Reason, that which is truly human and entirely free from the animal and coarser sides of nature, a state which for many is super-human. It is essentially the planet of rhythm and harmony, and therefore adverse positions or aspects to this planet disturb the reason and the higher and purer thoughts and intuitions in man. Its best expression is through the Airy and Mutable signs, with Virgo as a sub-influence, the most etheric of the signs. Its influence alone and apart from the signs can only be felt by adepts.

Venus is much more in affinity with the zodiac, although its influence apart from that of the other planets can only be experienced by the most refined and those who live cultured lives. It is in sympathy with Libra, the commencement of the zodiac in the human kingdom, the sign of balance and equilibrium. Venus is the planet signifying the "Grace of God," but to understand this term the influence of the planet Saturn has to be fully comprehended.

Although more potent in its action through etheric matter than physically, the manifestations of Venus through the creative arts and refinement of thought, feeling, and action bring its influence nearer to us than that of Mercury and Uranus.

Venus is the planet of equilibrium, representing the clear perceptions of the mind, which, having expressed all that can be perceived on the physical plane, turns the sight inward to perceive on the inner planes of being. It therefore represents the human soul.

The planet representing any Ego in manifestation may be ascertained and placed at the apex of the individual triangle by noting the following lines of development:

If on the Will line, Uranus; on the Wisdom line, Mercury; and on the line of Activity, Venus.

Of the seven planets in their relation to the seven principles of man, Saturn is the middle planet, ruling the critical stage between the individual and personal triads of consciousness. It may be termed the "Bridge" between the higher and lower expressions of Manas, the abstract and the concrete; it is therefore the *pathway* leading from the lower to the higher.

Saturn is the great sifter in human evolution. Metaphorically speaking, none may pass the influence of this planet who have not paid the debts of fate, or Karma, to the uttermost farthing. In every crisis, and in all critical stages of man's evolution, the influence of Saturn decides the issue. Saturn is, therefore, the planet of pure Justice, holding the scales of Libra, the perfect balance. This planet is Judge and Lawgiver and represents the Justice of God. None may be pardoned or forgiven until the sanction of Saturn has been received. As said, Venus represents the "Grace of God," and between these two mighty Angels every human being is weighed in the balance of Libra, symbolised so often in the Egyptian mysteries by the Scales, the Altar, and the Pillow of the neophyte.

In Christian teachings, Satan "The Tempter" is the personification of Saturn, the Tester and Sifter of the spiritual from material experiences. Saturn as the individualising planet makes all things permanent, binding all forms, controlling and restraining life's expressions by limitations which cause one lesson to be learned before the next is attempted. Saturn is the planet of "Dharma," duty or obligation, for every human creature. Saturn builds the scaffolding around the youth of every soul, protecting the edifice that is being erected until stability, perseverance, and self-control have been achieved. Apparently the lowest, the influence of Saturn is the highest to which mortal man may attain. In every psychic experience, Saturn makes definite the consciousness through realisation, and marks the epoch of every soul in its progress through Time to Eternity. Saturn is, therefore, the "Middle Principle," between the material and spiritual triads. Between each triplicity of signs there is a centre or point of balance, a point wherein two forces meet and balance. This is the neutral point in a centre, from which Forces emerge, into which they disappear. The recognised neutral states between solid, liquid, and gas, are Laya centres governed by the critical planet Saturn. Just as the physical planet Saturn is ringed, so does his influence mark the "ring pass not" between each plane of consciousness.

These Laya centres are the waters of Lethe, drowning the memory of the other side. They come between sleeping and waking, life and death, and but for this ring or natural barrier, there would be no break in consciousness. It is the bridge of Saturn that enables us to cross from one state of consciousness to another without passing through the swoon of unconsciousness, and this can only be accomplished by fully understanding the laws of one's being, and the occult methods of progress from darkness into light.

Below Saturn in the order of the planets is the Moon, which synthesises the fiery triplicities as the crown of the personality, for the Moon gathers up the personal consciousness through the head and brain, which it rules; it represents the psychic-intellectual man centred in the head with its seven gateways. That is why so much stress is laid upon mind control in order that the voice of the spiritual man, who is seated in the heart, may be heard when the restless brain is stilled.

We have said that the ray of the Monad is represented by the triple aspect of Uranus, Mercury and Venus, and have seen how few there are who respond to their influence, and that therefore the Sun represents the Individuality for the majority. The consciousness as represented by the Sun is focussed in the heart, the last spot in the body to die.

Now in the same way that the Sun, as representative of the Individual consciousness is centred in Uranus by the genius of the awakened individuality, so is the Moon, the representative of the personality, centred in Saturn, the planet controlling the path of discipleship or freedom from irresponsibility. It will thus be seen how important it is to study the position and aspects of the Moon in every nativity.

The next plane below the mental is that of the personal feelings, governed by the planet Mars. This represents the animal man in the fullness of his strength, a force not to be despised or ignored, but transmuted and wisely used, for Mars represents the consciousness of all the cells of the body, including the brain but excepting the heart. The control of desire is necessary before the animal can be conquered and made a useful servant. It is the cerebellum that is the store-house of all the Kāmic or passional force; and Mars, its planetary representative, furnishes the materials for ideation, while the frontal lobes of the cerebrum are the finishers and polishers of the materials, but not their creators. The affinity between Mars and Venus can now be seen, Mars governing the animal sense, and Venus the soul; so that when both are in harmony through attraction, affinity is the result; but when opposed, antipathy or antagonism exists between them.

We have now to conclude this brief survey of the planets by a consideration of Jupiter. This planet governs all the bodies of man included in his Aura, from the finest film of matter surrounding the " Divine Fragment " down to the physical body, and this it rules completely through the life blood and the senses. It is however not wise to think that Jupiter alone governs the physical body, for all the planets have influence over it; but as lord or king over the body, Jupiter plays an important and mysterious part, namely to give expansion to the limit of the Karma for the present life; and in this respect it has rule over the atoms and cells of the body.

So far as the actual physical consciousness is concerned, Jupiter governs, 1st, the sensuous; 2nd, the instinctual; 3rd, the physiological-emotional; 4th, the passional-emotional; 5th, the mental-emotional; and 6th the spiritual-emotional. The last will explain why Jupiter signifies orthodox religion, and any religious feeling in which the emotions play a prominent part. Here feeling is more active than intellect, and in this respect it must be remembered that the astral and the physical consciousness are interchangeable or reciprocal.

This part of our study will receive fuller treatment later on when we come to deal with the relation of the planet Jupiter to the Human Aura.

CHAPTER IV

The Significance of Caste and Social Distinctions

THUS every Race in its evolution is said to be born under the direct
influence of one of the planets, the First Race receiving its breath of life from
the Sun; while the Third humanity—those who from Androgynes became
male and female—are said to have been under the direct influence of Venus.

Secret Doctrine.

THERE are many ways of explaining the divine origin of man, and his
long pilgrimage from divinity though vast cycles of manifestation to a
self-conscious realisation of his immortality.   To understand them,
however, the eyes of the spirit must be opening to the realisation of the
divine spark within and the necessity of harmonising it with the without.

Esoteric Astrology teaches this truth of man's divine inheritance
through an ancient symbology which takes for its central symbol the
Sun. This Sun is seen to be mirrored through its innumerable rays as
myriads of miniature Suns, whose reflections are again mirrored in the
vast ocean of life.   Each individual is a miniature Sun shining with its
own light in the many forms of matter, and by the reflections thrown
back to itself comes to know itself as the light of that inner Sun.
Astrology points out these reflections upon the great screen of matter in
all its various forms in the signs of the zodiac, and their presence in the
planetary vibrations as so many modes of consciousness.   Through the
nativity it studies the manifold indentifications of the persisting life with
the ever-changing forms, and helps those who have begun the struggle to
return back to the parent Sun of which it is but a faint reflection.

In ancient civilisations the relics of which remain to-day in India,
the Chieftain of the race, the MANU, or Divine King, arranged groups of
men into what is known as Caste or as we would say in the West into
grades of society. By this means men knew where they stood in
evolution and until they had out-grown the Caste into which they were
born they fulfilled the duties belonging to it.

At certain periods of evolution there comes a time when all caste
systems appear to be broken up for a rearrangement, and this takes place

29

when there is a confusion as to duty, and a clamouring for "rights" which more properly belong to the form than to the life.

A Hindu can explain this confusion much more adequately than a Western Astrologer, owing to his perfect acquaintance with caste and its relation to Astrology, and we are therefore fortunate in having a simple and almost complete explanation of this subject in an admirable chapter on "Caste Confusion" in the first Volume of "Studies in the Bhagavad Gita," by The Dreamer,[1] from which we make the following lengthy extract in the belief that it will help western students of Astrology to see how the subject is viewed in the East.

The Dreamer is dealing with *The Yoga of discrimination*, and in Chapter II. he says :—

"Let us therefore understand what caste is, and find if there is any relation whatever between caste and duty. The Lord in the Bhagavad Gita describes caste or colour as being due to *Guna* and *Karma*. These form the differentiating factors in the division of castes. The caste is thus the expression, in the lower planes, of the karmic heredities and the inner qualities evolved by the Ego. In other words, in a normally healthy Society there is always a fixed rule governing the stages of individual growth, dependent on the qualities and limitations of the individual."

"If we study the origin of the individual we find something which helps to clear the ground for us. The individual, or, as it is sometimes called, the individualised Self, as it starts into existence, is a white spark of the Divine Light enclosed in a colourless film of matter. It is a spark emanating from the Divine Flame and having all the qualities of the parent evolved in it. The seed is cast into the soil of the phenomenal planes, that it may grow into the likeness of its sire. As regards the Spark of Light, *per se*, it is the same Divine Light everywhere—it is always of the substance of what is called in the Gita, the Daivi Prakriti.

"From the standpoint, however, of this Light, there is no differentiation nor evolution; we cannot posit any beginnings in Time to it, for It ever is. We must therefore seek for the root of evolution elsewhere.

"Though in essence it is colourless at the beginning, yet in its *actual* manifestation some change takes place. The Divine spark can only reach the matrix of matter through some intermediate agencies, Rays of the

---

[1] Published by the Theosophical Society, 161, New Bond Street, W.

Light, who are called the Sons of Mind. The Divine Light, in manifesting the Universe from the state of *pralaya*, acts on the vehicle of matter
not directly, but rather through what we may term definite 'rays.' These
rays, or the pencils of Light, catch up the image of the Logos of a
system and mirror It in the various *upadhis*.[1] The characters of these
rays are different and so too their functions. Thus the rays energising
and vivifying the matter of cosmos into several planes of matter of
varying densities are sometimes spoken of in Theosophical literature as
the First Life-Wave. So, too, the Devas who superintended the
building of the forms and the fashioning of the tabernacle of man come out
of the Second Life-Wave. When the tabernacle is ready, then there is
again a downpouring from the Logos called the Third Life-Wave. It
is the birth of the Individual.

"Now, if we look carefully into the Shastras, we find that this
incoming of the man, or rather the building of the vehicle of individuality,
is caused by the action of those Rays of the Divine Light known in the
Theosophical terminology as the Sons of Mind, the Manasaputras of
Brahma. These Mighty Beings of a past *Kalpa* having evolved their
individual *Upadhis*—having attained to individuality — become the
channels by which the one Divine Light becomes individualised for the
purposes of evolution.

" Each of these great Sons of Mind has His own individual characteristics. As the Perfect Man, He is seven-fold in nature, yet having
for his basic principle one particular principle, so to say, in which the
others come in and inhere without disturbing the basic harmony. The
basic harmony is expressed by a particular sound, colour, and other
correspondences. The basic colour may thus be called the colour of the
Ray when in manifestation. When these Primary Rays sub-divide, the
basic colour is not disturbed, while the other principles come in, in a
slightly different degree, yet without disturbing the harmony. These
great Beings, who had in the previous Kalpas evolved mind and consciousness, who had even attained to spiritual bliss in the full consciousness of a *gnanin*, are thereby made the link to connect the spiritual spark
and the material bodies, the bridge to connect matter with Spirit. So we
read in the Yoga Vashistha how They went to visit the Logos, and how in
the pride and consciousness of Their Spiritual freedom, They refused to

---

[1] Vehicles or " sheaths."

make Their obeisance to Him—and how They were cursed to incarnate
in man and to furnish him with well-ordered and well-stocked mental
bodies, with the forms and laws of thought.   It is They, the Higher
Pitris, who furnished the out-breathed human monads with what is
known as the causal body.   These beings are likened to the seven colours
into which the one white light is refracted in passing through the prism
of the Buddhi principle.   Distinct individual characteristics which are thus
imparted to the causal bodies of the outbreathed monads, impart to these
bodies, made of the delicate film of the causal matter, the soft lines of
differentiation.   The colours of the causal body thus furnished are
indicative of the lines of least resistance, so to say, the lines along which
the spark may best develop its latent powers.   The astrological planets
governing a man's life are but other names for the influences of these
Seven Lords of Light, and these signify the nature, the arrangement and
balance of the principles in that particular earth-life.   This colour is
thus the spiritual *plasm*, the basis of spiritual heredity of the spark
coming into existence, and, as already said, defines the limits of growth,
the lines of action and so forth, of the inner man.   It is, so to say, the
key-note of that man's life, all other notes being blended with it in such a
way as to produce harmony.   As differentiation proceeds, the basic
colour is played upon by the colours of the other principles, giving
rise to definite variety and play of colours, without disturbing the basic
harmony.   We can understand this by the analogy of music with its
seven principal notes.   Now in Indian music we have six manifested
Ragas or principal tones (with one unmanifest), each having its own
characteristic marks.   The Ragas sub-divide into sub-tones called
Raginis, each having distinct marks of its own and yet having something
to connect it with the original Raga from which it sprang, while differing
in external form and even in notes and sub-notes.   The subtle harmony
which exists between the Raga and the Raginis is not ordinarily perceived ; the basic identity is generally overlooked by the commonplace
musician who notes the external forms more than the inner essence.   As
the *Ragas* become differentiated into *Raginis* the basic harmony is
undisturbed, but within its limits the other notes are arranged in diverse
ways, giving rise to various melodies, having still for the basic harmony
the characteristic of the original Raga.   The Raginis themselves can be
interblended to produce further variety, by the arrangement of the notes
and sub-notes in infinite ways, yet resulting always in harmony.

"So also in the case of man. The Hindus are familiar, though without troubling themselves much as to their real import, with what are called the *gotra* and the *prabara* of the individual. Thus everyone has got a *prabara*, the root colour of his being, depending as is exoterically known, upon the particular planetary God, but really on the particular ray from the Central Sun. This root colour then differentiates, within the limits of harmony, till a particular Rishi is reached, who is the source directly of the *spiritual plasm* in man, and along those lines the individual must travel in order that the goal may be reached with the least possible dissipation of energy. This is, as may be guessed, what is called the *guna* of the individual and defines the law of growth of the individual up to the causal body. This is why, when a man has outgrown the limitations of the causal body, when he reaches the PARAMAHANSA stage that he gives up the characteristic caste marks ; and this is also why when thus fit to step out of the KARANA SHARIRA, he is transferred from one ray to another, in order that he, now developed in strength and balance may assimilate the qualities of every other ray, and thus pass again into the white light of the Sun from which he has emerged, enriched with the fruitage of evolution. Nature never works 'per saltum'— all her works are sequential.

"Thus far, then, as concerning the *guna*. And now we will consider the other element, the *karma* of the individual. *Karma* is the expression of life in a given plane. It is thus the order, arrangement and harmony between the six remaining principles which express the inner life of the Individual. It is the expression of that life in terms of the remaining principles. As in music the coming in of the secondary notes and sub-notes help the swell, and form the cause of harmony of the Raga or the Ragini, just as these notes and sub-notes help in the differentiation of the one Raga into myriads of secondary Ragas and Raginis ; nay, just as the harmonious arrangement of the notes helps in what the musician would call the portraiture and the expression of the Raga, so also the arrangements of the principles help in the differentiation of the Individual Root into various sub-groups—species and individuals. Speaking again in the terms of astrology, the karmic element is symbolised in the co-ordination of the other principles. As in music, the secondary notes are necessary for the purpose of producing by their harmonious arrange- ment a grander harmony, a sweeter melody than would be possible with the dull monotony of a single note, so also in any individual incarnation the secondary principles are always so arranged as to produce a harmony best suited to the individual, and adapted best to the true expression of real life. We have in astrology the Primary Key—under which a man is born—the natal planet, as well as other planets occupying different houses. The primary planets give the *Guna* of the individual—while the arrangement of, and places occupied by, other planets show the order and comparative 'motive power' of the remaining principles. The primary planet connects him with the spiritual source of his being, while the order and arrangement of the others express the stage of evolution, the capacities evolved, and in short the *Karma* of the individual. The harmonious arrangement of the planets helps towards the manifestation of the inner Life according to the lines of least resistence evolved in the past, and thus helps further the differentiation of the individual Ray. Thus several people may have the same primary planet as their natal star, yet it is the arrangement of the remaining ones that expresses their lives as individuals. This arrangement and order of the secondary planets show the Karma of the individual, show forth to a mind properly trained the physical, mental and higher potentialities as well as even the occurrences of a man's life. They are indicative as to the quality, power and capacities of the different bodies of the man, and thus help in the harmonious expression of the inner life in terms of these bodies.

" It may be noted here in passing that even in the forms of initiation by the family *Guru* prevalent amongst the Hindus, a man's horoscope is cast and the order and powers of the secondary planets are calculated ere he is given the MANTRAM. Each family has a special MANTRAM, but the form of the MANTRAM depends upon the order and arrangement of the secondary planets of the individual. Limitation as this may appear to be to many, in reality such limitations are necessary for the truest expression of the inner life ; and they further serve the Man within as instruments of growth by furnishing him with ready-made appropriate vehicles for the manifestation of the inner life.

" Thus we have got, over and above the original colouring of the Causal Body, the Body of the individual man formed of the matter of the ARUPA levels of the mental plane, the colours reflected in that body, the colours of the principles evolved by the man and the improvements in powers corresponding to the principles. As body after body disintegrates, as principle after principle is resolved into latency, the colouring matters are handed on to the Auric Egg where they remain in a latent state as karmic seeds from which will spring forth at the re-awakening of the Ego its lower principies and bodies; and hence it is that the Auric Egg is also called the Causal Body. All the powers evolved, all co-ordinations gained in an earth-life are thus preserved as colours playing through the Causal Body. The synthesis of all these when manifested in the lower planes as powers of consciousness, is what can be really and truly called the colour of the Individual— his Caste.

"A well-developed Causal Body, it may here be mentioned, is a gorgeous thing with the loveliest tints flashing through it, a thing of supernal glory ; while at the lower stages it sometimes appears as a mist, loose and unstable, with no life force manifesting—an inchoate something rather than a definite organism."

The writer goes on to say that, " Facts thus revealed by up-to-date Astrology are pregnant with momentous issues if pondered over."

He also wisely adds that " the infinite sub-divisions of castes, which we find in the India of to-day, are the result of necessities of evolution towards specialisation of the individual."

THE HINDU SUB-DIVISIONS OF THE ZODIAC

The Eastern astrologer recognises the remarkable correspondence between the various divisions of the zodiac, and the kinds of matter, and has done more to explain these divisions and sub-divisions of signs than many Western astrologers are as yet aware.

The Hindu astrologer considers the most minute division of the Lagna or rising sign, which is a certain fraction of a second in time, to be a seed cast in the cosmic soil or Ether to unfold its latent qualities, of which the individual then born is supposed to absorb more or less according to his powers of response and stage of soul evolution.

On the surface, the Hindu astrologer is apparently a fatalist, but individually he has a firm belief in free will within certain well defined limits. The very well established belief in re-incarnation and transmigration makes him a fatalist so far as the rewards and punishments of past lives are concerned, and it is to causes set in motion in a former birth that he traces the inevitable fate of the present life ; for he has a wider comprehension of the laws of Karma than the western astrologer.

There are, as already stated in previous chapters, three fundamental modes of matter and four distinct arrangements of those three modes, and this produces seven distinct types of characters. The modes of manifestation of thought, feeling, and action will be different in each type, even in similar circumstances; and this knowledge of law makes it possible to predict results from the various divisions of the Lagna, or rising sign.

The belief in fate and freewill is only partial, for a man is neither wholly fated nor wholly free, and the only way to measure the extent of his limitations is to endeavour to realise his condition of knowledge or ignorance; which, in a well organised society, would attract him to the caste or status in society to which he naturally belongs. A man with knowledge will endeavour to work with one who has power to help him, while a man who is ignorant may apply to a money lender charging a large percentage of interest, and thus make his conditions more and more hopeless.

The Hindu astrologer appears to have a remarkable knowledge of the value of sub-divisions of time and arc in connection with planetary influence. These are grouped under Trimsamsas, Dwadasamsas, Asterisms, Navamsas, Drekkanas and Horas; and they form a complete zodiac as illustrated in our diagram. (DIAGRAM III.: see Frontispiece.)

To the Hindu astrologer the heavens form the Macrocosm and man the Microcosm. Man is an exact copy of the universe, a little world or miniature of the great world around him.

Unfortunately the great difficulty of harmonising the Eastern and Western science lies in the exact measurement of the *Ayanamsa*, which is the difference between the first point of the zodiacal constellations, known as the *Nirayana Sphutam*, and the vernal equinox at the beginning of the ecliptic, known as the *Sayana Sphutam*. Hindu Astrology calculates the places of the planets in terms of the Nirayana sphutam; and the failure to measure correctly the length of the ayanamsa makes the Hindu's horoscope unreliable, when judged by the western standards. A few western astrologers have interested themselves in the attempt to apply the interpretations of the Hindu zodiac to the western system, but not with much success so far.

Now the author believes that this interpretation of the Hindu zodiac constitutes the hope of Esoteric Astrology being restored to its rightful place as a unique system of genethlialogy with methods of its own apart from the present unfavourable mixture with Horary Astrology.

Broadly speaking, in Hindu astrology there are three chief methods of classifying the zodiac and its divisions.

(1) The twenty-seven asterisms over which the Moon has chief rule ;

(2) The twelve signs and their numerous divisions over which the Sun has chief rule ;

(3) The nine planets in their relationships as rulers over the two previous classes.

In dealing with these systems of zodiacal classification, respecting which the Hindu interpretations are given, it must be remembered that, instead of starting from the supposed position of the fixed star Revati (said by some to be Zeta Piscium), we are starting from the first point of the sign Aries, from which the various degrees in the diagram have been measured.

At a first glance this diagram appears very complicated but it is in reality simple enough if looked at from the standpoint of a single sign only, and its divisions followed carefully, beginning from the centre and working towards the circumference.   Taking Aries, it will be found that this sign is divided into two halves, positive and negative, governed by the Sun and Moon.   A person born under the first 15° of Aries will be more positive than negative, more masculine than feminine, so far as this mode of expression is concerned, and the same applies if a planet occupies that sign at birth or moves into it after birth.

The positive half belongs to the centrifugal, electric, volitional, subjective, life side of manifestation ; and the negative to the centripetal, magnetic, formative, objective, and plastic side.

The sign Aries, has in the next place, three main divisions of 10° each, known as drekkanas or decanates, governed by Mars, Sun and Jupiter.

Then comes the classification according to navamsas of $3\frac{1}{3}°$ each, having the nature of the signs of the zodiac and their respective rulers.

This is followed by the asterisms, each containing $13\frac{1}{3}°$.

The next circle is that of the Dwadasamsas, wherein it is seen that a sign is divided into twelve equal portions of $2\frac{1}{2}°$ each, over each of which one of the signs of the zodiac presides with the lord of that sign, thus bringing the influence of the whole twelve signs into each one of them.

The outer circle is that of the Trimsamsas or degrees, which are considered most important. These are grouped irregularly somewhat after the fashion of the Ptolemaic " terms," and are not so easy to follow as the others. Outside the whole are found the signs with their Hindu names.

This complicated method of dividing a sign into numerous parts has induced Hindu authors to compile numerous slokas which embody in the form of aphorisms all the rules and ideas connected with each minute division of the zodiac ; but owing to the confusion caused by the various measurements of the ayanamsa mány of these slokas, particularly referring to the Lagnam and its divisions, no longer apply.

It is the hope of the genuine Hindu astrologer that his western brother will restore the ancient knowledge of the zodiac and its divisions by means of a more accurate and precise method of calculation.

The author of this work does not imagine that the constellation-zodiac can in any way directly affect human beings, except through National or Mundane Astrology, where a consideration of the constellations and an exact knowledge of the precession of the equinoxes is essential ; but in genethliacal astrology it seems to have little if any value.

The ecliptic is a reflection of the constellations considered apart from precession ; and until the ecliptic and the constellations again coincide, humanity will be involved in another of the innumerable cycles through which it is compelled to pass while on its way toward that goal of perfection which it is destined in the end to reach. By applying the Hindu system of dividing the zodiac to western methods, we may profitably add to our knowledge of its influence upon human life and destiny.

In the first place, we may reasonably utilise the division of each sign into positive or masculine and negative or feminine halves, governed by the Sun and Moon respectively. We may also accept the well tried system of decanates, but beyond these divisions we must still labour in the field of experiment.

If, accepting these important divisions of a sign into Horas and Decanates, we apply them to each degree of a sign, we shall have reduced our divisions as far as it will be safe to go at present, and even then the application will be unsafe unless the horoscope has been carefully rectified and all possibility of error in the time of birth eliminated.

There are 60' in each degree, which when divided gives 30' positive and 30' negative. Applied in the order of the signs, we shall find that the first half of the first degree of Aries is masculine and the second half feminine. The first half of the second degree will be feminine and the last half masculine ; and so on throughout the 30° of the sign Aries.

The first half of the first degree of Taurus will be feminine, and the last half of the first degree masculine ; while the first half of the second degree will be masculine, and the last half feminine, and so on. Thus we have the first half of the first degree of each positive sign masculine and the first half of each negative sign feminine throughout the zodiac.

With regard to the decanates, the first 20' of each degree will be of the nature of the sign itself and the next 20' will be of the nature of the second decanate of that sign, and the third or last 20' of the nature of the third decanate. These minute divisions, however, as previously remarked, cannot be relied upon unless the horoscope has been especially rectified ; and even then more than ordinary judgment will be necessary to understand their true value.

The astrology of the future will in all probability ascertain the exact value of each degree of the zodiac, and instead of as at present being content with the knowledge of certain degrees, every degree will be estimated at its true worth.

The value of the degrees of the zodiac taken singly and conjointly has been largely lost to astrology, and it will be the work of the investigator of the future to re-discover them and tabulate their influence for the benefit of genethliacal astrology.

WAVE LENGTHS

It will be a familiar idea to most readers that the ecliptic zodiac is the earth's aura, and that the quadruplicities, triplicities and signs are sub-divisions brought into existence by the electric, magnetic, and other subtle forces that play in the matter of that aura. We are told that there are many such forces of various orders and with diverse properties yet remaining to be discovered by science ; and it seems tolerably certain that any further sub-divisions of the zodiac as a whole or of the signs taken separately are based upon the vibrations of these forces in the etheric, astral, or other matter through which they pass.

Even the longest of these vibrations must of course be exceedingly small when compared with the whole circumference of the earth; but if a number of vibrations of differing rates pass through the zodiac together, these will be marked out into regions of harmony and discord. Where two or more rates of vibration synchronise there will be harmony, but where they clash or interfere discord will result. So that even if the matter through which these forces pass was uniform originally, it will become divided into regions varying in number and in their properties according to the nature of the forces, their rates of vibration, and the harmony or discord resulting from them.

The very minute sub-divisions of a degree are marked out by vibrations taken separately or only a few at a time. Larger sub-divisions, such as those of a sign, result from a great number of the smaller ones being grouped together and there establishing points of agreement and disagreement of their own, just as the very minute waves originally did. And when these in turn are brought together, there will be formed not merely signs but groups of signs, such as the triplicities and quadruplicities.

A few simple rates of vibration, if their numerical value were known, would therefore give us regions of space with varying properties such as we actually find in the zodiac. How many such forces will have ultimately to be taken into account we do not yet know, nor can we tell for certain how far it is practicable to divide and sub-divide signs and degrees ; but scientific theory presents us with a clear picture of vibrational nodes and internodes as not only possible but inevitable. The zodiac is a vast musical instrument, and the laws of musical harmony are observed throughout its whole extent, and will some day be correlated with the known properties of signs and planets.

The following illustration shows how sub-divisions would be made as soon as forces with varying rates of vibration were started in a previously uniform medium.

	Z	Y	X	W	V	U	T	S	R	Q	P	O
A	1	2	3	4	5	6	7	8	9	10	11	12
B	1	-	2	-	3	-	4	-	5	-	6	-
C	1	-	-	2	-	-	3	-	-	4	-	-
D	1	-	-	-	2	-	-	-	3	-	-	-
E	1	-	-	-	-	2	-	-	-	-	3	-
F	1	-	-	-	-	2	-	-	-	-	-	-

This represents six different systems of vibration of different forces. Force A travels at a certain uniform rate, and twelve of its waves are shown, signified by the numbers one to twelve along the horizontal line. Force B has a wave-length twice as long, and only six of its waves are included in the twelve of A. It harmonises with A at the vertical points marked, Z, X, V, T, R, P, but is discordant at the intermediate points. These harmonies and discords between A and B correspond to the distinction between odd and even signs.

Force C has a wave-length three times that of A, and the two agree at points Z, W, T, Q; and these points correspond to triplicities. Force C agrees with B at only two points, Z and T.

Force D has a wave-length four times that of A, and the two agree at only three points, Z, V, R, which in this diagram correspond to quadruplicities. D agrees with B also at these same points, but it is markedly inharmonious with both A and B at X, T, P.

The other two forces in the diagram, E and F, explain themselves. If the whole six forces are taken into account, four of them agree at T, which corresponds to the division of the zodiac into two halves, the northern and the southern.

If the diagram were arranged so as to represent the forces as travelling circularly and not horizontally it would symbolise the zodiac better. The number of forces also should be increased and should be represented as returning on themselves round the circle. In this way additional nodes and internodes, some of them of considerable complexity, would result, corresponding to sub-divisions of signs; but this would complicate the diagram in an undesirable manner, and a simpler representation such as this although incomplete will be easier to grasp.

It is practically certain that other sub-divisions of signs than those mentioned in the published Hindu books exist, and it is open to doubt whether those that are there given are classified correctly in all cases, especially as some of these classifications vary in the works of different authors. The division into seven parts links up with a system described in Book iii. of *The New Manual of Astrology* dealing with the Law of Sex, in which each zodiacal quadrant is divided into seven. The twenty-eight parts resulting from this coincide with the so-called Mansions of the Moon, which are referred to by some of the older authors, but which have fallen out of sight in modern works.

The whole of these sub-divisions are, in a sense, properties of the zodiac and its forces taken alone. Where any conclusion is drawn from the presence of, let us say, the ascendant in one of the sub-divisions, it is dependent upon the natural characteristics of that arc derived from the kind of force playing in it.   When in addition to this, the influence of a planet is taken into consideration the case is altered.   The vibrations of the force emanating from the planet will be either harmonious or discordant with those existing in that part of the zodiac taken alone. It will therefore follow inevitably that each planet will have its positions of strength or harmony and of weakness or discord; and that these positions for any one planet might, if the information at our disposal were sufficient, be graded in series, from perfect harmony (house) through partial harmony (exaltation, etc.) to partial discord (fall) and complete discord (detriment), according to the laws of musical harmony.

TRANSCENDING CASTE

While dealing with all the mass of detail belonging to minute divisions and sub-divisions we must not lose sight of the fact that behind the whole, the real self is an uncompounded and harmonious unit, eternally bathed in the sunshine of the Central Sun.   Caste confusion arises when the harmony within does not find its response in the outer world; or, as the Dreamer would say, when the Ego fails to discriminate between the Real and the Unreal.

In the exoteric rules of astrology we find a harmonious arrangement of the twelve houses of a nativity with the twelve signs of the zodiac and also with the planets as lords or rulers over their respective signs, and we can see how easily that harmonious arrangement is disturbed by a slight change in the arrangement.   But Exoteric Astrology utterly fails to find harmony amid the apparent inharmony of the sub-influences of signs, which seemingly adds to the confusion in disturbing the natural order of things, instead, as Esoteric Astrology seeks to show, of restoring that harmony with an added self-conscious realisation which the natural order did not impart to the individual.   It would be useless if Caste, or the various grades of society, held a man bound within its more or less rigid unwritten laws from which he could not rise by individual effort and merit. While man is developing in the early stages of his evolution Caste, or graded society, is necessary to keep him within the bounds of rightly ordered laws and customs; but when a man has become a law unto himself and has built within his own nature the desire to do right for right's sake only, then he is no longer bound to obey the rigid influence of the signs of the zodiac or, as is commonly said "his stars," but he willingly obeys those laws which he knows and understands; and consciously works with the influences he has realised as a perfect means to a perfect end.

Astrologically he has risen first above the bondage of the Cross of the twelve houses, then above the Cross of the twelve signs, and finally above the Cross of the planetary influences affecting those signs. His Sun now shines gloriously radiant, illuminating the Path before him, and no longer thrown back to him as a reflected light, for he has become that Sun, and shines now upon others to illuminate the dark places of doubt and despair which he has trodden himself. The Christ is born within him; matter no longer binds him; he is free, and seeks the way to triumph over life as he has formerly triumphed over death.

CHAPTER V

THE HOUSES AND THEIR IMPORTANCE

Know ye not that ye are the temple of God, and that the Spirit of God dwelleth in you ? If any man defileth the temple of God him shall God destroy, for the temple of God is holy, which temple ye are.

THE twelve houses are important because they have a more direct bearing upon the fate and fortune in the outer world, the Karma of the current life, than have the zodiacal signs or the planets when considered apart from the houses. The houses may be compared with the physical body, and planetary positions in the signs with the inner man, who inhabits that body. Zodiacal position from this point of view becomes highly important because it shows the powers and possibilities of the inner man, his capacities, his strong and weak faculties ; and yet in actual practice this is subordinate to position in the houses.

Whether the soul is strong or weak, wise or foolish, savage or civilised, it can accomplish nothing on this plane unless it possesses a physical body through which to act. This is certainly true of the average man ; for when disembodied he is so completely unable to prove his survival of the death of the body that large numbers of people doubt whether there is anything that survives, and whether the body itself is not the real man. It is equally true even if we take into account the phenomena of spiritualism and super-normal interventions into human affairs generally. In these cases either the disembodied being borrows the body of some living physical person, or he is able to gather round himself enough of the matter of this world to serve as a temporary body, and not until then can he perform physical actions.

Planetary position in the signs, therefore, while highly significant of inner powers and characteristics, is not necessarily equally important with regard to events and happenings in the outer world. This does not mean that such events are never signified by sign-position but only that they are not so inevitable as is house-position. For instance, if the Moon is in the seventh house in a man's horoscope, well aspected, and if nothing else contradicts, marriage is as nearly certain as anything can be; but if the Moon is in the seventh sign instead of the seventh house, marriage cannot be predicted with so much confidence, even if the aspects are the same. The man may wish to marry and may be suited for living happily in that state, but the sign-position will not have the inevitability of the house-position; and before a definite prediction is made, the influence of any planet in the seventh house should be noted, or, when there is none, the position of the lord of the seventh with relation to the Moon, Venus, and the ruler of the ascendant.

This distinction between signs and houses, however, varies somewhat according to the age of the soul, its position in its evolutionary career. As stated elsewhere, the youngest souls are now the most deeply immersed in body and are, therefore, the most subject to the influence of house-position; for the twelve houses correspond to the dense physical body, which, when taken only as body, may be that of a savage or a saint, an idiot or a genius, and the houses signify the body of the one as much as they do that of the other. In the case of the young and unevolved soul, house-position will be almost all-important, and a malefic or benefic influence will work itself out with practical certainty. In the case of the strong and highly evolved character, a genius of some kind or a saint, the circumstances will be more or less reversed. His strength of character or greatness of soul is much more likely to be signified by positions and aspects in the signs than by those in the houses. House-position will still enter into the problem even with him, but it will show how far the body is adapted to act as a vehicle for this type of soul, and how far the karma of the current life helps or hinders the inner powers of the soul; it will not exercise so much restriction and limitation, there will not be so much inevitability, as in the case of the younger soul.

The planets apart from signs and houses represent the individual spiritual man considered apart from both the temporary personality and the physical body. Those who have attained to the superman stage of evolution, who have passed one or more of the great initiations, will come more under the direct influence of the planets and will exhibit planetary characteristics apart from both signs and houses; although even these, when descending into manifestation, will have to take upon themselves zodiacal soul-vestures and mundane bodies, and must submit to some extent to the natural limitations. In such a case the sign-positions will show what soul powers have been incarnated in the

personality, and the house-positions will show the kind of work that has
been undertaken and the environment within which it has to be accomplished; for the body is adapted to and is a mirror of the world in which
it moves and the use to which it has to be put.   Here the position of the
planet to which the soul belonged would be the predominant factor, the
centre and heart of the whole, and all the rest would be subordinated to
this; body, events, and character would all alike be " ruled " by the
spirit within.

There are thus three stages of evolution.   The young and inexperienced soul is under the dominion of the twelve houses and can do
little but submit to the conditions they impose.   The stronger and more
experienced soul has a character and faculties of his own, indicated by
sign-position mainly; although the zodiacal signs pertain to every type
of soul and show all its moods and phases, from the animal to the highly-
evolved human.   Finally the planets apart from the signs represent the
super-human stage of evolution.

A horoscope is thus a blending of spirit, soul, and body, and the
twelve houses are the physical expression of the whole.

CLASSIFICATION OF THE HOUSES

Turning now to the classification of the houses, it is to be noticed
that they fall into three-fold and four-fold groups corresponding exactly
to the zodiacal signs.

Cardinal or Angular	Fixed or Succedent	Mutable or Cadent
I, IV, VII, X	II, V, VIII, XI	III, VI, IX, XII

Fire	Earth	Air	Water
I, V, IX	II, VI, X	III, VII, XI	IV, VIII, XII

It is rather strange that while the terms cardinal, fixed and mutable,
when applied to the houses are called angular, succedent, and cadent, no
substitutes for the terms fire, earth, air, and water have been proposed
for the houses, so that these four names have to be employed for signs
and houses alike.

In addition to these two groups there is also the obvious distinction
between the day and night halves of the circles; for the Sun rises on the
cusp of the ascendant, the eastern horizon, and sets on the cusp of the
seventh house, the western horizon ; so that the houses from the twelfth
round to the seventh belong to the day, and the remainder to the night.

The ascendant, although technically a part of the dark half, is included usually in the day because it is the house of morning twilight. These day and night halves divide the circle into two by the horizonal diameter, the line of the horizon.

Running across this is another two-fold classification, that of the rising and setting halves of the circle of the heavens. The cusp of the fourth house, or nadir, or midnight point is the lowest part of the circle, and the cusp of the tenth house, or zenith, or noon point is the highest. Any heavenly body moving from the fourth to the tenth is passing from a lower position to a higher, and in this sense is rising. Any heavenly body passing from the tenth to the fourth is going from a higher position to a lower, and in this sense is setting.

The day half of the circle is that of manifestation, unveiling, bringing to light, creation, openness, publicity, power, manvantara; and the night half is that of concealment, latency, withdrawal, dissolution, pralaya.

The eastern or rising half of the circle is that of Self, egoism, its increase, individualisation, separation from others, evolution, the gain of powers or faculties; and the western or setting half is that of Others, the rest of the world whether taken as friends or as enemies, union, decrease of Self, involution, altruism.

When these two diameters are taken both at the same time, there is formed the well known cross in the circle, dividing it into four quadrants. This is the foundation of the whole horoscope, in fact it might almost be said that this really is the horoscope and that the remaining eight houses are mere sub-divisions. How clearly these four parts of the circle possess the properties and characteristics attributed to them can be seen by examining their relation to the apparent motion of the Sun in its rising and setting.

The cusp of the ascendant is the point of sunrise; the cusp of the tenth, that of noon; the cusp of the seventh house, that of sunset; and the cusp of the fourth, that of midnight. Three out of these four points are concerned with day; namely sunrise, when day begins; noon, the middle of day and the point of fullest manifestation; and sunset, when day ends. The remaining point marks the middle of the night, and this is in a sense that out of which the other three emerge and come forth during the manifestation of day, and into which they return again when day ends and night resumes it sway. So that of the four points, one which is always hidden is the source of the other manifested three; and the four may be divided into a manifested three and a hidden synthetic one.

When the Sun is at the midnight point, darkness reigns over the world, the activities of day are at an end, and typically all men sleep. In the actual world, of course, especially in busy centres of human life, activities of some sort are going on during every hour of the twenty-four ; nevertheless this period obviously corresponds, cosmically, to pralaya, before a solar system has come into existence or after it has passed out of existence, while individually it indicates the similar state of unmanifestation before the soul has been born in a body in this physical world or after it has passed away at the death of that body. In terms of the lunar changes it corresponds to New Moon, when the satellite of our earth is invisible, withdrawn from manifestation, the middle of the " dark fortnight."

When the Sun is rising, day and its activities begin. Here the correspondence with the coming into existence of a solar system and the birth of a human being are too obvious to need dwelling upon. Something that before was latent is now becoming manifest. This is the angle of Self, the separate centre round which all subsequent experiences, actions, feelings, and cognitions gather. The *Pranava Vada* informs us that in terms of the Hindu sacred word Aum, sunrise corresponds to the letter A, the Self, and cognition ; and as the ascendant or first house is associated with the first sign Aries, with fire, and the mental plane, this is appropriate.

At noon the activities of day are at their busiest and fullest, the point of fullest possible manifestation has been reached, and there is an obvious analogy with the middle period in the life of a solar system, with the fourth globe of a chain, and the fourth race. The Self is putting forth its powers to the utmost as a separate being, and its capacities which were only possibilities in the beginning have now become actualities. The correspondence here is with the letter U, the Not-self, and with action; and astrologers will note that the tenth house signifies occupation, that is to say action in the outer world and the culmination of the powers of the individual. The earthy sign Capricorn, belonging to the physical plane and action, comes here.

At sunset the activities of the day are about to end. The Sun is now at the middle point of that decline which began as soon as the noon point was passed. The period of manifestation is ending and that of quiescence and cessation of activity is beginning. The Self, which was separate at sunrise and at noon, here loses its separateness and becomes indissolubly associated with and merged in others, and in doing so acquires characteristics and faculties appropriate to that state for good or evil; that is to say love and hate, friendship and emnity, and all the emotional and intuitional powers that are associated with these are called forth. This is the angle of Others, and it corresponds with the letter M, with the relation between Self and Not-Self, and with desire in the personality or buddhic consciousness in the individuality.

Although these four points have here been referred to the Sun, the same principles apply to the rising, culminating, and setting of any other of the heavenly bodies. When any planet rises, it comes out into manifestation as a separate self; when it culminates it is in the most prominent position possible and is at the middle period of manifestion; when it sets its separateness is lessening and union is beginning; and when it is on the lower meridian it is completely withdrawn from manifestation.

This fourfold division of the circle gives the four triplicities of fire, earth, air, and water. When the equilateral triangle is inscribed within the circle, the three quadruplicities of Cardinal or rajasic signs, Fixed or tamasic signs, and Mutable or sattvic signs result. This classification as applied to sub-divisions of the day is not so familiar, and for the most part is used as a mere sub-division of the fourfold system, by which each quadrant is divided into three parts, giving the twelve houses in all. The division of the day into three periods, apart from its use by King Alfred the Great, was actually employed by the ancient Egyptian magicians, however, and a short account of it is given in Dr. E. W. Budge's *Egyptian Magic*. Experience shows that parts of the heavens that are in mundane trine with each other, or that are situated at the points of an equilateral triangle, have many properties in common and that this classification is a reality.

The three points of this triangle with their correspondences must not be confused with the manifested points of the cross. There is a temptation so to confuse them, and in some respects there actually is an analogy. If instead of representing the day and the night as two halves of the circle, each were represented as a complete circle in itself, the analogy would be complete, and sunrise, noon, and sunset would form a triangle similar to that of the quadruplicities and with similar correspondences. As things are, however, especially in practical astrology, midnight is a fourth point which forms a cross when joined to the points of sunrise, noon, and sunset, so that the latter are three angles of a square and they do not form an equilateral triangle as do the quadruplicities.

The three quadruplicities are also subtler than the four triplicities; for the latter correspond to fire, earth, air, and water, which are states of matter, all fully manifested and objective; whereas the triangle corresponds rather to qualities and modes of motion, to things abstract rather than things concrete, to the soul rather than the body, even though in this world that soul is always manifested in a body. The triangle is a group of three, and the unity or synthesis of them makes in a sense a fourth; but this is entirely different from the cross in which the fourth, although also in a sense the source and ultimate of the other three, is only another point within the same circle, distinct from each of them. In short, the one carries with it the symbolism of the ternary and the other that of the quaternary.

The Influence of the Houses

The four Angular houses I, IV, VII, X, come first in importance in a horoscope; indeed they are so much the essential part of the map that the other houses, as previously remarked, look like little more than subdivisions of these four. The influence of the angles is similar to that of the cardinal signs; they are concerned with making manifest and concrete, with bringing out into the open, unveiling and manifesting whatever may be latent in the personality and everything that is denoted by the signs and planets connected with the angles.

The four houses that are classed as angles are not all on an equality in this respect, however. We have already seen that the day half of the map, including the ascendant, has to do with bringing out of latency into manifestation; and that the houses below the earth tend to veil, preserve, protect, hide, and retain in latency. But the secrecy and reservation surrounding the lower houses is only relative, not absolute, because they are all concerned with various activities of life; their quiescence is not that of total unconsciousness. Generally speaking each house in the night half of the map reflects its opposite in the day half, so that the two become complementary; the first and the seventh, the second and the eighth, the third and the ninth, and so on.

Of the angles, the ascendant and mid-heaven are the most potent and active, and it is scarcely an exaggeration to say that everything signified by planets in those houses must inevitably be expressed in some way and cannot be avoided.   Hence planets in these two angles denote what may be called a typical life from the astrological point of view, that is a life that neither greatly exceeds the average through unusual will-power or rapidly maturing genius, nor falls short of it in any remarkable degree through weakness or inexperience.   There are some cases in which an unusual fate is to be experienced rapidly and the life is filled with incident to an abnormal extent, but these we pass by for the time, and the above generalisation refers to ordinary persons.

The seventh house is nearly as open, prominent, and inevitable as the first and tenth, although to a less extent ; and whereas Self, in some sense, dominates both the latter houses, the experiences of the seventh come through Others.   It may be said to be between latency and activity, and the same is true in a much greater degree of the fourth house, relating as it does to such matters as home, domesticity, parentage, old age, seclusion ;   nevertheless they both usually bring forth into activity that which they denote.

The first house is quite personal in its influence and depends upon the strength of the Individuality behind it to give expression to its powers. Self, in either the restricted or the enlarged sense, is dominant here.   The same is true of the tenth house, but here a wider field is provided for the utilisation of the talents of the Self.   The seventh is connected more with experiences related to the Not-self, taken in the sense of Others ; friends, partners, associates, all whose interests are blended with those of the native, whether in love or hate, help or rivalry ; and experiences gained through this angle come quite as much through actions started by Others as through those begun by Self.   The fourth house may be said in a sense to be neither personal nor individual, for here separation tends to be lost or obscured ;   in the young or weak soul because of the lack of strength to break through the bonds, and in stronger souls through voluntary submission to the needs of others.

These four angles are directly connected with the physical and external world, and represent outgoing activities originating in the Self but affecting the Not-self very directly.   They generally show the nature of things that must be openly expressed, and therefore denote the fame, reputation, public position, and general activities more clearly and definitely than any of the other houses.

The Succedent houses, II, V, VIII, XI, are connected with desire, feeling, emotion, and with the guna tamas. They are not so open, expressive, and full of action as the angles ; they are less on the surface and also very much less changeful. Experiences and characteristics based upon planets in these houses tend to continue unchanged or with the minimum of alteration for long periods, sometimes all through the life. Faults of character that arise out of planets here are far harder to over-come than in the case of the angles, and the good qualities are never lost. Evil aspects to the hyleg from these houses have more serious effects upon health, and cause diseases that are long lasting and intractable ; but good aspects give great power to resist disease.

The second and fifth houses are rather more conservative and their effects are somewhat less open than are the eighth and eleventh, these two latter showing desire more externalised in action.

The Cadent houses, III, VI, IX, XII, are mental and show how thought guides and directs both action and desire. Events that are denoted by these houses taken alone are based upon and originate in cognition rather than feeling or action. The state of the native's mind is concerned here, the workings of his thought, and his power of mental response. These houses are somewhat lacking in initiative and are at their best when working under a superior or when obeying the will of another, although the natives do not always realise this and are sometimes inclined to resent it and to endeavour to grasp power and authority for themselves, but they are not at their best or most fortunate when they do so. The third and the ninth are the most definitely intellectual and also the most positive ; they give many and varied interests, sometimes two or more lines of activity carried on at the same time, and mental versatility. The sixth and the twelfth houses relate more to workers and occupations carried on in connection with masses of people ; they are also more quiet, reserved, slow-moving, and less ambitious and independent ; events that arise out of them are either personal and private or are often surrounded with mystery and secrecy.

These divisions of the heavens, angular, succedent and cadent in their direct analogy with action, desire and cognition have a special interest for those who understand the law of action and re-action, or karma, and who accept the theory of reincarnation, since they reveal the conditions through which each person has to work out his own destiny.

The rapidly moving Moon and the energetic, impulsive Mars are the two most characteristic heavenly bodies that belong to the cardinal angular cross, although in saying this it must not be supposed that they rule the quadruplicity in any restricted and limited sense, for that is not the case. Any planet whatever may be acted upon and influenced by Rajas, if placed in one of these four houses, and the nearer it is to the cusps of the houses, the four points of the cross, the stronger will be the influence brought to bear upon it and manifested through it. The characteristics of this cross are—rapidity of motion, frequency of change, restlessness, separation, individualisation, and many other features that follow of necessity from these and that vary according as to whether they are used wisely and unwisely, for good or for evil.

The fixed succedent cross marks off one angle of the base of each of the four triangles, namely those which form the cusps or first points of the second, fifth, eighth and eleventh houses and signs. The Sun and Saturn are typical members of this fixed quadruplicity, the characteristics of which are :—fixedness, slowness of motion, infrequency of change, self-centredness, strength to resist outside influences, will-power, tenacity and steadfastness. Like all other powers these can be used either for good or for evil, and they vary according as they act through fire, air, water, or earth.

The common cadent cross marks off the second angle of the base of each of the four triangles, namely those which form the cusps or first points of the third, sixth, ninth and twelfth houses and signs. Mercury and Jupiter are the two planets that have rule here. The characteristics of this quadruplicity are rhythmical motion, adjustment, balance, transference of force, the establishment of relations, order, coherence, the shaping of form, the building of vehicles, the drawing together of otherwise separate units, whether in matter or in consciousness.

THE RELATION OF SIGNS AND PLANETS TO HOUSES

Having grasped the idea that the houses are the concrete expression of life in the physical body, it will be readily understood that their natural significance and strength can be either increased or lessened according to whether the signs and planets are similar in nature to the houses in which they fall, or the contrary.

Any sign may fall on the cusp of any house, but for our present purpose it is sufficient to confine the attention to the three crosses or quadruplicities, in regard to which the following table shows the possible number of variations.

Angles	Succedents	Cadents
Cardinal	Fixed	Mutable
Fixed	Mutable	Cardinal
Mutable	Cardinal	Fixed

Cardinal signs on angles will considerably increase the tendency to activity, mental or physical, or both; will bring the native before the public for good or ill through his own doings, his own self-expression. Should the majority of planets be here also, a life of extreme activity and full of interests and varied experiences will result; but if the aspects are malefic there will be much strife and contention, rivalry and opposition, friends lost, ties broken, and enemies made.

Fixed signs on angles bring desire forward into activity; states of consciousness motived by desire pass outward into action, and it must be remembered that the word desire includes an almost endless series of feelings and emotions, high and low, simple and complex. In addition, there will be manifested the aversion to change, and the display of more or less obstinacy, steadfastness, rigidity, conservatism, or indolence, that are characteristic of this quadruplicity.

Mutable signs on angles indicate that cognition and action are being brought into touch; actions are performed from motives that originate in thought rather than in feeling; and there will be displayed features that belong to this class, dualism in thought or feeling or action, adaptability, the judicial attitude, indifference, and so on.

The man of action, whose thoughts and feelings are chiefly concerned with practical results in the outer world, finds easier expression if cardinal signs are on the angles. An organiser, a statesman, a merchant, a philanthropist would benefit more by coming under fixed signs. A writer, a clerk, a publisher, an editor, a traveller, a divine, a physician, a nurse, will be best if associated with mutable signs on angles.

In all these cases planetary positions are highly important. If they corroborate the indications of the rising sign the horoscope will be greatly intensified, but when the two contradict each other the result may either be a blend of both or the planetary quadruplicity may outweigh the ascendant in importance.

It is not necessary to consider here all the combinations that can be brought about. Cardinal signs and angles are more directly concerned with events and happenings in the outer world that seem either very self-initiated or else inevitable.   Fixed signs and succedent houses have more to do with desire or will and the movement towards action.   Mutable signs and cadent houses have more bearing upon thoughts than upon actions.

Signs and planets that were in succedent or cadent houses at birth are more or less latent in the early years of life, and they pass outward into action as they progress towards the angles by the directional motion of the horoscope.

This makes the angles the most important part of the map from the outward point of view, and perhaps the most desirable also until we realise that actions produce environment, ill as well as good.   This may be illustrated by watching the two extremes shown by Saturn, the planet of limitation and resistance.   One man with Saturn rising may treat all difficulties and obstacles as opportunities for the exercise of his will and resourcefulness, and by exhibiting the virtues of patience and perseverance may achieve success and honour.   Another man, resenting his limitations and brooding over his wrongs, may allow himself to be checked and thwarted, and will sink into depression and despair.   Character, as shown by zodiacal position and aspects will account for these differences. Opportunities for action will come to both, but the attitude of mind will decide the use that will be made of them.

The following classification of signs is based upon suggestions contained in the *Pranava Vada*.

Self	*Not-Self*	*Relation*	*Summation*
ARIES	TAURUS	GEMINI	CANCER
LEO	VIRGO	LIBRA	SCORPIO
SAGITTARIUS	CAPRICORN	AQUARIUS	PISCES

Let us conclude by emphasising that there are two chief ways in which the signs and houses may be classified.   They may be regarded as consisting of three crosses, or four triangles.   When taken as four triangles, these are compared with the four so-called elements or states of matter, earth, water, air and fire ; giving the triangle of fire with its apex to the east, that of air with its apex to the west, that of earth with its apex at the zenith, and that of water with its apex at the nadir—an idea which is further elaborated in our next Chapter.

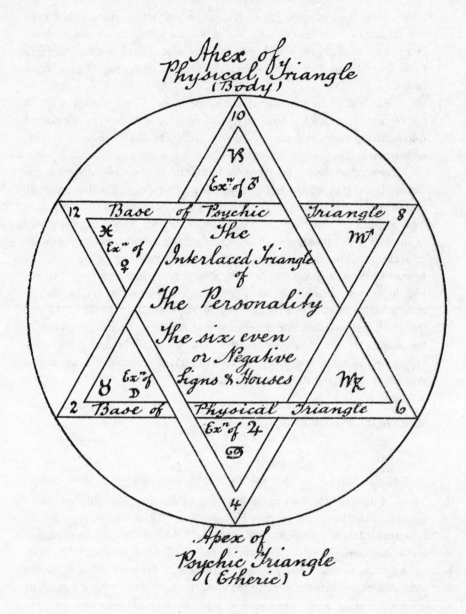

DIAGRAM IV

CHAPTER VI

THE HOUSES (*Continued*)

THE Virgins of Light have their clothing in (i) Kingdom, (ii) Wisdom, (iii) Victory, (iv) Persuasion, (v) Purity, (vi) Truth, (vii) Confidence, (viii) Patience, (ix) Frankness, (x) Goodness, (xi) Justice, (xii) Light. These twelve virgins correspond to the twelve signs of the zodiac.

IN the present Chapter we shall pursue the subject on the same general lines as in the former, but with special attention to the practical application of the ideas there put forth.

From a geometrical point of view each horoscope may be regarded as composed of four interlaced triangles, the apex of a triangle appearing at each of the four points of the cross in the circle.

The Earthy Triangle has its apex in the tenth house, and its base from the second to the sixth. This is the purely physical division representing fame, honour, reputation and the whole of the physical or bodily well being; its limitations are worldly renown and either world-wide fame or notoriety. It represents through the second house, physical possessions, wealth and the accumulation of money; and through the sixth house, work, employment, food, servants and service of all kinds.

The Watery Triangle, representing the psychic and emotional nature, has its apex in the fourth house, the house of the home, infancy, feeling, the reception of sensations and all psychic experiences. It has its base from the eighth to the twelfth house; the eighth representing the generative and re-generative tendencies, the fixing of feelings and the influence of others, and the twelfth representing purification of emotions, realisation through feelings, and self-undoing through the misuse of personal feelings.

The Fiery Triangle has its apex in the first house, the house of the brain and mental outlook, and has its base from the fifth to the ninth house. These houses are said to represent the past (5th), the present (1st), and the future (9th). This is owing to the mental states represented by them; the fifth, Fixed-Fire or inherited mental qualities—past karma; the first, the house of the new and unformed mind, liable to change like the quality of rajas, Cardinal-Fire; and the ninth, the house of that which

57

is to be, Mutable Fire.   The ninth therefore shows the introspections, aspirations towards the future, and the possibilities of the higher mind. Apart from the houses, the rulers of the fiery triplicity of signs denote this; the Sun, ruler of the fifth sign Leo, representing the accumulated character of the past, the Individuality; Mars ruler of the first sign Aries, the present Personality; and Jupiter, ruler of the ninth, philosophy and the storing of the fruit of this life in the aura and as future Karma.

The Airy Triangle has its apex in the seventh house, the house of union, perception and refinement.   It is the triangle of Intuition and has its base from the eleventh to the third, the houses of Reason and Memory.

The interlacing of the triangles denotes that they are complements or counterparts.   In those nativities where the sign Aries rises at birth, the signs will follow in the same order as their corresponding houses; in other horoscopes, however, some difficulty may arise in interpreting the signs at the apex of each triangle.

The simplest and least complex horoscopes will be chiefly those in which Aries rises at birth, but secondarily those in which any fiery sign rises.   They become more complicated when other signs are found upon the ascendant, the most complex being those in which Libra rises, for Libra inverts the natural correspondence of signs and houses more completely than does any other sign ; it brings the naturally western influence into the east, and carries the fiery Self of Aries into the altruistic Other-self of the seventh house.

THE INTERLACED TRIANGLES OF THE PERSONALITY

In Diagram IV. the interlacing of the physical and psychic triangles is illustrated, showing the houses with the signs naturally corresponding to them.   In cases where Aries is on the first house, Taurus on the second, and so on, in regular order, the houses and signs agree quite regularly.   In cases where the signs and houses do not coincide in this order, the houses permanently represent these triangles; the tenth, second and sixth, representing the physical, and the fourth, twelfth and eighth the psychic. Planets in these houses are affected by, and operate on, the planes represented by them.

The apex of the physical triangle is the tenth house; this represents the summarised physical conditions; and that part of the physical body ruled by the sign upon the cusp of the tenth will be the most sensitive, for it represents the critical or turning-point of the life currents. Planets in this house have a more or less independent action, and are less subject to the sign they are in, than any other house. This rule is modified when planets are in the first or seventh house, and more so still when any are in the fourth, for the angular position of the planets is freer from sign influence than is the case with the other houses.

The Sun has much strength in the tenth, and gives abundance of life. It blends the influence of the first with that of the tenth, because the Sun is exalted in Aries, the normal first house sign. The Moon in the tenth blends the influence of the second with the tenth, because the Moon is exalted in Taurus, the normal second house sign, showing fame and money. By similar reasoning it will easily be deduced that Mercury in the tenth blends the sixth with the tenth house influence; Venus in the tenth blends the twelfth with the tenth; Mars in the tenth blends the eighth with the tenth; and Saturn in the tenth blends the seventh with the tenth. Uranus in the tenth increases the flow of nervous fluids through the body, and denotes a strong mental magnetism, while Neptune in the tenth accentuates the personal physical conditions.

The second and sixth houses are dependent upon the tenth for expression, and, if not supported by a good tenth house influence, produce an indifferent Karma so far as the physical and outer expressions are concerned. This will not apply when the signs and houses agree in regular order.

The fourth house is the apex of the psychic triangle.

The magnetic forces in the body are polarised either upwards or downwards. Life and all outward expression of force and vitality stream upwards to the apex of the physical triangle, and life indrawn, or all internal tendencies, manifesting through feeling and emotion, stream downward through the apex of the psychic triangle. In other words, the tenth is the electric pole, and the fourth is the magnetic pole of the life currents streaming through the body.

From this it will be seen that greater physical activity goes on through the tenth, second and sixth houses, and greater psychic energy is poured through the fourth, twelfth and eighth houses.

These triangles are the objective and subjective manifestations of the two states of being, and they represent the two halves of the human being in the two sexes, the male and female elements interblended.

In any nativity where the earthy signs appear on the physical

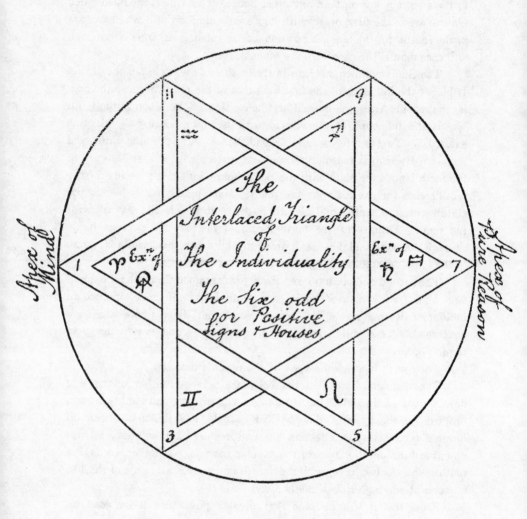

DIAGRAM V

triangle, in whatever order, there will be a harmonious expression of force on the physical plane. The same applies to the watery signs and the psychic plane.

Mars exalted in Capricorn and the Moon in Taurus in the physical triangle show that they have affinity with the purely physical mode of life, and generally denote a harmonious blending of the physical with the etheric sheath. In the case of the Moon, ruler of the psychic triad, the physical and the astral are shown to be well knit together, and not easily separated; a strong physical heredity is denoted, and usually the fact that family ties are strong and not easily broken. It generally gives a well-balanced personality.

The exaltation of Mars denotes that the body will not be easily dissolved.

Planets in the fourth house affect the psychic triangle. Saturn, to a certain extent, is inimical to it, tending to make it too concrete and too much affected by physical conditions. Mercury and Uranus are not well placed here, the nervous system being too sensitive. Mars here is not good for health, being disruptive and disintegrative. Jupiter having exaltation in the fourth sign is favourable here, giving expansion and fullness. It will be noted that the benefic planets Jupiter and Venus are the strongest in this triangle, both having sympathy with the emotional and psychic nature.

THE INTERLACED TRIANGLES OF THE INDIVIDUALITY

In Diagram V. we have the interlacing of the higher and lower mental triads. They are concerned more with the individual, and represent the objective and subjective states of the mind, also the masculine and feminine expression of the human being.

The first house is the apex of the mental body or the mind, as it manifests through the brain. The triangle itself may be said to represent so much mind-stuff, which receives its colouring from the signs at its apex and base.

The houses show the flow of the mind stuff, limited by the brain and its ramifications. It is primarily affected by the self in the first house, is expressed in generation through the fifth, and as creation through the ninth. The planets in these houses have a direct influence upon the mind of the native; the Sun in the first illuminating the mind in the brain, in the fifth giving much generative force, and in the ninth stimulating the creative faculties; for the Sun gives life to whatever triangle it occupies. The Moon in either of these houses gives a psychic type of mind, and increases mental receptivity.   Uranus gives originality to the mind, and Neptune makes it dreamy.   Jupiter expands it, Saturn contracts it, and Venus refines it, while Mars tends to make it assertive and forceful. Any of the fiery signs coming in the order of this triangle favours the mind in its normal evolution.   It has a subordinate affinity with the airy signs, but not with the earthy or watery.

The airy triplicity having its apex in the seventh house is concerned with the higher or spiritual mind.   It is the triangle of refinement and unity and is more directly connected with the Higher Ego than any of the other triangles.   While intertwined with the fiery triplicity, it represents the subjective and objective types of mind, the one re-acting upon the other.   It has a sub-affinity with the watery triangle, but little, if any, with the earthy.

The airy triplicity has more affinity with Uranus than with any other planet and Saturn has its exaltation in Libra, the apex sign of this triangle.   When the concretions of the lower mind are dissolved, the individuality of every human being is weighed in the balance of Libra, the sign in which the personality is finally merged into the individuality.

CHAPTER VII

THE ZODIAC ESOTERICALLY CONSIDERED

THE descent and re-ascent of the Soul cannot be disconnected from the zodiacal signs, and it seems more in accord with the fitness of things to believe in a mysterious sympathy between the metaphysical soul and the bright constellations, and in the influence of the stars upon that soul than in the absurd notion that the creators of Heaven and Earth have placed in Heaven the types of twelve Jewish tribes.   *Secret Doctrine.*

IN Esoteric Astrology the zodiac is the boundary line of the earth's sphere of influence, and the picture gallery of what is known as the astral light, the subtle form of existence at the base of our material universe. In this astral light the whole of the world's history is pictorially represented, from the beginning to the end of its cycle, and the zodiac is the synthesis of the world's substance in which the record of all events, past, present, and future, are preserved and retained as the eternal memory. It is the book of life that is read on Judgment Day. The esoteric zodiac is, therefore, a sensitive plate forming a link between the subjective and objective sides of nature, connecting Heaven and Earth, or spirit and matter.

Although the zodiac is the Astrologer's Alphabet, from which he obtains the words of power to interpret his astrological symbolism, it is a circle of mystery more profound than the planets. The vital importance of the zodiac has long been established, and its nature is so far revealed as to leave no doubt concerning its influence upon human life and destiny. It is said, however, that the key to unlock the mysteries of the zodiac has to be turned seven times, and the truth of this statement is obvious when we know that each sign is an ideograph, a number, a colour, a tone, etc., the whole combined representing nature's perfect sounding board.

Mathematically the zodiac is one in the completeness of its circle, but in its inherent nature it is divisible. It is the womb of the earthly

universe in which the germ of the eternal substance is placed, and out of
which all forms and shapes are born, each character containing within it
an essential quality from the sign of its birth.

Just as the Sun's rays illuminate and vitalise each degree of the zodiac,
so do the rays of the Monad passing into the womb of the earthly
universe, give to each Ego its own peculiar tone and colouring ; and
although those rays are eternally pure and immaculate, they become
attached to forms or vehicles of expression, which, absorbing other
tones and colourings, produce confusion for the Ego, thus leading him
into conditions that account for the peculiar nature of his destiny.

Each individualised self coming into separate existence is a pure ray
of the Divine Light, enclosed in a colourless film of immaculate substance.   It is a seed cast into the phenomenal worlds, in order that it
may grow like unto the Father in Heaven.   Before, however, it can
reach these worlds, this seed must pass through one of those rays that are
directly connected with the Lords of the zodiacal signs, for without this
connecting link no intelligent ingress can be made into the earthly
universe.   These rays are known as the "Sons of Mind," each having a
particular sound and colour which they impart to the individuals under
their protection and guidance.   They are the eternal links between spirit
and matter, and through these Sons of Mind man has derived his
thinking principle.   Man's spiritual heredity is therefore derived from
those seven Lords of Light who are the seven spirits before the throne of
God, and they guide him, through the influence of the seven planets, to
the sign under which he is born.   In essence, as a " Divine Fragment,"
man's spirit comes down from the plane of the Logos with His possibilities unexpressed.   Through the agency of the Divine Rays he draws
around the spirit on the upper mental plane matter to express himself,
and thus creates as his vehicle a causal body, having within it the
primary colouring of the Father in Heaven.   Within this causal body
evolves the Ego, the consciousness in man, which knows itself as " I am
I " ; and from this causal body a ray is cast into the physical body at birth,
known in the physical world as the Personality.

On the physical plane we view man as a composite being of Spirit,
Soul and Body.

The Spirit of man is a centre in the universal consciousness—a unit
of consciousness.

The soul of man is spiritual, human or animal, according to the plane or quality of matter with which his consciousness is, for the time being, identifying itself.

The body of man is the vehicle with which he directly contacts the plane upon which he is functioning; thus, to express himself on the physical plane he requires a solid physical body, on the Soul plane an astral body, and on the Spiritual plane, a refined, or pure mind body.

It is these bodies or vehicles of consciousness that we trace in the zodiacal signs, the physical body being the vehicle on the physical plane for the expression of all that can be manifested through it of the subtler or more refined states of consciousness; for every human being is in essence divine. It is, therefore, a question of individual unfoldment through a variety of forms, in which temperament and quality of matter play their most vital and important part.

The divisibility of the zodiac provides a choice of suitable vehicles for every conceivable type of Ego, and although the fundamental principles are the same for all, each individual has plenty of scope, within certain limitations, to express himself freely where method is concerned. He has much longitude within a certain latitude, so to speak.

These fundamental principles are allied to the Will, Wisdom and Activity aspects of consciousness and have their lines of least resistance for expression in the worlds of form, through the fixed, mutable and cardinal signs respectively; each sign belonging to these qualities having a sevenfold expression, thus producing innumerable sub-influences. These signs of quality also give to each body its stability, flexibility, and responsive power. They compose the three main quadruplicities of the zodiac, out of which the four triplicities of elements are formed. It is through these seven distinct groups that each simple zodiacal sign, as an ideograph, colour, sound or number, obtains its greatest complexity. This complexity begins when the circle of the zodiac is divided into two halves of positive and negative signs, forming, by their alternating positions, the two great dragons of life and form indissolubly entwined.

Each sign, positive or negative, is an ideograph of enormous importance in unravelling the secrets of nature when its hieroglyphic is correctly interpreted, and it is with these inner interpretations that Esoteric Astrology is chiefly concerned. The tones and colours are related to the triple arrangements of signs, primarily in the Cardinal, Fixed and Mutable signs, producing violet, indigo, and blue, respectively, with green as the middle colour; and these, reversed again,

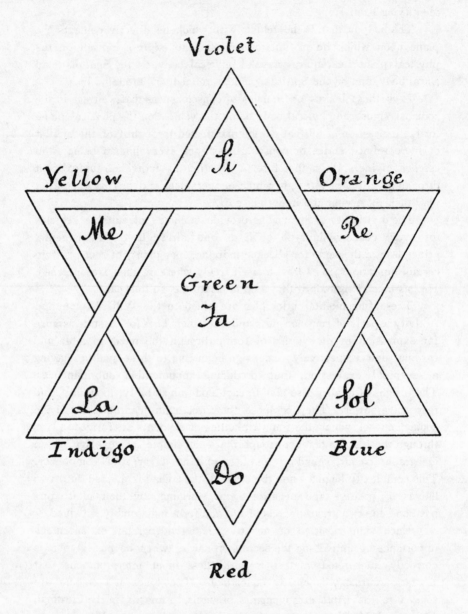

DIAGRAM VI

produce the Mutable, Fixed and Cardinal triplicities, yellow, orange and red : (DIAGRAM VI). The tones are in the same order, but as numbers are interchangeable according to the rising sign at any given moment, there is no *direct* order in which they can be placed. We may tabulate this arrangement for future reference as follows :

Sign	Characteristics	Colour	Tone
♈	Intuition	Red[1]	Do
♉	Secretion	Indigo	La
♊	Reason	Yellow[1]	Mi
♋	Feeling	Violet	Si
♌	Faith	Orange	Re
♍	Circulation	Yellow	Mi
♎	Perception	Indigo[1]	La
♏	Attachment	Red	Do
♐	Introspection	Blue[1]	Sol
♑	Absorption	Green	Fa
♒	Memory	Green[1]	Fa
♓	Emotion	Blue	Sol

Esoterically we may consider man to have an exact correspondence with the circle of the zodiac, each part of that circle having its uppermost point in turn, the signs and triplicities of signs revolving from light into shadow, and refinement into density. The circle, when divided at its four cardinal points, produces all the extremes that are to be obtained out of the primary three qualities, that are constantly foreshadowing the possible fourth, in this mystical squaring of the circle. They each rise, culminate, and set in turn. Dividing these four triplicities of fire, earth, air and water, we find that each triplicity and the three qualities are inseparable, producing a complexity of expression in which the consciousness of man has become bewildered, and his divine origin forgotten.

The knowledge of the divine origin of consciousness has been lost to the majority of the earth's inhabitants through the materiality of the age, corresponding with our passage through the lower arc of the circle, and Astrology, although it has survived through the darkest periods, has also suffered in materialisation, until its exponents have had to be satisfied with an exoteric, or objective exposition, which falls as far short of the truth concerning Astrology, as the lake is from the highest mountain peak.

---

[1] *Overtones* of sound and colour.

It is the hope of Esoteric Astrology that by a simplification of its metaphysical interpretation, man's divine origin will be traced backwards through the grosser forms of manifestation to the most refined, until it is not only seen that there is but one life permeating the wonderful diversity of existence, but also how truly Astrology has emphasised the statement " In Him we move and live and have our being."

Each sign of the zodiac has its Light, Primary and Dark expression, which is equivalent to saying that the three qualities are locked up in each separate sign.   This has been recognised by the Hindus' partition of one sign into many sub-divisions, far too minute for us at present to examine.

Astrology as a science does not recognise good or evil, it simply deals with qualities of matter, and states of consciousness.   What the three qualities are *in essence* we are not able to describe, but it is enough to say that there is behind those qualities a divine substance in which the three inhere as a homogeneous whole ;   and their disturbance into a triple expression produces all that can be made manifest ;   " What can be must be."   These qualities are :   Stability, change, and harmony or rhythm, being known to science as the inertia or resistance of matter, motion, and vibration ; or they may be expressed as the three modes of motion, rotary, translatory and vibratory.

The four grand divisions of elements, each division a triplicity in which all three qualities are always combined, have a correspondence to certain states or divisions of consciousness, which they may be said actually to represent from an astrological point of view.

The airy signs come first in these divisions.   They are composed of the finest and most important of the humane signs ; Aquarius—the Man ; Gemini—The Twins ; and Libra—the Scales or the balance.

These three signs harmonise and synthesise the other three triplicities of signs.   They also represent the three qualities in their most subtle form, and are, therefore, the elementary signs of the zodiac, the least complex, and yet the most difficult to interpret, being elusive and inexpressive signs for the undeveloped, and the most elastic and expressive for the developed or regenerate man.   These signs correspond to what is known as intellectual self-consciousness, the Manasic state or Manas, from Man, to think.

It is thus clear that the less a man thinks independently, and apart from others, especially where stereotyped and concrete thoughts are concerned, the less likely is he to respond to these signs ; but the more he thinks, originates and displays the Genius of himself, by thinking in the abstract from within, the more likely is he to find his consciousness on this level.   This airy triplicity then corresponds to the ideal of abstraction and refinement, comprising as it does the signs of true art, Libra ; music, Aquarius ; and literature, Gemini.   They are the signs of exalted latitudes offering the greatest longitude.   It is also through these signs that the steps are found to the higher planes of wisdom, and to the unification of the individual Will with the Will of the supreme.   They are balancing, fundamental and spiral signs of the zodiac, upon which all the other signs hinge, or turn, between the objective and the subjective sides of the nature ; the signs in which the zodiacal spheres are reversed, and the higher planetary spheres opened up to the enlightened vision of the seer.   They are for every one the signs of Memory, Pure Reason, and clear Perception.   In each triplicity they represent the three permanent and subtle qualities of matter permeating the whole of the world's substance.   Each triplicity has, in common with each sign, a light, a primary, and a dark division : the primary being the hinge, or turning point, always denoted by the Mutable sign separating the fixed sign, representing the dark, from the light Cardinal sign.   This division of signs must not be looked at from the standpoint of good and evil.   The term " dark " is meant to imply potentiality, concentration, concealed force waiting opportunity for expression ; and the term " light " that which is volatile, willing, spontaneous and easily expressed, or precipitated. They are the signs of the past, present, and future in the eternal NOW ; representative of Sanchita, Prarabdha, and Vartamanam Karma.

A chart or diagram will now be necessary to study the further divisions of the four triplicities.   (DIAGRAM VII, overleaf.)

It will be seen in this diagram, that the Airy triplicity has been entirely separated from the other triplicities below it, by " The Bridge," to be explained later.   This is not meant to imply that they have no connection with the other triplicities ; on the contrary, the airy signs are the most connective and relative of the signs ; the other triplicities, to a great extent, being reflections of them, as will be seen by the letters A, B and C.

The triplicities of fiery, earthy, and watery signs may be taken for all practical purposes to represent the ordinary man of the world in his composite being of spirit, soul and body, and for physical plane manifestation

ESOTERIC ASTROLOGY CHART

	Character and Tendency	Element and Quality	Tattva and Guna	Expressed in Consciousness	Triple Divisions or Decanates			House
					0-10	10-20	20-30	
	SPIRITUAL BODY							
	SPIRITUAL	AIR	VAYU	PURE OR ABSTRACT MIND *synthesised by* Venus INDIVIDUALITY	0-10	10-20	20-30	No.
♒ a	Memory	Fixed	Tamas		♒	♊	♎	11
♊ b	Reason	Mutable	Sattva		♊	♎	♒	3
♎ c	Perception	Cardinal	Rajas		♎	♒	♊	7
Critical State	SATURN, *the individualising planet, separates the higher from the lower, the air from the fire "Triplicity," and represents The Bridge, where the Ego touches the Personality through the*							
	MENTAL BODY							
	MENTAL	FIRE	AGNI	LOWER MIND *governed by* The Moon PERSONALITY				
♈ c	Intuition	Cardinal	Rajas		♈	♌	♐	1
♐ b	Introspection	Mutable	Sattva		♐	♈	♌	9
♌ a	Faith	Fixed	Tamas		♌	♐	♈	5
Critical State	*The ☽ governs the Astral plane, the link between fire and water through the :—*							
	BODY OF FEELING AND EMOTIONS							
	EMOTIONAL	WATER	APAS	SENSATIONS *governed by* Mars PSYCHIC BODY				
♋ c	Feeling	Cardinal	Rajas		♋	♏	♓	4
♓ b	Emotion	Mutable	Sattva		♓	♋	♏	12
♏ a	Attachment	Fixed	Tamas		♏	♓	♋	8
Critical State	*The ☉ governs the "Prana" or Vitality through the Etheric and Physical, or :—*							
	DENSE BODIES							
	PHYSICAL	EARTH	PRITHIVI	PHYSICAL *synthesised by* Jupiter				
♑ c	Absorption	Cardinal	Rajas		♑	♉	♍	10
♍ b	Circulation	Mutable	Sattva		♍	♑	♉	6
♉ a	Secretion	Fixed	Tamas		♉	♍	♑	2

a. The Physical *reflects* the Spiritual, or Will aspect of Consciousness.
b. The Emotional *reflects* the Sub-Spiritual, or Wisdom aspect of Consciousness.
c. The Mental *reflects* the Pure Mind, or Activity aspect of Consciousness.

DIAGRAM VII

they will be sufficient to describe his desires, cognitions, and volitions and all that is normally expressed through his personality, over which the Moon, exalted in Taurus, is the presiding genius.

The three signs of the earthy triplicity are the synthetic physical signs, affecting honour through action, Capricorn; possessions through desire, Taurus; and the serving attitude as well as the bodily health, Virgo. The etheric, the counterpart of the physical body, is governed by Taurus, the sign of the vocal organs, and all the concealed motive powers. The link with the astral or psychic body, is made by Virgo governing the cerebellum and the sympathetic nervous system. The framework and the bony structure are governed by Capricorn, which is related to the mentality and the finer nervous system, through volition, giving motives for actions. Therefore desire, Taurus; cognition, Virgo; and volition, Capricorn; are through this triplicity expressed physically as action. It is through Capricorn, *absorption*, that the personality is individualised. The five senses are summed up in this triplicity in smell, and the physical method of opening up the inner senses is through ceremony and ritual.

The watery triplicity synthesises the sensational and emotional side of Man's nature. It governs all instincts, feelings and emotions, from the most limited personal susceptibilities to the highest and deepest expression of devotion. It is the triplicity which represents the soul in all its varied modes of expression, from the animal to the human, even to the border-land of the spiritual. Taken separately, each sign answers to a note of feeling in which colour is especially pronounced. In Cancer the feelings are changeable and ever actively expressed, and in this sign pleasure and pain alternate in unerring succession. The colour of this sign is pale mauve or violet, becoming more beautifully pale and delicate as the feelings are refined. In the sign Scorpio, the sign of attachment, the feelings are pronounced in attraction and repulsion, and either love or hate is active, rarely are they weak, being more often deep in affection and unforgiving in hate. The colour of this sign is a deep dark red, with all kinds of lurid and bright red clouds. The desire nature of Scorpio is very potent, this being the sign of the zodiac in which feeling is concentrated into permanent moods. In Pisces the emotions are profound and extensive; and although dual, loving romance, they are more impersonal, and the love element is more pronounced, and hatred is rarely found in this sign; hence we find love for all dumb and helpless creatures and a widely extending sympathy expressed through Pisces.

The derelicts and wastrels of this sign are those who have failed to raise their emotions beyond a self-centred or superficial state. The watery triplicity represents the most important factor in our present daily life; for as incentives, these signs are the propellers, or the steam stirring into activity.

In Cancer the feelings are related to the self, whether personal or individual, therefore selfish where one's self alone is concerned. In Scorpio the feelings are always affected by others, particularly one's equals, and in Pisces they go out to either inferiors or superiors as pity or reverence. All pleasure, in these signs, is due to expansion of feelings, and pain due to their contraction. The earthy and watery signs are linked together, both having to do with the form side of life, these being the negative, or formative signs of the zodiac. When affected from without, or moved by external conditions, they are personal; and when moved from within, or subjectively, they are individual and much more highly evolved. Cancer never holds feeling very long, Scorpio carries it into Hell, and Pisces into Heaven. The watery signs are therefore the most impressionable signs of the zodiac. They are just like water in all its conditions, reflective, like the mirror of a lake; restless and changing like the running river, and ever full of motion like the ocean. This is why psychic phenomena are so unreliable, unless interpreted by a trained psychic, who has pure reason developed to enable him to see beneath the surface of things.

Representing the Kamic Astral or desire region, ever tending in the direction of feeling and impulse, they are the signs of Kama-Manas; and because the mind is mixed with desire in all things personal, they are signs to be purified and refined in the fire of love and knowledge, before the personality can hope to be saved.

The fiery triplicity in its connection with thought, or manas, and the mental activities, is the prime mover of the human being—as a thinker. It is the crown of the personality, and through it the dross of Kama-Manas is burnt out by the fire of knowledge, for knowledge puts an end to pain. The fiery triplicity holds a peculiar relationship to the other signs, through Aries leading the circle; and from its vital position within that circle, it affects the whole considerably, being opposed to the airy triplicity, and squaring the watery and earthy signs. Into the human body through this triplicity, a ray of consciousness is reflected directly from the complementary airy signs, and its perfect expression depends upon a good brain—Aries, a sound heart—Leo, and a pure nervous organisation—Sagittarius. The most the brain can do is to receive intuitive flashes from the higher planes of being. The highest the heart can attain to is to have faith in the divine ray that is centred in it; and then the personality, through Sagittarius, can by a wise introspection link the Lower to the Higher Manas.

In ordinary manifestation the consciousness reflected through Aries is a changeable mind, reformative, and pioneering, the mind often going in advance of the man's present capabilities. In Leo the self-reliance and stability of the Will allow the inner voice of the mind to speak. In Sagittarius the flexibility of the mind allows the man in meditation to catch an inspiration of his higher self.

The best of this triplicity expresses a developed reason, and the self-conscious knowledge of right and wrong, or the discrimination between the real and the unreal. It is in this triplicity that responsibility is realised. These signs, however, are those of great danger, in which Black Magic may be chosen instead of White; for these alone are the signs of choice. They may produce giants of intellectual development, and yet the Higher Self may be entirely dormant, the whole of the man's consciousness being drawn into the personality, and his knowledge used solely for the personal selfish ends and not for the good of others. Seeing the importance of a correct understanding of what the fiery signs represent, with regard to consciousness, I cannot do better than quote, with a few modifications, the words of our revered Teacher :

" The Higher Ego is, as it were, a globe of pure divine light, a unit from a higher plane on which is no differentiation. Descending to a plane of differentiation it emanates a Ray, which it can only manifest through the personality which is already differentiated. A portion of this Ray, the lower Mind, during life may so crystallise itself and become one with Desire that it will remain assimilated with Matter. That portion which retains its purity forms (the bridge). The whole fate of an incarnation depends on whether (Saturn) will be able to restrain the Kama-Manas (Desire-Nature), or not. After death the Higher Light (purified through Saturn) which bears the impression and memory of all good and noble aspirations, assimilates itself with the Higher Ego, the bad is dissociated in space, and comes back as bad Karma awaiting the personality. The feeling of responsibility is the beginning of Wisdom, or proof that (Saturn) is beginning to fade out, the beginning of the losing of separateness."

The intuitive student of Esoteric Astrology will now perceive that the fourfold division of the zodiac represents the various bodies or vehicles of consciousness required when functioning upon the different planes of manifestation.

The earthy triangle, having its apex in the M.C., represents the physical sheath. The Watery, having its apex in the fourth house, corresponds to the astral or psychic body ; the fiery triangle, with its apex in the Ascendant, to the mental body ; and the Airy, with its apex in the seventh to the Buddhic, intuitional rays.

These bodies are not separate, the one from the other, they interpenetrate one another as the signs of the zodiac make up the circle in this triangular form ; but in sleep or at death, when the consciousness is withdrawn from the physical plane, the earthy triplicity is latent and inactive ; and the same occurs throughout the circle of signs. When the astral consciousness is withdrawn, the watery triplicity is latent ; and it is not until the consciousness is again spiritual, that the whole of the circle has passed into latency. But this is a subject for another study, that which concerns the Aura and the Auric body.

CHAPTER VIII

THE MEANING OF ASPECTS

MATTER is the vehicle for the manifestation of Soul on this plane of existence, and Soul is the vehicle on a higher plane for the manifestation of spirit, and these three are a trinity synthesised by LIFE, which pervades them all.
Secret Doctrine.

THE aspects between the planets from the various signs and houses in the zodiacal circle modify their influences by establishing a relation which changes the nature of the vibrations to a remarkable degree.

The Planets represent spiritual influences affecting consciousness in its vehicles. The Signs of the Zodiac represent the senses and the vehicles through which consciousness is working. The Aspects denote the relation between spirit and body, or the attitude of the soul or self towards its environment; they represent the varying and changing moods and points of view of the soul.

The Sun, Moon and Mercury are the chief factors with regard to aspects, for they act as translators and direct communicators between spirit, soul and body. The Sun representing the life and energies in the body, denotes the interaction between a healthy body and the mind, and it governs the heart, the will, and the moral attitude.

The Moon represents the lower part of the brain, the spinal cord and the sympathetic system, and is thus closely connected with the senses. It denotes the interaction between thought and feeling, or the psychic nature with all its rapid and fluctuating moods and changes of consciousness.

Mercury represents the cerebro-spinal nervous system, especially the more recently evolved portions of it. This planet is therefore more rapidly responsive to those conditions and relations that are signified by the aspects of the planets. It translates all aspects in terms of the mind, and its influence is more or less pronounced according to the sign and position it occupies at birth.

The Sun translates the aspects of Mars and Venus more rapidly

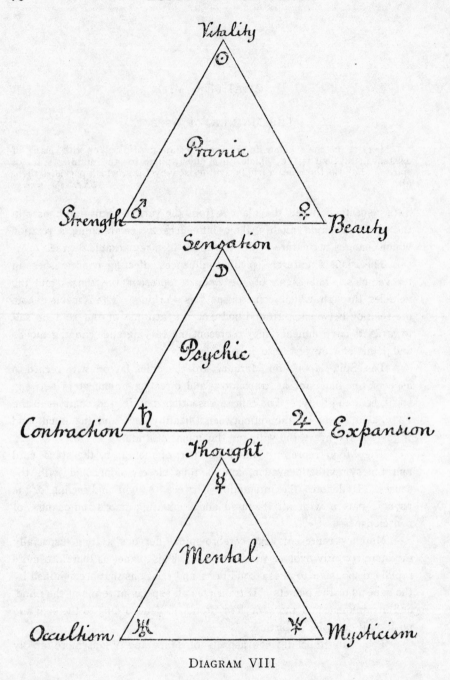

DIAGRAM VIII

than those of any other planet and does so in terms of strength and beauty. The Moon translates the aspects of Saturn and Jupiter more easily than the other planets, and expresses them in terms of expansion and contraction or the ebb or flow of both psychic and physiological life.

Mercury translates the aspects of Uranus and Neptune in terms of the occultist and the mystic outlook on life.

These three centres form the apex of three triads governing the life of the vehicles, the sensations and feelings, and the thought both concrete and abstract : (DIAGRAM VIII).

It is because of the modifying influence of the aspects of the planets one to another, from different signs and houses, that all the complications arise which make it so difficult to follow the unfolding of the spiritual side of Man's nature. The aspects represent the *changing attitude* toward all the passing phenomena of life and form. The soul may either repeat over and over again the same experiences, running round and round like a squirrel in a cage, or pass from one to another in succession, as a bee passes from flower to flower, gathering the wisdom and experience necessary for its evolution.

Each aspect has a special quality, a major or minor import, with a corresponding influence from that planet to which the aspect may be said to belong, as shown in the following table : (DIAGRAM IX).

The Opposition is either a complementary or a separative and opposing aspect.

It denotes the ending or finishing of fate, or Karma, and is of the nature of Uranus and the Sun. It completes or terminates a system of vibrations without necessarily unifying. This position accentuates the two poles of the positive and negative signs in which the opposition occurs. From Aries to Libra it accentuates the fiery and airy qualities and causes either the Cardinal-fire or Cardinal-air characteristics to be pronounced. In the nativity of King George V., Uranus is in opposition to Jupiter from the mutable, airy and fiery signs Gemini and Sagittarius. This denotes mental and social *reforms* in which the *mind* of the King will be concerned. From Taurus to Scorpio the opposition would accentuate the earthy and watery influences ; and so on throughout the zodiac, acting differently according to the fixed, mutable or cardinal qualities.

In the remarkable nativity of Prince Rudolf of Austria, born 10.15 p.m., 21st August, 1858, at Vienna, Mars and Uranus were in opposition

Nature of positions and Aspects	☉ and ♅	(Mental) ☿	Western Angle and ♀	M.C. and ♄	and ♆	North Angle and ♂	Ascendant and ♃
Complementary *and* Opposing	☍						
Humane *and* Selective		⊼					
Harmonious *and* Rhythmic			△				
Critical *and* Conflicting				□			
Vibratory *and* Combining					⚹		
Natural *and* Contesting						⋁	
Completing *and* Unifying							☌
Nature of Aspects	Major position	Indifferent aspect	Major aspect	Major aspect	Major aspect	Indifferent aspect	Minor position

DIAGRAM IX

in air and fire signs, from the 1st to the 7th houses. This opposing force produced the tragedy in the Prince's life, for the *attitude* of his mind, Mercury opposition Neptune, was separative and conflicting. In this case the mundane squares of Saturn, Uranus and Mars are very significant also.

The Quincunx aspect of 150° is of the nature of Mercury. It is humane and selective, and is disturbing only when in aspect with Saturn or Uranus; but being an indifferent aspect, it partakes more closely of the nature of the aspected planet than is usually the case. It assimilates two contrary influences, such as earth and fire, or air and water, and such elements do not readily combine. The influences of the planets in aspect are modified considerably by the quincunx, or even partly neutralised, so as to produce an attitude of mind similar to that known as "sitting on the fence," an indecisive non-committal frame of mind which tends to hold things in abeyance or to put them off to a more fitting occasion.

The next aspect is the Trine, which is of the nature of Venus, harmonious and rhythmic. It blends the influence of the planets in aspect harmoniously. If formed between Saturn and Mars, the extremes and contrasts of these planets are modified and made to act more after the nature of Venus than either Mars or Saturn. It harmonises the bodies, or vehicles, represented by the signs occupied by the planets.

Through watery signs it influences the astral or emotional body, and through fiery signs the mental body. In this respect it is a fortunate aspect, for it establishes harmony between the influences without and the attitude of mind within, so that its nature is without friction, antagonism, or harshness, and is peaceful, forgiving and charitable. This aspect does much to improve an otherwise adverse nativity. When occurring between the luminaries it is more fortunate than any favourable aspects to the benefics alone, especially if one of the benefic planets joins in the triangle.

The Square is the most critical and conflicting of aspects. It never fails to give an attitude which is disturbed, prejudiced or adverse to the conditions or circumstances accompanying it. It is also, like Saturn, a *separative* aspect, usually affecting the moral tone of the nativity. It is known as the angle of pain and sorrow, bringing remorse and a perturbed state of mind and feeling with worry, anxiety and despondency. Illnesses produced by the square aspect are often slow and lingering, but when acute they are never so quickly over as the opposition.

Every condition or event arising out of this aspect is critical and turns the tide of fortune one way or another definitely with more or less permanent results.

The Semi-square and Sesquiquadrate aspects must be considered along with the square; they are of the same nature but less defined, less critical and conflicting. Nevertheless they are both of the same nature as Saturn, and indirectly affect honour and moral states. The square is probably the only aspect that may be considered as positively evil, although even here good may arise out of the apparent evil. It involves all the four triplicities, fire, earth, air and water by position or by polarity, and through them is liable to affect any matter governed by them; so that it can be easily seen how much the mind and feelings may be in conflict when a square occurs from fiery and watery signs; and how inharmonious thought and action may become, when the aspect occurs from airy and earthy signs.

Although the square gives a saturnine tinge, the nature of each planet participating in this aspect is usually more accentuated, and the *attitude* of the spirit, mind and feelings is usually one that tends to produce a crisis.

The Sextile aspect is more combining in its nature than any other, in the sense that the influences of the planets forming the aspect are mutually blended. As a vibratory aspect it is more or less colourless and depends chiefly upon the planets and signs between which it occurs. It is often more potent and favourable than the trine, as it seems to blend two influences of a more or less like nature such as fire and air, or earth and water. In this respect the trine may be said to denote negative goodness, while the sextile is *positively* good; or, in other words, there is more activity and change shewn by the sextile than by the trine.

In the horoscope of King George V., the trine of Neptune and Mars is passively benefic, so far as the aspect is concerned and through it he may be easily influenced for good; while Mars sextile Moon is an actively good aspect in which the attitude of his mind will be more energetically expressed. The trine may be likened to the reward of the past, while the sextile contains the potentiality of the future.

The Semi-sextile aspect is often more important than it seems; for it brings two neighbouring signs into active relation in which the positive and negative elements are both concerned. In this respect the Sun sextile Neptune in King George's nativity is less complex than the Sun semi-sextile Venus, the former sounds only one positive note while the latter gives both a positive and negative vibration. Semi-sextile aspects are worthy of especial notice in some nativities, because they are natural but contrasting, and bring into action two forces which may be somewhat contrary in nature, such as fire and earth, or earth and air, or air and water; and yet include the positive and negative influences. Thus the semi-sextile and the inconjunct have a similar vibration, both being favourable.

The Conjunction is more or less expansive, completing and unifying. In some cases it tends to neutralise the effects of the planets that form the conjunction, and it often produces an attitude of indifference or suspense. The conjunction of Jupiter with any planet never fails to expand its influence and to bring to completion that which it denotes in the nativity. The conjunction of Saturn, on the other hand, rarely fails to contract and limit the influence of the other planet. Mars disturbs the influence of the planet it conjoins, and Uranus makes it either definitely opposing, or complementary; Mercury humanises, and Venus harmonises.

The Parallel must be judged according to the nearest aspect formed by the planets in parallel; apart from this it is similar to a conjunction with benefic planets and an opposition with those termed malefic.

Aspects Philosophically Considered

When the universe is classified under the heads of Self, Not-self, and the relation between them, it is easy to see that aspects belong to the third of these, for they represent forces flowing along definite lines between the various bodies, bringing them into relation with each other.

In dealing with any horoscope, and from the point of view of the native or owner of the horoscope, aspects come between the two departments of the world within, or the Self, and the world without, or the Not-self, and bring them into touch. Each acts upon the other and is reacted upon by the other; and the aspects indicate the modes of action and reaction, whether smooth and peaceful or discordant and provoking opposition.

Considered in this way as mere relations, good aspects show that the attitudes of the man and the world to each other are harmonious and pleasant. It does not necessarily follow that the man is unusually wise or good or strong ; this may or may not be the case.   He may be all that these words imply, but, on the other hand, benefic aspects may only signify that his good Karma has surrounded him with favourable conditions in which he is sure to prosper and to avoid serious temptation and failure.

Similarly, bad aspects show that the attitudes of the man and the world to each other are inharmonious and unpleasant.   Here, again, it does not follow of necessity that the man is weak or bad ; he may or may not be so.   It may be the case of a strong soul placed amidst uncongenial surroundings for the purpose of doing some special kind of work, some reform or pioneering work in which opposition would be inevitable ; or, whether the man is strong or weak, malefic aspects may indicate the working out of some piece of unpleasant Karma.

But this does not exhaust the problem of aspects.   Planets signify character ; that is, states of consciousness in the Self, as well as objects and conditions in the world without.   For instance, in the world within, or the Self, Mars rules courage, energy, positiveness, desire, and so on ; and in the outer world, or the Not-self, it signifies soldiers, war, weapons, iron, fire and many other objects.   Therefore, because the mode of operation of a planet is conditioned by the way in which it is aspected, aspects may be interpreted in terms of character, on the one hand, and of conditions in the outer world on the other.   *Both these lines of interpretation are secondary in importance and subordinate to the primary signification just given, namely that aspects are mere relations between the Self and the Not-self;* nevertheless it is as well to mention them.

When aspects are taken as relation between the different states of consciousness or departments of character in the man himself, good aspects indicate thoughts, feelings and actions that tend to a favourable and harmonious development of character ; while bad aspects imply such as are inharmonious, contradictory, or provocative of discord and opposition.

When they are taken as relations between the parts of the environment, or world without, good aspects indicate peaceful surroundings productive of happiness and prosperity ; while bad aspects show that some of the things or persons in the environment are contradictory or discordant with other things or persons ; a state of affairs that is likely to result in sorrow or discomfort to the owner of the horoscope.   For instance the parents may quarrel with each other, and yet the native may maintain a friendly attitude to both of them.

CHARACTER, OR ENVIRONMENT?

In no horoscope are the aspects between the heavenly bodies all good or all bad, with no admixture ; and because of this, as well as because of the considerable number and variety of possible aspects, the question arises as to whether we can know along which of these lines any given aspect should be interpreted.

It is by no means easy to give a definite reply to this, for all three methods of interpretation are vital so far as they go, and if used wisely. It is known, however, that some of the heavenly bodies have a better claim to represent the owner of the horoscope than have the others. The Sun, Moon, and Ascendant (including under this term the ruler or lord) are the three that are more directly related to Self ; and of these the ascendant and the ruling planet are the most immediately significant. Therefore—passing over the further question of which is the real ruler of the horoscope, whether it is the rising planet, or the strongest and most prominent planet, or the lord of the rising sign—we may certainly assume that while all the heavenly bodies may produce effects both within and without the man, there is one that has predominant claim to represent him as the Self, or the world within ; and that all the rest although possessing subjective correspondence in terms of character belong preponderantly to the world without, and represent objects and persons in the environment which will produce their due effect upon the man.

It would be intereresting to enquire whether aspects indicate actual right or wrong, good or evil ; but the question is too complicated to enter upon here ; and all that need be said now is that their primary meaning is probably nothing more than relative harmony or inharmony.

The further question of the strength or weakness of the soul, its stage of evolution, is also outside the scope of this chapter. Strong and weak characters may both alike have either propitious and pleasant or hostile and unpleasant surroundings. If the ruler of the horoscope is weak or obscure by sign and position but is well aspected, it might indicate a commonplace or a weak character who would drift through life easily and comparatively happily ; while a ruler strong and prominent but with bad aspects in the horoscope might point to a strong (but not necessarily perfect) character in a hostile environment, with some difficult work to do.

There is one other point of view from which aspects may be

considered.   Those who have studied the subject of crystallisation will be
aware that all substances which crystallise do so in accordance with
definite geometrical systems, and that the same substance always
crystallises in the same way if the conditions remain unchanged.
Common salt forms cubes, alum forms octohedrons, while the dodeca-
hedron is found in some preparations of copper, silver and gold.   The
fact that different chemicals yield differently shaped crystals, shows that
difference in shape implies a difference in the inner properties or qualities ; that is to say, that for each variation of the life within there is a
corresponding variation in the form without.

This conclusion is not only justified by science, it is corroborated by
clairvoyant investigation, which has shown that different chemical
elements all have differently shaped and constituted atoms.   All these
different crystalline and other forms, whether simple or complex, are built
up round axes, which are arranged at various angles to each other ;
But astrological aspects are also formed of lines inclined at various angles
to each other ; and here we have a clear correspondence between form,
axes, angles, and inner properties or characters.

This is a great subject in itself, and we can do no more than indicate
it ; nearly every astrological aspect or angle implies some definite power,
quality or characteristic ;   and that justifies the attempt made in this
chapter to give some general indications of what these characteristics are
for each aspect, considered apart from the planets forming the aspect.
To study the subject at all fully, even from the exoteric point of view, it
would be necessary to investigate the many possible shapes of crystals,
their angles and axes, the variation of chemical and medical properties
with variation of crystalline form, and so on; but this is obviously quite
beyond our powers now even if sufficient information were at our disposal.
It must be left to scientific investigations of a future date.

CHAPTER IX

FIRE

THE elements now known have arrived at their state of permanency in this Fourth Round and Fifth Race. They have a short period of rest before they are propelled once more on their upward spiritual evolution, when the ' living fire of Orcus' will dissociate the most irresolvable, and scatter them again into the primordial One. *Secret Doctrine.*

THE four so-called *elements* of antiquity, fire, earth, air, and water, with the fifth, æther, the quintessence of the four, have been the source of some little confusion for modern readers; partly because of doubt as to the correct order in which they should be enumerated, and partly through uncertainty as to the precise meaning intended to be conveyed by them.

The use of the word *element* in this connection need not, of course, give rise to any trouble; for it does not bear the same connotation here as when employed by the chemist, who speaks of some eighty chemical elements; and its use by occultists, astrologers, and alchemists long antedated that by the modern man of science.

The five elements are the types of the ultimate atoms of the five lower cosmic planes out of which all the matter of these planes is constructed by combination. They have correspondences in the five lower sub-divisions of each plane and their archetypes are apparently the five regular or platonic solids.

On the familiar physical plane the known states of matter are solid, liquid and gas, beyond which lies the mysterious ether; and the first difficulty arises when we note that fire is not enumerated in this list and that there seems no particular reason why it should be. The old name "earth" evidently means solid, and "water" means liquid, in our physical plane correspondences; but why any special state should be called fire is not very evident. Solids, liquids, and gases can all three be made to burn under suitable conditions. Whether the state beyond the gaseous will do so we do not yet know, although since it will certainly conduct light and heat there seems nothing very unreasonable in supposing that its particles, whether electrons or what not, might be made to enter into that combination called burning.

Moreover there is an absence of agreement among authorities as to the position of fire in the list.   It has been given sometimes as the second and at other times as the third or fourth counting from below upward.

Dr. Anna Kingsford in *Clothed With the Sun*, gives the order of the Elemental Divinities in her hymns as Hephaistos, fire ; Demeter, earth ; Poseidon, water ; and Pallas Athena, air.   Fire is taken first apparently because the lowest sub-division of the astral plane is said to be actually beneath the surface of the earth, although the remainder of that plane extends many thousands of miles beyond the surface ; the idea of the "descent" of the dead into Tartaros, Hades or Hell is very common. So that fire here really applies to the astral plane and refers to the fire of desire, purgatorial in its effect.   Water here refers to the heaven-world and may perhaps be intended as a contrast to the lower fire of desire which has been extinguished in the soul that has reached the higher plane ; and also while water signifies matter in general, the first garment of matter put on by the soul on its descent into incarnation is the mental body on the lower mental plane.

In the case of the zodiac we have fire, earth, air, and water, three times repeated in this order, to make up the twelve signs.

The more prevalent view is that fire is separative and individualising and that it corresponds to the heaven-world or mental plane upon which individualisation takes place.   This plane is the third from below, and answers apparently to the state of gas on the physical plane.   An objector might urge that there is no reason why the term fire should be applied to the third plane exclusively ; because as the three lower states of physical matter will all burn, therefore the three lower planes might all be called fire indifferently.   The answer to this seems to be that the molecules of solid and liquid substances always pass into the gaseous condition even though only for a fraction of a second before they burn, and that the term fire is therefore rightly applied to the gas and not to the solid or liquid.

A rather more serious objection may be brought against the idea that fire is separative and destructive on the ground that this is only half a truth.   If a piece of wood is burned it is certainly destroyed as wood, and the chemical elements of which it is composed are wrenched asunder from their combinations and scattered ; but this is only half of what takes place.   If instead of looking at the piece of wood as a whole we pay attention to its chemical constituents, we shall see that union is going on all the time side by side with the separation. The carbon in the wood unites with oxygen in the air to form carbonic acid gas, hydrogen in the wood combines with oxygen in the air to form water; and similarly with any other elements that are capable of combination.

The problem is simplified if instead of looking at a complex material like wood we study the burning of a simple chemical element like hydrogen gas. When a light is applied to this gas and it burns, the process of burning consists in the hydrogen entering into combination with oxygen in the air, with the formation of water which is composed of two volumes of hydrogen united to one volume of oxygen; and no burning can take place without this combination. This may be illustrated thus :—

$$4H + 2O = 2H_2O$$

At first sight it seems as if there were no separation, no destruction, here; for pure hydrogen unites with pure oxygen, and the process appears to be wholly one of combination, synthesis, integration. Nothing is destroyed, but something, namely water, is created. It is true that, in a sense, the hydrogen and the oxygen may be said to be destroyed as separate gases when they unite to form water, but this not quite on a par with the destruction of wood by burning. Science tells us, however, that atoms of hydrogen never exist alone; that when they are not united with some other element they combine with each other, two atoms of hydrogen uniting to form a molecule of hydrogen; and that the same is true of oxygen.

The burning of hydrogen therefore takes place in two stages. The molecule of hydrogen is first destroyed by its two atoms being driven apart, and the free atoms are then combined with oxygen to form water, the oxygen molecules being themselves split up in the process, thus :—

$$H{-}H \quad O \qquad H \qquad H$$
$$\qquad\quad + \quad | \quad = \quad |{>}O + |{>}O$$
$$H{-}H \quad O \qquad H \qquad H$$

This seems to provide us with a description of what takes place when a substance is burned or raised to the state of fire. The molecules of the substance are first separated into their constituent atoms, and these are then recombined in various ways so far as they are capable of it, usually by means of atmospheric oxygen.

A definition of fire might, therefore, run somewhat as follows :—Fire is that state during which atoms are in the process of separating from one combination and entering into another.

The word "atom" is here used as it is by modern scientific chemists, who speak of atoms of solid, liquid, and gaseous elements; and not in the sense in which it is employed by occult observers, who only apply the word to matter on the seventh and highest sub-division of a plane.

It must also be noticed that atoms floating about loose and uncombined are not necessarily in the state of fire. Such an uncombined condition is said to be normal with some chemical elements, especially some of the rarer gases in the atmosphere, the atoms of which cannot be made to combine even with each other. An atom is only in the state of fire during such a time as it is in the act of separating from one combination and entering into another, and not while it is drifting about uncombined.

If there is any truth in this hypothesis, additional light is thrown upon the correspondence of fire, and Agni the fire-god, as well as Tejas the tattva of fire, with the mental plane. This plane is the abode of the Ego, the permanent soul, in the causal body; from it the descent is made into the matter of the lower planes at each new incarnation; and to it the soul returns when each incarnation is finished. If we note the condition of the Ego at the time when one incarnation has completely finished, all its energies having been fully withdrawn into the causal body, and when the creative impulse that will go to form the next personality has not yet begun, it will be seen that such an Ego is, at that moment, in a state precisely analogous to that of an atom in the condition of fire. It is just in the act of separating from one combination, namely its past personality, and of applying to another, which will be its next personality.

Any Ego at such a period may be said to be in a condition corresponding to that state of matter called fire. The utmost possible degree of separateness, of individualisation, has been attained; for the past combination has been destroyed (Shiva, Tamas, Fixed), the next combination has not yet been formed (Brahmâ, Rajas, Movable), and the Ego is balanced or rather is moving rhythmically between the two (Vishnu, Sattva, Common).

When taken in this sense, therefore, fire would seem to correspond to *Self*, which, at our stage of evolution, shows in us as intellectual self-consciousness, the awareness of the separate self, shut off from other selves and also from the Not-self. But its correspondence would seem o be primarily with self, and only secondarily with intellect.   Intellect is the means by which man becomes aware of self, but self is not intellect.

In a much higher application the Logos is the great cosmic fire, because He passes from the disintegration of one universe to the creation of another, just as the Ego passes from the disintegration of one personality to the creation of another.   So we read in the *Secret Doctrine* (III. 589) : " Fire is Divinity in its subjective presence throughout the universe."   Moreover this transition from one condition to another, whether that which is moved is an atom of hydrogen, a human Ego, or a Logos, bears an obvious analogy to the passage of the electric spark between the two poles of the battery ; and this generalises the idea of fire as that universal cosmic energy which is known under the names of Daiviprakriti, the Light of the Logos, Fohat.   " Under other conditions, this Universal Fire manifests as water, air, and earth.   It is the one Element in our visible Universe which is the Kriyâshakti of all forms of life.   It is that which gives light, heat, death, life, etc."

It is, therefore, the source of all forms of energy, on every plane of nature, whether appearing as attraction, integrative, upbuilding, or as repulsion, disintegrative, breaking down.

This might have been inferred from the definition of fire previously given, namely that it is the state intervening between the separation from one combination and the formation of another ; for atoms can be transferred chemically from one combination to another while in the liquid condition, without visibly burning, and without showing any flame.   If a solution in water of any soluble chloride is added to another solution in water of nitrate of silver, the silver will be torn asunder from its nitrate combination and will unite with the chlorine, forming chloride of silver. While it is passing from the one to the other, the silver will be undergoing a change similar to that of an atom of carbon in wood when burning, but the process will take place in water, and neither light nor flame will be manifested.

In correspondence with this it may be noted that, although the human Ego finishes one process of disembodiment and begins another of re-embodiment upon the mental plane, yet analogous changes in the animal and vegetable kingdoms go on upon lower planes than the mental, and possibly upon all planes.   The triads that are passing through the group-soul condition in the lower kingdoms, mineral, vegetable and animal, must pass through similar processes of separation and reunion many hundreds of times, and this will not take place upon the mental plane in most cases. Whenever and wherever it may take place, the entity concerned is in the state of fire for the time being; and we must apparently recognise an actual or potential state of fire on every cosmic plane.

The idea that fire is individualising is supported by the position of Aries, the most fiery sign in the zodiac. This corresponds to the ascendant or first house of the horoscope, and signifies the self or person to whom the horoscope belongs, a physical self in its lowest application but really the spiritual individual self animating a physical body through its personal ray. Considered apart from the mundane houses, Aries is the self of the zodiac, the Cosmic Self; and accordingly Subba Row writes in his essay on *The Twelve Signs of the Zodiac* that Mesha, Aries, signifies the supreme Brahman, " the self-existent, eternal, self-sufficient, cause of all." In saying this he gives the idea of self its highest possible cosmic application; but "as above so below," all smaller selves are strung on the one supreme Cosmic Self like beads on a string, down to the limited and restricted self of the physical body; the thread of self-hood is continuous through them all.

The same writer gives the meaning of Leo, the second fiery sign, as the perfected man, the Christ, the Buddha, realising himself as the son of the Cosmic Self, Aries; the fifth house, which corresponds to Leo, representing the child of the first house. Sagittarius, the third fiery sign, is said to represent the builders of the material universe, the common or sâttvic quadruplicity being upbuilding and integrative, so that sâttvic fire is a name for the intelligent forces that build and shape the solar system, and especially its body of fire. In the human application this becomes the cohesive, vitalising energies that hold together man's physical and other bodies; the power of growth of the cells physically, and the power of the Hiranyagarbha or radiant shining body spiritually, signified by Jupiter, the ruler of Sagittarius. The reader will remember that in ancient times as well as in modern astro-meteorology Jupiter was the producer of lightning, one form of fire.

Fire, therefore, may be taken as either energy, or consciousness, or a form of matter. As energy, it is polarised and concentrated and is the cause of all changes of state, all separations and reunions in matter, both physical and superphysical, and is the animating and moving cause of all things. As consciousness, it represents a precisely similar state of concentration into a limited self, and of polarisation entailing movements of separation and combination. In the case of man, this self belongs to the mental plane, and its movements manifest as death and rebirth; but units of matter and of consciousness passing through analogous changes occur on every cosmic plane.

Planetary Colours and their Sub-Divisions

		Sub-influences				Sub-influences
JUPITER	♃	Blue	SATURN	♄	Green
		Red			Indigo
		Violet			Yellow
BLUE		Green	GREEN		Orange
		Indigo			Blue
		Yellow			Red
The Auric envelope		Orange	*Mental*		Violet

		Sub-influences				Sub-influences
MARS	♂	Red	VENUS	♀	Indigo
		Violet			Yellow
		Green			Orange
RED		Indigo	INDIGO		Blue
		Yellow			Red
		Orange			Violet
Astral and Passional		Blue	*Manasic or Abstract Mind*		Green

		Sub-influences				Sub-influences
MOON	☽	Violet	MERCURY	☿	Yellow
		Green			Orange
		Indigo			Blue
VIOLET		Yellow	YELLOW		Red
		Orange			Violet
		Blue			Green
Etheric		Red	*Buddhic or Intuitional*		Indigo

		Sub-influences
SUN	☉	Orange
		Blue
		Red
ORANGE		Violet
		Green
Prânic (Uranus golden		Indigo
Jiva-atmic)		Yellow

DIAGRAM X

CHAPTER X

The Human Aura and its Significance

When Kronos is represented as mutilating his father Uranus, the meaning of this mutilation is very simple : Absolute Time is made to become the finite and conditioned ; a portion is robbed from the whole, thus showing that the father of the Gods has been transformed from *Eternal Duration* into a limited period. *Secret Doctrine.*

It was stated in Chapter III. that the planet Jupiter represents the body, which term is here meant to include the etheric double as well as the dense physical ; and its relation to the human aura was also mentioned in connection with other vehicles of consciousness besides the physical.

For many centuries all knowledge concerning the aura that envelopes every human being has been surrounded with profound mystery, probably owing to its being invisible to all save those possessing clairvoyant vision, and it was not until recent years that astrologers were able to understand the statement that Jupiter was concerned with the aura in all its various divisions.

Roughly we may divide the human aura into four main parts, closely corresponding to the four states of matter that are to be found on and surrounding our globe. These are the well-known tattvas of the Hindu astrologer, Vayu or Air, Agni or Fire, Apas or Water, and Prithivi or Earth.

The last of these, the Prithivi tattva working in etheric matter, forms the etheric or health aura surrounding the physical body ; it is, in fact, the etheric mould upon the pattern of which the body has been built. This Etheric Aura is governed by the Moon in its sub-influence under Jupiter.

It is not easy to follow these sub-divisions without applying to them the colour language, so often used by clairvoyants and those who wish to judge planetary influences dispassionately ; therefore the following table of planetary colours and their sub-divisions will now be useful. (Diagram X.)

From this table it will be seen that the colour connected with the Moon is violet, and that the Moon's sub-influence under Jupiter—blue—

is a violet sub-ray of the blue.   This lunar etheric mould is laid down in
the womb of the mother at the prenatal epoch, and it is fructified by the
permanent physical atom, projected by the father at the time of coition;
conception taking place when the two elements have completely fused.
The position of the Moon at the prenatal epoch is all-important, because
the etheric mould is attracted to the mother when the magnetic vortex is
set up by the parents who are drawn together at the time by either
passion or love, animal or human feelings.   The Moon's place at epoch
decides the ascendant at birth, hence the importance of the prenatal map,
which needs to be more fully understood by astrological students.

The etheric mould is new at each rebirth of the Ego into the
physical plane of manifestation.   It is practically obtained from the
dregs or lower emanations of the permanent auric envelope of the Ego
itself; and it becomes, at the time of the prenatal epoch, the pattern for
the etheric double and the dense physical body.

This etheric double of the physical body may be said to act as the
vehicle for influences handed down from the astral and mental planes;
therefore the Moon governs the whole of the personality—seated in the
lower quarternary of the mortal man, which is made up of *personal*
activities; *personal* feelings; and *personal* thoughts.

When the Moon represents the vitality or health aura, it is the
sub-influence of the Sun-Prâna; and is shown as the Central Violet
sub-ray of the Orange ray.

When it influences the personal feelings and desires, it is the Violet
sub-ray of the Red Ray, representing the astral body.

When concerned with the personal thoughts, or the lower mind, it is
the Violet sub-ray of the green-ray; representing the Mental body.

It can now be easily seen why, in Esoteric Astrology, aspects to the
Moon are so important to a correct rendering of the nativity.

The Moon in good aspect to the Sun denotes good health, good
recuperative power, and much vitality; while adverse aspects hinder the
flow of the life-giving prâna, lower the vitality and delay the recuperative
process.

The Moon in aspect with Mars increases the response to feeling;
and stimulates the impulses of personal attractions.

The Moon in aspect with Saturn makes the mind concrete, and
limits the thought to practical personal ends, until the violet sub-ray may
even become absorbed into the green.

Before passing on it may be well to remark that the purer the violet ray shewn in this aura the nearer will the mortal man be to freeing himself from personal desires and thoughts which bind him to the lower or grosser influences of matter.

All the colours of the planets may be said to be complementary or interchangeable; for instance Red and Green are complementary colours, and so are Blue and Orange, and Yellow and Indigo. Green will absorb red; and as man advances in evolution each colour will be refined and manifested more through the higher vehicles of consciousness.

THE DIVISIONS OF THE AURA

The most important division of the human aura corresponds more or less to the tattva Vayu, and is that which is connected with the Ego or Individuality. It has to do with that part of the aura which is in touch with the essence or aroma of the personality,—all the purified thoughts and emotions which have ascended into heaven. Speaking of consciousness working in this division, the Esoteric teaching says: " The Higher Ego is, as it were, a globe of pure divine light, a light from a higher plane, on which is no differentiation. Descending to a plane of differentiation it emanates a Ray, which it can only manifest through the personality which is already differentiated. A portion of this Ray, the Lower Manas, during life may so crystallise itself and become one with Kâma that it will remain assimilated with matter. That portion which retains its purity forms Antahkarana (*Saturn*). The whole fate of an incarnation depends on whether Antahkarana (*Saturn*) will be able to restrain the Kama-Manas (*Mars*) or not. After death, the Higher Light (Antahkarana) which bears the impressions and memory of all good and noble aspirations, assimilates itself with the Higher Ego, the bad is dissociated in space, and comes back as bad Karma awaiting the personality"; or in other words is worked into the Etheric mould or lowest portion of the aura, and is shown in the rising sign at birth as well as through the ruling planet and its aspects to the other planets.

This teaching goes on to say that: " The feeling of responsibility (*Saturn*) is the beginning of Wisdom, a proof that Ahamkara is beginning to fade out, the beginning of losing the sense of separateness."

This portion of the aura is often spoken of as the Auric Egg, wherein is " the preserver of every Kârmic record." " It is the storehouse of all the good and evil powers of man, receiving and giving out at his Will—nay, at his very thought—every potentiality, which becomes then and there, an acting potency; this aura is the mirror in which sensitives and clairvoyants sense and perceive the real man and see him *as he is*, not as he appears."

Its power to reflect everything that is imprinted upon it makes it the record of the whole of a man's past life. It is the body of Manas or the pure abstract mind considered as apart from desires and practical concrete thoughts, and through it the pure mind represented by Venus shines whenever the lower vibrations are stilled and the passions are transmuted. The Auric Egg itself, regarded as vehicle, is under the dominant influence of Jupiter, as are all the finer substances composing the inner vehicles of Consciousness; but it is also subject to the binding influence of Saturn, and it is here that the main influences of Jupiter and Saturn are experienced; expansion and contraction being continually at work increasing and diminishing the boundaries of consciousness at various stages of man's evolution.

This portion of the Aura is under the blue ray, and it is affected indirectly through the green and indigo sub-rays. The green ray will act as a kind of scaffolding protecting the individuality within the aura until it is ready to stand alone after having been slowly built up through the ages under the individualising action of Saturn.

Saturn acts as the bridge between the personal, mortal part of man and the higher spiritual and immortal; thus Saturn may be said to purify, refine, and spirtualise the essence of the Moon and Mars, and transform their colours from dark red into rose pink and from the darker shades of Violet into the most refined and subtle hues of that colour.

In this division of the aura come all variations between the extremes of optimism and pessimism, of hope and of depression.

So far as the tattvas or vibrations in æther are concerned, we have now reached the highest division, that of Âkâsha, of which the Causal or spiritual body is composed. If we divide the aura into its active components and colours, we shall find that the prithivi tattva affects the physical body through the Prana or Vitality which is ever streaming through it so long as it continues to be a living body in which the *animal life* is constantly manifesting.

The Apas or watery tattva affects the Etheric Double or mould upon which the physical cells are built.

The Tejas tattva corresponds to the Astral Body, or that portion or colouring of the aura through which the passions and animal desires are working and in which the lower mind is largely involved.

The Vayu tattva, over which Saturn has chief rule, represents the critical state between the more homogeneous æther, Akâsha, and Tejas; the dividing line so to speak, between the mortal and the immortal man.

Over the Akâsha tattva Venus may be said to have chief sway, for she is lady of heaven, the true Isis, and here is the Veil between spirit and matter.

The Esoteric teaching deals with two more tattvas which are quite unknown to ordinary students, but Astrology enables us to understand them through the planets Mercury and Uranus; they are known as the Anupâdaka, and Âdi tattvas.

The portion of the aura which may be said to extend beyond the individual Auric Egg is composed of the spiritual essence, out of which the spiritual soul is formed, although in reality form as we know it does not exist on these planes. It is known as the "Buddhic Ray," and is under the influence of the planet Mercury, the Ray of Wisdom. Its colour is yellow, it exists as a sub-influence in all the other rays, and all the other rays exist within it as sub-rays. To reach it through the Etheric body we must understand the Moon's fourth sub-ray in the order of the Violet sub-rays; through the astral body, or the devotion of Mars, by understanding the reason of devotion, or by direct contact with the object of devotion through purified emotion, by way of the fifth or Yellow sub-ray of the Red ray; and through Venus and pure intelligence by way of the second or yellow sub-ray of the indigo ray.

The pure influence of Mercury is that of intuition, spiritual understanding, a direct knowledge of spiritual things, an immediate reflection of the Cosmic and super-human consciousness.

It is the plane of the heaven world, and to reach this portion of the aura all earthly things must disappear and the consciousness function directly through the yellow Ray, apart from any sub-division of it; or in astrological terms, man must reach to the plane of consciousness in which the planet Mercury revolves, apart from any touch of the zodiacal signs.

The mirror of the true Mercurial consciousness must reflect nothing but itself and that which is in the likeness of itself.

The next and last tattva of which we can have any consciousness is the Âdi tattva, under the rulership of Uranus. In speaking of the influence of this planet upon the aura, the Esoteric teaching describes it as opalescent, the whole aura shining with a beautiful iridescent light like mother-of-pearl. No words can describe the golden light shining through this aura like the Sun, making it a most glorious picture to behold.

PAST AND FUTURE

The most remarkable thing about the whole aura surrounding a man is that it contains the results of all former lives and the potentialities of the future. Each of the human tattvas is centred round a permanent atom, in which are stored all the vibratory possibilities accumulated during past incarnations; and because of this each man comes forth into rebirth with the vibratory energies of these atoms prompting him to act in certain ways along what, for him, is the line of least resistance. When we consider that each cosmic tattva has a spiritual Intelligence or Lord as its head, and source, and a host of minor intelligences working in that particular field of æther, it can easily be seen how the vibrations of each atom respond to its own particular planet, and how the consciousness of the man within responds to the matter without himself.

A careful study of the aura, and its relation to the higher and lower or finer and denser planes will afford a clue to a considerable amount of knowledge concerning the three definite stages of a man's evolution. The highest and most refined portion of the aura is under the influence of Uranus, the planet of Will, which is used in Esoteric Astrology as a symbol of the monad, the real Self. The middle portion is under the influence of Saturn, the individualising planet, which is the symbol of the Ego or Individuality. The lower portion, or that which more or less directly contacts the physical, is under the influence of Jupiter.

In the ordinary man, who is still Animal-Man unregenerate, the Moon is the symbol of the personality, which is limited to the brain and sensations for expression; but when regenerate the expansion of consciousness caused by Jupiter moves the centre from the brain and the sensations to the heart, and a moral sense is born, which is tested and tried by the responsibilities imposed upon the man by the Saturnine influences, and he then passes into a more fully individualised state. For a long period the Sun is a representative of the ordinary individual, who is not self-consciously established in the Causal or spiritual body; but when the moral sense is fully developed and the heart is freed from the attractions of the senses and the promptings of the lower mind, the

expansive influence of Jupiter is too wide to come within the scope of
Saturn's restricting limitations, and his bonds are broken, so to speak.
Then the Uranian influence begins, the man learning to transcend the
individuality and to realise that humanity is but one great Entity of which
he forms a part. He is then the real student of human nature, who,
understanding all, forgives all. He is then treading the path of freedom,
and becomes the houseless wanderer in the true sense of the term, having
no zodiacal sign more prominent than another, the whole circle being his
field of manifestation and not an isolated part of it. In the ancient
mythologies, Uranus, Lord of Space, was dethroned by Saturn, God of
Time, who finally gave way to Zeus, Lord over form and matter; and in
Hindu mythology these symbols are again expressed in Shivà, Vishnu
and Brahmâ.

CHAPTER XI

The Planets in Relation to Consciousness

MERCURY as an astrological planet is still more occult and mysterious than Venus. He was the leader and evoker of Souls, the 'Great Magician' and Hierophant. He is the 'Golden-haired Hermes' whom the Hierophants forbade any to name. *Secret Doctrine.*

IT should now be clear why all our ideas on Esoteric Astrology should be based upon an understanding of the real difference between the Individuality, which is the permanent part of our nature, and the Personality, which is the fleeting part, and which only exists as a very small ray of the Individuality.

Each planet has a definite connection with consciousness in all its grades, from the lowest to the highest. There is only one supreme consciousness, but each "sphere of influence" represented by a planet shares a large portion of this consciousness, and uses it in connection with the many and various departments of nature. From the standpoint of the evolution of the soul, these are connected with the seven principles or aspects of human consciousness, such as the Will aspect, the Wisdom aspect, and so on, each planet being concerned in the evolution of one of the principles; for we evolve or unfold in consciousness in the same way as we do in body, and we possess a physical, an emotional, and a mental body, for the expression of the corresponding states of consciousness.

The highest and most subtle states of consciousness are those which find expression only through the Individuality, or permanent soul of man, namely the Will, Wisdom, and Love aspects. These three high and exalted states of consciousness are, according to the rules of Esoteric Astrology, governed by Uranus—Will, Mercury—Wisdom, and Venus—Love. They are connected with what is often termed in Eastern philosophy the immortal triad, and in the West the trinity of perfection. We may think of these states of consciousness as representing Spirit, Spiritual Soul and Human Soul, or three aspects of that which in its highest sense is the one Individual Soul.

In reverse order there are three reflections of this higher consciousness closely connected with the Personality, and these have more to do with limited embodied life in matter; mental matter, astral matter, and physical matter.

They represent firstly the life of the physical body, in which all the cells of the body have a consciousness of their own, and this is governed by the planet Jupiter. Secondly, there is the life of the personal feelings, the Animal Soul, as the sum total of all our varying moods, sensations and feelings, the consciousness of our emotional body ; and this is governed by the planet Mars. Finally, there is the life of the mind, our own peculiar personal mind, giving us opinions, bias, and prejudices. It is the mind that fills our brain-cells, giving them life and consciousness of their own, animating the phrenological organs in the head and making us see all things concretely and practically ; this is governed by the Moon.

When these three states of consciousness and the vehicles through which they work are all combined in the one physical body, they are vitalised by the Sun, which supplies Prana or vital force ; and when this Prana is withdrawn from the physical body, death ensues. The cream of the lower or personal consciousness is then gathered up into the Individuality according to the following pairs of opposites :—Uranus and Jupiter, representing respectively the Will aspect in consciousness and the stability of the body; Mercury and Mars, representing the Spiritual Soul and its opposite the Animal Soul ; Venus and the Moon, the Human Soul and the personal mind of the brain.

THE RELATION OF INDIVIDUALITY AND PERSONALITY

Saturn forms the Bridge, or the straight and narrow way, between the Individuality and the Personality. This planet is the divider and separator of the gross from the fine, the impure from the pure, and hence is the great source of sorrow and pain, the chastener, and also the individualiser.

We may now represent these states of consciousness and their governing planets in tabular form :

⊙ Spirit   expressed as Will ♅.
☿ Spiritual Soul   ,,   ,, Wisdom ☿.
♀ Human Soul   ,,   ,, Love ♀.
♄ The Bridge or Individualiser.
☽ Personal Mind   expressed through The Brain ☽.
♂ Personal Feelings   ,,   ,,   The Animal Soul.
♃ Physical Cells   ,,   ,,   The Etheric and Dense Body.
⊙ Vitality or life of the body.

The Sun is both spirit and life, the highest and the lowest.

Just as Aquarius is the astrologer's ideal sign, so is Uranus his ideal planet, and those who can pass the vibrations of all the other planets may hope to contact and respond to Uranus. Some can only respond to Mars, and some only to Saturn, but those who can respond to Uranus, even in its lowest expression, are few and rare. This then is the true meaning of living up to one's horoscope—making a full response to the highest vibrations operating.

These are the physical plane planets that are used as representatives of the seven states of consciousness and the seven pathways of evolution. Every Individuality is evolving under the care and guidance of one of the great Beings represented by these planets, and every incarnated Personality is born under the rulership of one of them; but whereas the Individuality, or permanent soul, remains constantly in touch with the same one of the Seven, normally at least, throughout the whole of its long series of incarnations, the Personal ruler changes from life to life.

The Relation of the Personality to the Body

When the time for birth comes, a body is chosen of a special type, suitable for the soul's acquirement of the experience needed at that special time. The upbuilding of that body is not a matter of chance, it takes place in accordance with a pre-determined plan, and the very structure and composition of the body are arranged to suit that plan. The various kinds of chemical elements of which the body is composed as well as the way in which they combine are all expressive of the operations of the planetary rulers, and birth takes place when the planets are in the positions they ought to occupy according to the pre-determined plan which constitutes the horoscope. The type of body and its upbuilding, therefore, are arranged to suit this plan, and it is upon this plan that the very fabric of the body is built; and this is the truth that underlies such sciences as physiognomy, phrenology and palmistry. It is not that the body by long-continued effort is wrought into the likeness of the soul, though there is some truth in this view also, but that the type of body is arranged beforehand to suit and express the type of Personality which requires manifestation during this earth life. In short the body is made to fit the Personality just as a suit of clothes is made to fit the body; and since this is the case, it is not to be wondered at that the shape, size, structure and contour of the body and its parts should show the character of the person who uses that body as a vehicle.

At birth, therefore, the planetary positions are a perfect index to the type of body that is born and of the Personality that will inhabit it for one life-time.   But probably the birth moment is the only time during the whole life when the planetary positions will exactly indicate the type of body, for the planetary positions and aspects in the heavens without are then in perfect agreement with the life currents in the body and with the potentialities of the Personality ; for the body changes very slowly, whereas the planets quickly move away from their birth positions and are never exactly the same again, even in the longest life.   It is this agreement that gives the horoscope an importance it could not otherwise possess, and makes it a guide to the type of Personality as shown in the body and to the character of the soul that dwells within.

Each personality is, in a sense, a new evolution that is to function in a body which has been pre-arranged to call forth a certain type of character from the consciousness within ; and the body does this by shutting out some faculties, partially shutting out others, and allowing the full development and free play of the rest.   This is chiefly determined by the structure of the nervous system which, according to the composition of its various parts, either permits the free action of consciousness, or hinders it, or wholly obliterates it.   Those faculties which have free play are very easily called forth in the course of education or through the influence of parents or companions, and they will generally give pleasure in their exercise ; in most, if not in all cases, they represent powers that have been slowly growing through many past incarnations, and they will be shown to be the strongest, but not necessarily the best aspected planets in the horoscope.

Those faculties that are partially shut out will be acquired with greater difficulty during life ; they will not give so much pleasure in their use, and the person will have but imperfect success at any occupation depending upon them ; they are generally represented by planets that are weaker or less prominent in the horoscope.   They may be faculties that the soul has never yet properly acquired in any of its past lives ; but in a few cases they are deliberately shut out in order that the person may pass through a particular kind of experience or pay some karmic debt that is due ; for nearly all our actions depend upon our character, and with a given type of character the appropriate actions and experiences will follow when the environment is known.

Similarly with faculties that are almost wholly shut out, they are either naturally lacking or are purposely prevented from expressing themselves for karmic reasons.   The planets that signify these are either very weak or in obscure parts of the horoscope, or are seriously afflicted, and often they have all three drawbacks.   The horoscope of the Earl of Arundel shows how very heavy the afflictions can be when many faculties are shut out.

Therefore some faculties are called forth powerfully, some partially, and some not at all ; and when placed in a given environment, previously chosen by the divine guiders of the soul's destiny, the pre-arranged type of Personality results.   Actions are performed according to the kind of character conditioned by the environment : experience is acquired, a new view of the world is presented to the soul for the space of one life, and sooner or later after death the whole of this is gathered up into the permanent Individuality, which is the richer, fuller, and stronger for its acquirement.

SUCCESSIVE INCARNATIONS

Personalities succeed each other, each one representing the same Individuality, but no two of them quite the same.   If we take as an example an Individuality that is evolving, let us say, under Saturn, all the seven rulers will be represented within that Individuality, but Saturn will be the strongest.   When it incarnates in a Personality that is born under Jupiter, this planet and Saturn will both be strong in the horoscope, although they will not necessarily be well aspected, for that is a matter of karma.   For one lifetime the soul will see everything from the point of view of Jupiter, and after death its experience will go to enrich the Individuality, making stronger within it the influence of Jupiter.   Another Personality will follow it after an interval of rest in the heaven world, born under a different planet, intended to enrich another aspect of the Individuality ; and when, after a succession of lives the time comes for that soul to be born again under Jupiter, there will again be that planet and Saturn acting in some way as the two strongest influences in the horoscope, but the remainder of the map of this Jupiter personality will be unlike that of the former one, because the soul will have grown, evolved, changed somewhat in the long interval, will have worked off some of its old karma, and will have made fresh, and the Divine Guardians of man will see that it is born in a different environment for the sake of obtaining increased experience.   Therefore its horoscope will necessarily be different in many respects, although in a succession of such Personalities we may expect to find some strong resemblances, like those that generally exist between members of the same family.

There is no other difference between souls than that which is due to the varied kind of experiences they have had in the past.   The greatest sinner and the highest saint do not differ except in this, and in the fact that the saint is an old and experienced soul, whereas the sinner is relatively young and inexperienced as a soul.   Birth in successive Personalities under new combinations of signs and planets, provides, astrologically speaking, the experiences required; and this will ensure that the sinner of to-day will be the great saint of the distant future.

CHAPTER XII

PLANETARY INFLUENCE AND GESTATION

RELATIONS with others complicate man's karma on the physical plane, and the particular physical form that he wears during a particular life-period must be suitable for the working out of this complicated karma.

A Study in Consciousness.

THERE are many points of view from which the universe may be studied and classified, in the endeavour to understand its mysteries and to explain the unknown or only partially known in terms of things we know. Every science constitutes one such point of view from which a little of the truth of things is seen, for each investigator adds new facts to the universal store and tries to explain them by correlating them with other facts and principles already known. Every religion, so far as it appeals to the understanding, is another point of view, looking out upon quite a different region of the universe, but following the same rule of bringing that which is strange or far off into relation with that which is familiar and near, and so explaining the one by means of the other.

At first, and especially from the scientific point of view, this method seems to be wholly objective in its scope, and we are engaged in explaining one portion of the outer universe by means of other portions of the same outer universe. A botanist who discovers a new plant understands it sufficiently from the botanical point of view when he has determined its order, genus, species, habitat, and similar facts, all of which relate to the outer world. The same holds good of the other sciences; and even religious people, in so far as they think of a life after death, always contemplate it as definitely located somewhere in space and having as much objective reality as this world although doubtless built of a different order of matter and obeying other laws.

Many philosophers go to the opposite extreme and resolve everything into states of consciousness, refusing to acknowledge the independent existence of an outer material universe. They point out that the only knowledge we have of an outer world is what passes within our own consciousness; that when one or more of the five senses is exercised, the result is a modification of consciousness, which is all that is really present to us and all that we can really know; and that the argument by which we seek to prove the existence of something other than consciousness is itself only a series of modifications of consciousness and cannot be shown to be anything more.

This resolves the whole universe into consciousness and its states, and denies the existence of anything else. The process of understanding then consists in bringing some new or relatively unfamiliar state of consciousness into relation with some older, more familiar, or more comprehensive state, so that the two blend and interpenetrate within the total consciousness, and the one is understood by means of the other.

The materialist or realist regards consciousness or spirit as a bye-product of the activities of matter. The complete idealist goes to the opposite extreme and looks upon matter as only a mode of manifestion of spirit; that degree of spirit which constitutes consciousness in each of us is so far removed from that other degree of spirit which constitutes matter that an impassable gulf seems to intervene between them, and even when regarded as ideas only they refuse to blend, they seem to remain separate like oil and water, but they are only two different modes of manifestation of the same underlying spirit. As Mrs. Annie Besant puts it, spirit is God's activity, matter is God's stillness.

This division of the universe into the world of spirit or consciousness and the world of matter, separated from each other by their relative but not absolute degrees of unlikeness, leads on to the consideration of man as similarly constituted. Man, like the universe in general, is essentially consciousness or spirit surrounded everywhere by matter. In man consciousness is aware of itself, has attained to self-consciousness; and it has to be noticed that if, avoiding the closer examination of the problem as to whether matter has any independent existence of its own, we accept matter and spirit for what they may be worth, matter is always without and is manifested while consciousness is always within and is hidden. Matter in a vast variety of forms we see around us on every side, but spirit or consciousnes or self we never see, for it is always hidden behind a veil of matter. Anyone exercising the ordinary five senses can perceive matter but no one perceives consciousness either through these senses or through any others analogous to them. All we ever perceive is the material veil that hides the self within it.

If the examination is carried on to the next higher plane of the universe, the astral or desire world, precisely the same holds true. Anyone who functions on that plane or who examines it clairvoyantly from the physical plane will perceive various objects and bodies animate and inanimate formed of astral matter, but he will no more perceive consciousness there than he will here. In either world all we ever perceive are the outer manifestations of consciousness working underneath and within matter. The same is true again in the mental world which lies beyond the astral; matter is always open, on the surface, and perceptible; consciousness is always hidden, beneath the surface, and imperceptible. When a clairvoyant tells us that he sees a spirit, the expression "a spirit" is used in a loose popular inaccurate sense and what he really sees is some of the matter of the astral plane organised into a human form. That form is animated by a human consciousness just as our physical forms are in this world, but he no more sees the consciousness as such than we do here; he sees astral matter and we see physical matter, and that is all. Subba Rao writes that even the Logos does not see Parabrahman; he sees Mulaprakriti, root-matter, like a veil thrown over Parabrahman.

The Function of Body in Relation to Consciousness

Man may therefore be regarded as consisting of consciousness or self, which is always within, and body, which is made of the matter of whatever world he is functioning in; and both these are surrounded outwardly by the rest of the world. Taking the ordinary physical plane as typical of the whole, we have, firstly, the world at large, the environment; secondly, the physical body; and thirdly, the self, the man, who uses that body as his vehicle for so long as it lives. The environment here includes not only the immediately visible, tangible, and audible surroundings, but also everything that is outside him and that produces any effect upon him by its aerial or ethereal vibrations, no matter from how great a distance, such as the heavenly bodies.

The inner or real man is brought into touch with his physical environment by means of his physical body. That is the purpose for which body exists, to bring the man into these surroundings, to enable him to receive impacts from objects animate and inanimate in the physical world, and thereby to become aware of them, to like and dislike them, and to have his inherent powers called forth in the pursuit or avoidance of them; so that, beginning with a state of complete ignorance of it, he ultimately becomes wise in the wisdom of this world and full of experience of men and things.

If it were not for body, this physical world would be non-existent for us. The not-yet-incarnate soul, descending towards birth, requires a physical body to bring it into touch with the physical world, and until it has acquired one the physical side of things can make no impression upon it. And similarly after the death of the body, the strictly physical plane ceases to exist for the man; the memory of it remains and the desire for it may be very active, but he no longer possesses any senses through which physical matter can make any impression upon him, and he no longer has any powers that can enable him to affect it and to bring about changes in it. He still sees the astral counterparts of all physical objects whenever he turns his attention to them; and, because they answer exactly to the physical objects themselves, to perceive the astral counterpart of, say, a house, serves the same purpose as perceiving the physical house; so that the dead man can easily become aware of what is going on in this world. Nevertheless it is true that for him physical matter as such has ceased to exist; he is influenced by astral matter and influences it in his turn, both that which exists in inanimate objects and that which is built into the vehicles of living persons; but purely physical combinations of matter are practically non-existent for him, just as he himself has become invisible and imperceptible to ordinary persons who are clothed in a physical body and who are only fully conscious of the vibrations and responsive to the impacts of physical matter.

The possession or non-possession of a body, therefore, decides whether a man is able to come into touch with this world, to affect it and be affected by it. If we adopt the classification of (1) the man, (2) his body, and (3) the surrounding world, body is the key to the whole situation, and enables the other two to influence each other.

If character belongs to the soul, the real man, its ability to express itself in this world depends entirely upon body. The soul brings its various faculties with it when it is born upon this earth, but its possibility of using them efficiently depends upon the kind of body that is given to it; and because character determines fate to a very large extent, the type of body decides what the man's career will be, his good and evil fortune, his successes and failures. That this is true in part is obvious; for a feeble and sickly body will make it impossible to succeed at an occupation requiring muscular strength and endurance ; a coarse and heavy body will ensure failure if the man tries to pursue a calling that needs refinement of touch and delicacy of manipulation : a weak and overstrained nervous system will make impossible many experiences and situations that demand great self-control and strong nerves.

These and other similar cases that will occur to any thoughtful person are self-evident ; but astrology and occultism as well as scientific theories on the subject of heredity require us to carry the subject very much further. We have apparently to see in body a kind of physical epitome or expression for the whole of the soul's character, or rather for so much of it as succeeds in manifesting during the space of one life-time. We have to recognise that character, and therefore fate, varies with the body, not only along the broad lines and in the obvious ways just mentioned but also in more subtle fashion and with regard to faculties that are not so much on the surface or so self-evident. Special types and qualities of body, and especially of brain and nervous system, go with special types of character ; or, to reverse the proposition, each distinct kind of character requires a distinct kind of body to express it, and could not manifest without it. Body and mind fit each other like hand and glove. Body is a kind of living mask which hides, and yet at the same time expresses, the man who wears it. A man with a pink mask cannot play the part of a negro successfully ; and the soul, whatever it may be in itself and apart from this world, is similarly limited in its possibilities by the type of body received from its parents.

Phrenologists, physiognomists, palmists, and similar investigators of human nature are familiar with the idea that the body, or at least that part of it which they study, expresses the character and through this to a large extent the fate of a man. Astrology, occultism, and the problems of heredity compel us to recognise the fact that this is true not merely of head, face, and hands only, but of the whole of the body, within and without, from head to feet.

HEREDITY FROM A SCIENTIFIC STANDPOINT

Taking the subject of heredity first, the most recent and widely accepted theories of men of science affirm that within the body are certain generative cells which are handed down from parent to child unaltered. Two of these, one from the father and the other from the mother, unite, and the fertilised ovum that results from their union sub-divides, producing many new cells. Some of these cells are handed on unchanged to the child to form its generative cells; and only one of them, by continual subdivision, forms that mass of material which is built up into the body of the child. This one cell contains all the potentialities of the future body within it. It is the physical basis for the expression of the character of the child that is to be born, and in its small compass are the whole of the complex forces of heredity.

Every part of the body that is capable of varying as a whole, is believed to be present as a factor within the nucleus of this one cell. Weismann, who has brought this theory much to the front, considered, we are told, that the ultimate physical elements of heredity within the nucleus of the cell are—" a colony of invisible self-propagating vital units or *biophors*, each of which has the power of expressing in development some particular quality. He supposed that these biophors are aggregated into units of a higher order, known as *determinants*, one for each structure of the body which is capable of independent variation. These determinants are supposed to be grouped together in *ids*, each of which is supposed to possess a complete complement of the specific characters of the organism and also to have an individual character."

This is the scientific version of the way in which the potentialities of the whole physical body are contained within the one cell from which that body originates. Simple in apparent structure without, it is exceedingly complex within, and it contains the kind of material which will express the forces of heredity and will result in the complete new body with its various possibilities and limitations.

OTHER CONSIDERATIONS

Turning next to the occult teachings on the subject, we find that the scientific theories require supplementing by two important factors. The first of these concerns the plan or architecture of the body, and the second the influence of the incoming soul that is to inhabit and animate that body.

The body does not form itself and grow in a mechanical automatic manner, like iron filings clustering round a magnet. Certain lofty spiritual Beings, the Lords of Karma, give a model of the body that is to be, and create an artificial elemental whose task it is to build it in accordance with the model. The plan of the body varies according to the kind of character to be expressed by the soul and the kind of experience it is destined to pass through during its life-time in the body. Not all the character and powers of the soul are expressed in the physical body, for some are definitely shut out, sometimes because that is the fate the man has earned for himself by his past career in other lives, and sometimes in order that he may turn his attention to other aspects of his character which need to be developed.

This brings us back to the principles previously expressed; that a given type of character can only be expressed by means of a body exactly adapted for the purpose; that a body which is a suitable vehicle for one kind of character would be unsuitable or impossible for expressing a quite different kind ; and that fate and fortune to a large extent vary according to character. It is not that body causes character, for this with all its strengths and weaknesses inheres in the soul ; but the type of body and the environment ensure certain experiences being impressed upon the man within, and, by the reaction, call forth the latent powers and faculties, some of them easily because they are well developed and free from hindrance, others with difficulty or not at all because they are weak or are partly or wholly shut out by the formation of the body.

Here we have a clear sequence of principles. The plan of the body and the environment into which it will be born are decided by the Lords of Karma. This determines the general type of character and consequently also of the events and occurrences that will be experienced during the life history. The plan of the body is expressive of both character and fate ; in fact the horoscope is built into the very fabric of the body, and if we knew enough of occult anatomy and physiology we should be able to see the Sun, Moon, planets and zodiacal signs expressed in the constitution of the body and varying for good or evil according to its strengths and weaknesses.

THE THREE FACTORS AT WORK ON THE EMBRYO

The soul does not enter into the body until a considerable time after birth, but is in touch with it unconsciously from an early period of antenatal life, various currents of energy flowing down from the soul and playing a part in the shaping of the body. There are therefore three factors at work upon the embryo ; firstly, the forces of heredity, contained in the fertilised ovum ; secondly, the plan given by the Lords of Karma in accordance with which the artificial elemental builds the body ; and thirdly, the influence of the incoming soul, generally exercised unconsciously.

PLANETARY INFLUENCE DURING GESTATION

The average length of human gestation is 40 weeks (280 days), but a good deal of variation from this is possible. A child born at 28 weeks may live, although it does not usually do so. The longer the period of gestation lasts beyond the 28 weeks the more likelihood there is of the child living if prematurely born.

A week is one quarter of the Moon's revolution. Birth both in men and animals is regulated by the Moon. The following synodical revolutions, if taken in certain simple proportions, measure close to the period of gestation, 280 days.

Planet	Synodical Revolution	Proportion	Days
Moon	29·530 days	$9\frac{1}{2}$	281
Mercury	115·877 „	$2\frac{1}{2}$	290
Venus	583·920 „	$\frac{1}{2}$	292
Earth	365·256 „	$\frac{3}{4}$	274
Mars	779·936 „	$\frac{1}{3}$	260
Jupiter	398·867 „	$\frac{3}{4}$	299
Saturn	378·090 „	$\frac{3}{4}$	284
Uranus	369·656 „	$\frac{3}{4}$	277
Neptune	367·488 „	$\frac{3}{4}$	276
	The Average of the whole		281

The first of these columns gives the name of the heavenly body; the second gives the period of its mean synodical revolution in days and decimals of a day, the sidereal revolution being given in the case of the earth; the third gives the proportion of the revolution that is used; and the fourth gives the result to the nearest whole day, ignoring fractions. A synodical revolution is the time intervening between two conjunctions with the Sun, or the time that elapses before the return to the same relative position in the zodiac with regard to the Sun, as seen from the earth. In the case of Mercury and Venus, if the count is made from superior conjunction, the revolution ends with the return to the superior conjunction and not the inferior.

This table shows that $9\frac{1}{2}$ mean synodical revolutions of the Moon measure 281 days (more exactly 280·54) or within one day of the normal period of gestation. $2\frac{1}{2}$ synodical revolutions of Mercury measure 290

days.   Half the period of Venus gives 292 days.   The other planets
give either a little more or a little less than the normal ; the average of
the whole being 281 days, a very close approach to the 280 demanded
by medical science.

With regard to the proportions used, it will be noticed that the only
fractions are halves, quarters, and thirds, all of which are astrologically
legitimate because they are actually employed in the calculation of
aspects.

This table speaks for itself of the close relation between gestation
and planetary revolution, and of the supreme importance of the Moon
especially.   The fact that the revolution taken is synodical, *i.e.*, position as
seen from the earth, shows the geocentric nature of the whole and is,
therefore, in harmony with the rest of astrological science ; for birth takes
place upon this earth, and it is the influence radiated from the planets on
to human beings living on this earth that has to be taken into account.

Even the odd half in the proportions of the Moon, Mercury, and
Venus has significance, for these are the only known bodies that can come
in between the earth and the Sun.   In the case of the Moon, if conception
be supposed to take place at New Moon, birth will occur at about a Full
Moon, normally.   Taking the Sun as symbolising the Individuality and
the Moon the Personality, at New Moon these two are at one in the
higher heaven world.   The separation of the two orbs during the waxing
of the Moon symbolises the separation of Personality from Individuality at
the descent into incarnation ; and embodied life on the physical plane is
symbolised by Full Moon, when the Moon is half the circle distant from
the Sun.   The waning of the Moon stands for the departure from the
physical plane and the return of the Personality to its source.   The half
revolution, therefore, has its appropriateness.

In the case of either Venus or Mercury, the superior conjunction,
when the planet is on the further side of the Sun from the earth, symbolises the unity of personal and individual consciousness in the higher
heaven ; the same as New Moon.   If conception takes place at a
superior conjunction, birth will normally result at about an inferior
conjunction, when the planet is between the earth and the Sun, which
position symbolises the descent into incarnation.   These two planets,
however, vary from the mean too much to be taken as standards like the
Moon.

If the column headed " Synodical Revolution " is added up and an average taken, it will amount to 376·514 days; and then $\frac{3}{4}$ of this average is 282·386 days, which is again a very close approach to the average of 280 given by medical men.   So far as the writer is aware this is the first time these planetary averages have been pointed out; and when it is remembered that the Synodical Revolutions vary from $29\frac{1}{2}$ days in the case of the Moon to 780 days in that of Mars, it is truly remarkable that so close an approach to the scientific estimate of 40 weeks should be possible.   The fact speaks loudly of the close connection between the heavenly bodies and the period of gestation.

The reason for taking $\frac{3}{4}$ as a proportion is, of course, because nine months is this fraction of a year.   The proportion $\frac{1}{3}$, used in the case of Mars, measures from the cusp of the 1st house to that of the 5th (the child).   The proportion $\frac{3}{4}$ measures from the cusp of the 8th house (generation) to that of the 5th.

SUN, MOON, AND ASCENDANT

The clearest evidence with regard to the influence of the Moon upon birth is obtained in the study of what is called the Pre-natal Epoch. This proves that the Moon and the Ascendant occupy a definite relation to each other during the successive months of gestation up to the time of birth, so that the Moon's place or its opposition on the day of the Epoch, about nine months before birth, becomes either the Ascendant or Descendant at birth.   The Sun stands for heredity through the father and for his relation to the child as well as for vitality ; the Moon for heredity through the mother and for her relation to the child, as well as for the living material basis of the body ; and the Ascendant stands for the child itself.   The successive months of gestation repeat in little the various stages of human evolution in the past, and also correspond to the human Principles that have been in process of evolution throughout, a process still unfinished.

CHAPTER XIII

STRONG AND WEAK CHARACTERS

THE *Sidereal* 'prophecies' of the Zodiac, as they are called by the Christian mystics, never point to any one particular event, however sacred and solemn it may be for some portion of humanity, but to ever-recurrent, periodical laws in Nature, understood but by the Initiates of the sidereal Gods themselves. Why see in *Pisces* a direct reference to Christ—a Saviour but for his direct followers, a great and glorious Initiate for all the rest—when that constellation shines as a symbol of all the past, present and future Spiritual Saviours Who dispense light, and dispel mental darkness. *Secret Doctrine.*

ONCE in every cycle of Twenty-Six Thousand Years, the time taken for the whole of the zodiac to revolve round a given point, a superior MAN is born; to many he is known as the MANU, the divine man, or law-giver, striking the note of the whole cycle.

Again, every Two Thousand Years a human being is born in whom every human principle is personified, and he strikes the note for the sign of the zodiac which HE represents, for HE is a race Teacher, striking the note of a new religion to suit the race born under that particular sign.

Every Century a man is born who stands ahead of the race, and again every Decade sees a particular man born who is superior in expression to those who follow him.

Every Year one man is born who strikes a note higher than the ordinary note, and again every month, and every day, there is born a man or woman who is at the apex of the time in which he is born.

These special periods afford opportunities for the births of those souls who are above mediocrity.

The geometrical figures caused by the motion of the heavenly bodies are eternally changing, and although they express the mathematical calculations upon which astrological laws are based, they are never repeated in the same form during the cyclic revolution of the whole of the zodiac.[1] The aspects of the planets one to another are also based upon

---

[1] It has been shown that in 23892 years the Earth, Venus, and Mars complete an exact number of revolutions, after which the series of solar and mutual aspects formed between them would of course be repeated. In order to include Jupiter this period must be multiplied by 5; if Uranus also is to be included, by 30; and if the whole of the planets ☿ ♀ ⊕ ♂ ♃ ♄ ♅ ♆, by 90. Thus the complete series of possible planetary aspects cannot be repeated until after the lapse of about two million years.

this law. This axiom helps us to catch some glimpse of the value of the new moon preceding any birth-time, or the Sun's ingress into the zodiacal signs prior to that time, although our studies of Natal Astrology have not as yet advanced sufficiently to enable us to understand their importance completely.

This implies certain limitations beyond which souls cannot evolve if they are to retain the body moulded upon the pattern of the geometrical figure to which it is related. It also implies the necessity for Initiation into that state of consciousness represented by the 'beyond' of that particular form.

Looking at the seven planetary rays from below, at the head of the group of individuals belonging to each ray there stands a Master, or perfected human being, who has blended within himself all the contradictory influences of the other rays, as sub-influences of His own ray. That Master of life and form, who is living in the Eternal, is the ideal for every human being; for as nothing disturbs the harmony of His perfected human expression, so must we seek to transmute all the warring elements in our own nature, and sound forth, clearly and distinctly, the note of the present physical existence. The celestial pattern upon which the vehicles we inhabit have been moulded, may have limited the expression of our consciousness, but it does not bind us either to the physical, emotional or mental bodies separately, for we can transcend one and all, and yet not outgrow the limitations of higher modes of consciousness than those vehicles express. We may be mediocre so far as physical actions are concerned, and yet burst forth into genius through thought, feeling, or spiritual unfoldment.

The phenomena of what are called "conversions," and other less common religious experiences, to say nothing of those flashes of intuition which nearly all have experienced, prove clearly enough that we are not bound to one side of our nature alone, to the exclusion of other sides as yet undeveloped. It is the persistent identification with one planetary vibration to the exclusion of others that generally produces those lopsided developments and extreme contradictory influences we find in many horoscopes; and more often than not the apparently mediocre horoscope has some benefic influence that has been entirely overlooked by the native, who remains indifferent to it through what he is apt wrongly to term the force of circumstances.

How to Judge

There are so many factors to be taken into consideration when attempting to synthesise a horoscope, that to overlook the fact that each figure fits into some other figure, may throw the whole of our judgment out of a true focus; therefore, we must endeavour to understand from whence many of the contradictory influences arise.

A child is born into a family with which it is either in harmony or the reverse; in other words, the geometrical figure fits in with the horoscopes of the other members of the family, or it is impossible to find even the semblance of a fitting. Many of these cases have been examined, and no explanation has been found save that of the theory of Reincarnation, or the soul's successive re-embodiment into conditions necessary to work out its destiny. The people we meet in daily life have a larger influence over us than we at first imagine, and it is not until we learn to look upon ourselves as parts of the great human family, that a true sense of proportion is obtained.

We often resent the words, feelings, and actions of others, and cause a reaction upon ourselves that might have been avoided had we understood the motives or the temperaments of the persons affecting us; and we fail to sympathise with and to understand others so long as we do not realise the contradictory nature of the elements forming the mould of expression through which our consciousness is working. Mars and Saturn are apparently contradictory elements, but in their own place they work harmoniously, and without real conflict. The Martial and Saturnian temperaments cannot understand each other so long as each expects or demands that the other shall express similar vibrations.

The Martial colouring is the first and most powerful vibration in the lives of the majority, and this vibration ranges from very coarse to very fine, according to the sign, house position and aspects of Mars.

The ultimate of the Martial vibration is expressed in that of Venus.

The Saturnian colouring may be said to be the last prevailing influence for the majority, and to range between the very gross and very subtle; its ultimate is expressed in Uranus, or for those who cannot reach that subtle influence, in Jupiter. The Uranian vibration can only affect the very few who have worked through all lower influences, and now respond to that which may be said to synthesise the whole.

THE HIGH WATER MARK

There is in every horoscope the "high water mark," up to which the tide of the life is flowing; it may be Mars or Venus, Saturn or Jupiter, or possibly Uranus or Neptune; and toward this high water mark each individual is more or less striving, and his power of responsiveness to any particular vibration may be seen on carefully weighing up all the possibilities. The Moon's position, the place of Mercury, and the angles, are the most sensitive points in all nativities. The Moon's aspects denote ability to respond to the influences of those planets that aspect it. All aspects should be interpreted impartially and irrespective of the so-called 'malefic' or 'benefic' influences, but the sign and house should never be overlooked.

Persons who are strongly individual are inclined to be less responsive to the devotional side of life, and are generally affected through the positive signs. The Sun, Moon and Mercury in negative signs denotes too much receptivity and responsiveness, and an inclination to be too easily affected by sensations and feelings, or by circumstances; the reverse is the case when they are in positive signs. It is usually a safe rule to judge the power of response by planets in the negative signs as follows. The Moon, general responsiveness, modified by the planets aspecting it; Mercury mental, Venus emotional, Mars passional, Jupiter social, Saturn resisting.

Enfolded in the innermost of everyone is the life force upon which is based the ideals of consciousness we conceive to be wisdom, love, and the power to act; and we all are seeking with more or less ability to give expression to that inherent life force. As pointed out in a previous Chapter each soul is a pure white ray of its parent, or Father Star, and this ray shining out upon the kaleidoscope of material existence is coloured by the prevailing pictures at that special stage in evolution in which the soul or ego finds itself. The pictures are the same for all beings, and evolution goes steadily on, regardless of the sinner or the saint.

THE AGE OF THE SOUL

What then makes the great difference between souls born into the material world, while the pictures are running through the lantern of time?

It is the age of the soul and the nature of its past experience, and the consequent attitude that the soul takes toward the ever-changing panorama of Life, that causes it to identify itself with one picture while ignoring others.

Some souls are receptive and impressed by the colour of the pictures, while others are indifferent and lack sufficient receptivity to be much impressed; others again fix their whole attention upon one particular picture, and become absorbed by its influence.

The ray from the Ego is directed to the baby body, which gives it the first material colouring. The child grows into youth coloured by the environment in which he grows. He awakes to view the great drama of life, and is more or less conscious of a great play of which he knows little or much according to his hidden memory of the past, his powers of responsiveness in the present, and his ideals regarding the future.

The World Drama

The planetary spirits are the players, and the principal actors in the great world drama. The zodiac is, for our earth, the stage on which all the scenes are constantly changing, and from this stage the strong lime-light is reflected upon the lives of men and women who perform their parts in miniature upon the stage of daily life.

The play of human life has been written by wise and perfect beings. The scenes may change with each revolution of the scroll of time, but the acts are much about the same, although they may appear to vary with the centuries and the civilisations. With each birth into the material universe every human being has the opportunity to play his part thoroughly or indifferently, and the only limitation to his scope and efficiency is made when he identifies himself with other planets or with lesser parts than the one he was meant to play. The period of influence that each planet is said in turn to exert over the life of every human being may well be given here.

When a child is born it comes directly under the influence of the Moon for the first four years of its life, and this corresponds to the development and definite formation of the etheric mould as a receiver and collector of astral and physical vibrations. Now although the body grows and thrives more or less as life advances, this lunar influence may continue beyond the four years, indefinitely, if there is no response to the next influence which is around the child. This is the influence of

Mercury, extending from 4 to 10 years of age, and dependent upon the position of Mercury and the Mercurial signs in the horoscope.   During this period the intellectual faculties should expand through perception and observation, and a great deal of this mental development will depend upon parentage, environment, and the impressions made upon the young mind.

The influence of the planet Venus plays upon the generative system, and the emotions are stimulated by association with the opposite sex and the uprising of feelings and sensations affecting the Venus nature. These three periods are the youthful stages.

The maturing period begins under the influence of the Sun at 18 years of age, and lasts until the period of the Sun ends about the thirty-seventh year of life, during which time the vital forces are strengthening and vitalising the body.   From 37 until 52 the body is in its prime; the chief work of the world is then done and ambition succeeds or fails under the influence of Mars, the planet of strength and positive energy.   From 52 to 64 the period of Jupiter extends and brings wisdom and sober judgment.   The remaining years of life are usually under the influence of the planet Saturn.   These are the *general* influences governing the various periods of life, and making it good or ill according to the positions, aspects, and directions of the planets ruling those periods.   But they are general periods only, ruling over all in a general sense.

We have, it is true, heard of prodigies coming forth from time to time, and of precocious children who have transcended the periods and apparently risen superior to them.   We have also known old men in the prime of life and youthful men in old age, and we need to look deeper into the mysteries of Astrology to account for these and all abnormal cases.   Esoteric Astrology teaches that the rising sign, and particularly the decanate of that sign, is a focus for personal and individual characteristics expressed in the nativity.

CHAPTER XIV

THE ANGELIC HOST

THE verse, " For though there be that are called Gods, whether in heaven or on earth, as there be Gods many and lords many," shows at any rate the recognition by Paul of a plurality of " Gods " whom he calls ' daemons ' (' spirits,' never *devils*). Principalities, thrones, dominions, rectors, etc., are all Jewish and Christian names for the Gods of the ancients—the Archangels and Angels of the former being in every case the Devas and the Dhyân Chohans of the more ancient religions. *Secret Doctrine.*

THE more thoroughly we enter into the study of Esoteric Astrology the nearer do we approach the realm of the Angelic Host, of whose evolution humanity knows so little although it lies at the root of all things connected with both science and religion.

The ancient astrologers appear to have made a special study or at least to have had a deeper knowledge concerning this evolution, which runs side by side with the human although invisible to our physical senses. Remains of knowledge have been handed down to us in what we have been taught about the five " Elements " connected with the signs of the zodiac, known as Æther, Air, Fire, Water and Earth.

Modern astrologers have confirmed the usefulness of this classification, and have rediscovered the inner meaning of these divisions in connection with the types of matter through which the modifications of consciousness are constantly working. We may, however, apply the well-known Hermetic maxim " As above so below " to these " Elements " and extend our knowledge so as to discover more potent forces working through a host of entities belonging to the planetary spheres. These are specially connected with the manifold sub-divisions of the seven great rays that are constantly streaming through the seven planetary spheres of influence. The fact that there is a great evolution beyond the human in which there are grades of those Beings called angels, from the mighty archangels down to the minor elementals, should surprise no one who has even a faint knowledge of religion, since all religions teach that the work of creation began with the calling into existence of a vast host of intelligent Beings of varying power and authority, into whose care was entrusted the special work of guiding and controlling the activities of nature.

If we could look into the angelic world we should be amazed at the wonderful evolution that is going on there in a realm that is as real and as important as the other divisions of nature of which we are more fully conscious, namely the mineral, vegetable, animal, and human kingdoms. Each angel has his place in that world as humans have in this, but they are moved by one will, that of the supreme Intelligence who is both the heart and brain of all ; and although they have far greater power than any human being they are limited and restricted to their own particular sphere of operations.   Many names have been applied to these angels, but the Hindu Astrologers have always termed them Devas, which means Shining or Radiant, owing to their bodies being formed of the bright luminous matter of the plane to which they belong.   We shall, therefore, give them their eastern name of Deva to avoid confusing them with the modern ideas associated with the word angel.   All the Devas are more or less concerned with the matter side of evolution, and in the main they are either constructive or destructive ; that is, their work is to guide and build the forms required for the purposes of evolution, and also to destroy them when their time of usefulness has ended.

THE DEVAS

Now it is a fact that many human beings think they are working when all the time it is the energies of the Devas that are operating through them, for these are the agents of the great planetary spirits under whose influence they work.

A great deal of the so-called good and bad "luck" is due to the invisible working of the Devas who have power, within certain limits, to facilitate or hinder the working of planetary influences.

Many a scientific invention or great scheme of reform is brought about by them in the course of their work of applying practically the primary influences connected with events.   This does not imply that there is any favouritism in the Divine plan but merely that a man may earn the right, through merit, skill, or energy, to be the physical means by which small or great events are brought about.   It is true that a Deva may be drawn to some special person through his prayers and sacrifices : but to do this consciously one must be acquainted with the laws of occultism, which are higher than those ordinarily connected with mortals. The help of the Devas, however, like that of men is only transient, so that to attract their attention and win their good will is not the end for those who are seriously treading the path of occultism. The names of the principal Devas connected with the evolution of humanity are as follows:

Indra, who is connected with the planes of Ether; Vayu, the Deva of Air; Agni, the Fire Deva; Varuna, the Water Deva; and Kubera, the Earth Deva.

Each has a counterpart or female aspect but with these we are not at present concerned. There are also other lesser Devas whose names are known and who work directly under the Five, but to deal with them now would take us too far from the subject in hand. In Chaldean Astrology the functions of the Gods or Devas were well-known, and the priests of Chaldea were chiefly concerned with invoking these great Beings, and the whole study of Astrology appears to have been turned in this direction. Indra was known as the God of the Firmament, or the King of the Sidereal Gods; Vayu was the God or sovereign of the air; Agni, the God of Fire; Varuna, the God of Waters; and Kubera or Kuvera, the God of Hades, and king of the earthly elementals.

These have a deeper meaning, however, for each was a protector of mankind, some being connected with life and some with death, but all acting as guardians and helpers of humanity. We cannot know directly what actually goes on in the Deva kingdom, but we do know that they are directly concerned with the helping of all forms in manifestation toward a perfect expression of the consciousness within. Not a single human form comes into existence but a Deva is concerned with its building, and therefore, if for nothing more than their aid in our evolution we owe them a debt of gratitude.

It is possible to divide the Devas into separate classes, and this has already been done by students who are not working directly along the astrological line; the two classifications, however, coincide closely and throw light upon each other, so that aid in this direction may be obtained from such works as *A Study in Consciousness*, *The Secret Doctrine*, etc.

We learn that there are three classes of Devas who came over with the Logos of the Solar System from a past universe, and knowing the plan of the whole Solar System work consciously in its upbuilding. The first of these three classes includes the great Devas connected with the elements of ether, air, fire, water, and earth; and there are two more of these elements not yet manifested, seven in all. Then there are the architects, who are known as the Planetary Logoi, who have definite departments in which they work out the plan or scheme of the great Solar Logos, and finally there are the third class, who are the Lipikas, or Recorders, connected with the Karma of the whole system and all in it. These great Beings live on the highest planes, and we only see the last results of their activities on the planes below. Each Deva in the first of these classes may be said to have as his body the whole matter of the plane to which he belongs, and he controls the hosts of lesser Devas working on his plane ; so that when our consciousness is on the plane of any particular great Deva we are actually living and moving in his body. It may be as well to state that the names given to these Devas are only those of the offices they hold, and any such name is applied generally to whatever lofty Being may occupy that office at any time.

We must also remember that what is a world to them may be composed of many worlds so far as our consciousness is concerned, just as our body is a whole body to us, but is nevertheless composed of many parts making up that body. They are connected with the chains of worlds, of which there are seven in our Solar system, the whole making up the grand man of the heavens, the heavenly man or the Adam Kadmon of the Kabala.

The Architects, of whom we can know very little, are the Builders of each chain ranging from those who do the highest work connected with the building down to the nature spirits who are working in quite the lower kingdom of nature.

The Recorders can only be known to us by name. We read of them in the book of *Revelation* as the Scribes of the Solar system concerned with " the book of life." They have to do with the Law of God and are chiefly connected with the collective karma of nations and the universe generally.

In connection with and under the rule of these great Beings there are a large number of still great but nevertheless subordinate Devas. Connected with the Devas of the Elements are the rulers of the nature spirits and the nature spirits themselves. In connection with the Architects are the Builders and those who shape the mineral, vegetable, and animal kingdoms, also those concerned with the human forms.

Also connected with the Recorders are those Devas who have to do with the administration of the karmic law in its relation, firstly, to whole nations, and secondly, to individuals. Finally the Lunar Pitris are also included here.

Deva Worship and the Great Religions

From this it will be seen that what we term natural forces are nothing more or less than the activities of the Devas who work directly or indirectly in connection with some special sphere of influence. Astrologically, all the Devas connected with Kubera and the earthy element are working in the sphere of influence of the planet Jupiter.

If we would enquire further, we may find that the religion evolved under the influence of Jupiter is actually that of Deva worship, and that the element of ritual and ceremonial in any religion is directly or indirectly aiming at the control of or co-operation with these Devas. We are, therefore, taught that the forces involved in the operations of chemistry, alchemy, astronomy, astrology, electricity, and magnetism are all inspired by the Spirit of Jupiter, the great Lord of Form.

The chain of worlds to which the earth belongs, and which includes Mercury and Mars, is connected with Agni, the God of Fire. In a separate chapter we have dealt more fully with the element of Fire and its relation to the signs of the zodiac.

All fire-worshippers, such as the Parsis, come under its influence, and it ranges from the worship of common fire, ruled by Mars, to the great magnetic fires connected with the sun.

Varuna, the God of Waters, is closely connected with the astral plane and the fourth race. It governed the religions of Egypt for the worshippers of the Nile. It is also connected with all those religious teachings concerning the Fish-Deity, such as Oannes of the Babylonians, etc.

In Vayu, a power yet to come more prominently into manifestation, the real mercurial influence will be more active; while through Indra will come the potent influence of Uranus.

The following interesting account of Deva influences is from a lecture delivered many years ago by a well-known occultist :—

The planets which you see have no influence themselves, except the microscopic influence of gravitation; no one supposes otherwise. But there *is* an influence of some kind not coming from the planets themselves, but working in connection with them.

The planets may perhaps be said to represent certain centres in the physical body of the Logos.

The Sun is used chiefly as His representative, but all the planets of our system, being in reality but fragments of the Sun, are connected also with the physical body of the Great Logos.

It has been said that these planets mark certain centres in that body and when speaking of it we must remember that it possesses more dimensions than we generally know of. Its physical plane motions indicate the movement of still higher spheres of influence than we have any knowledge of, and it is the movement of those spheres which produces what is called planetary influence.

Our own physical bodies have centres, each of which deals chiefly with one class or sub-division of etheric matter. When any one centre is called into activity, it points to the fact that the man is able to respond to the particular vibration of that portion of etheric matter. In all conditions of matter, whether astral, etheric, or otherwise, there are existing elementals of all kinds. Certain parts of the surrounding elemental essence are set in motion when any centre is called into activity. Man is then acted on in two ways; part of the elemental essence within him is set in motion—and also the activity of the elemental essence outside him is intensified, and that reacts on him.

By the position of the physical planets we can tell where the planetary influence is working, at any particular time. If, however, we were clairvoyant we could see the influence for ourselves, and we should not need the indication which the physical planets give us. They are like the hands of a clock, pointing out what is happening in those other invisible spheres, without being themselves the causes of the influence.

In the action of the spiritual influences of the planets, three classes of entities are spoken of as the "spirit of the planet."

1. There is an entity, not very far advanced in knowledge, which is called the "spirit of the earth."

2. A special part of the elemental essence, which is called into activity by the action of the particular planet, and which is called the "spirit of the planet."

3. A far higher kingdom, called the Deva-kingdom, which has its divisions corresponding to those in the human, animal and vegetable kingdoms, the influences of which are spoken of as the "spirit of the planet," and which resembles the Christian idea of Angels. These have great influence.

The worship of the Chaldæans to the planetary spirits was not of the same kind as our worship of God. It was rather in the form of affection and veneration for these Star-Devas.   What the Chaldæan had in his mind might have been an exaggerated idea, but undoubtedly there was truth in it.   The idea of the Archangel of the planet was certainly a true one.

This kind of worship is not necessary for us now ; but it might have been necessary for even the great Adepts at that time, in their then phase of evolution.

The religion of Chaldæa had a great effect on the daily life, even in the minute actions of the people, as all religions ought to have.   The Chaldæans were greatly affected by the teachings of their priests and astrologers ; with some of the highly developed ones there were shown to be possibilities of getting into very close touch with even the hierarchy of the Devas themselves.   (We must always remember that though we are not taught to worship the Devas of the Stars, there are other lines of occultism besides the particular form to which Theosophy has introduced us.)

And there was a higher possible development still, by which a man could get himself re-born on another sphere, standing clear away from this world.   But there were very, very few capable of attaining it.

Astrology, now, is not taken up as a religion or means of worship and of prayer ; but it was so considered in ancient Chaldæa.

Among the priests various departments in connection with the influences of the stars were studied.   With some it was the study of medicine and healing, so that they could offer prescriptions suitable to the planetary conditions of their patients.

With another class, the study was in agriculture ; the effect of planetary influences was noticed on different classes of plants, so that the people could be advised of the best time to sow or gather in their crops. Other priests made a study of the breeding of animals, and so on.

Another class studied the weather department, having a kind of weather bureau.   The Government was mixed up with this part of the study, so that the weather prophets were made responsible for failures, and dismissed from their posts if the predictions did not come true.

A very important feature of the Chaldæan religion was the personal dealing of the priests with the people.   They would tell a man what were the predominating qualities in his aura, and they would thus be able to indicate to him what planetary conditions would be likely to influence him most.

ESOTERIC ASTROLOGY

———

SECOND PART

EXPLANATORY DIAGRAMS AND
ILLUSTRATIVE HOROSCOPES

THE DIAGRAMS

All the Diagrams, Map-Blocks, etc., in this book have been so arranged as to come on the left-hand page of book, and therefore any Diagram or Horoscope can be compared with any other, or with the descriptive letterpress, without the disadvantage of having to turn pages backwards and forwards in order to see what is on the reverse side.

The Star Maps on pp. 134 to 162 are explained on p. 169; but Chapters XV-XVII should preferably be read before that explanation is studied.

The Horoscope of Mrs. Besant was taken as an example in a Series of Special Lessons, and for this purpose was carefully rectified by events to 5.29 p.m., 1/10/1847; it therefore differs slightly from the map published in her "Autobiography," which shows ♈ 10° ascending. Mrs. Besant has herself stated that the time was 'somewhere between 5 and 5.45 p.m.'

ESOTERIC ASTROLOGY

Second Part

CHAPTER XV

ESOTERIC VALUE OF THE POLARITIES

THE Sun is the external manifestation of the Seventh Principle of our Planetary System, while the Moon is its Fourth Principle, shining in the borrowed robes of her master, saturated with and reflecting every passionate impulse and evil desire of her grossly material body, Earth. The whole cycle of Adeptship and Initiation and all its mysteries are connected with, and subservient to, these two and the Seven Planets. *Secret Doctrine.*

IN Esoteric Astrology the luminaries are taken to represent Positive and Negative centres, and the plan upon which the Soli-lunar combinations have been delineated is based upon the positions of these centres in relation to the zodiacal signs, first from the stand-point of the three qualities, and then from that of the triplicities to which they belong. This can be best illustrated by taking as examples a few of the Polarities published in the Text Books of Astrology.

Aries is the cardinal sign of the fiery triplicity and it therefore represents fiery activity. The Sun is exalted in Aries and thus makes active all the qualities of this sign from the positive or electric standpoint. The Sun represents the growing individuality or the more permanent life forces of the individual, and it has primary importance in all matters connected with the polarity of the two luminaries, being normally positive. In a positive sign the Sun may be said to be wholly electric, or the centre of an electric aura from which a continuous current of individualising forces is circulated or polarised ; and the Moon then forms the negative or collecting centre of the magnetic forces. The whole of this has been reduced to terms of Individuality and Personality as represented by the luminaries.

Taking the Sun as the individual centre, when in the sign Aries it would appear to be most active in the head, ruled by Aries, and would apparently find the line of least resistance through all the different vibrations in matter represented by Aries, which are astrologically synthesised as cardinal-fire or mental activity. Taking the Moon as the personal centre and the representative of the magnetic or collective

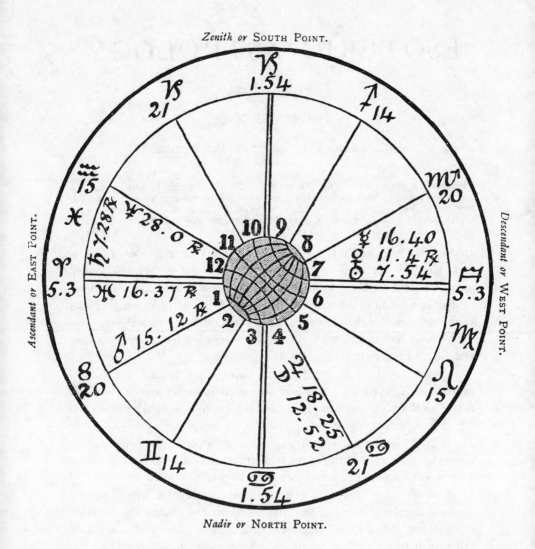

THE HOROSCOPE OF MRS. ANNIE BESANT

Orator, Reformer, Occultist

(See Note on p. 130.)

tendency, the energies that it signifies will tend to be polarised outwardly or to express themselves chiefly in the material form through which the combined soli-lunar forces are manifesting.

If we suppose the Sun and Moon to be both occupying the sign Aries, the polarity will be entirely Aries in its mode of expression, affecting the head and mental activity.

Taking the Sun as centre when in any part of the sign Aries, and holding the idea that the life forces are being individualised through the head and mental activity, the Moon in each successive sign will then draw out the energies of the Individuality towards whatever secondary centre is denoted by the sign through which she is passing. We will take for example Sun in Aries, Moon in Taurus. We have in the background the life force of the Sun seeking expression through the intellect, and drawn toward the lunar centre in Taurus, and this imparts stability, the power of resistance, concentration, firmness, and conservative qualities; in fact it blends the cardinal-fire of the one with the fixed-earth of the other, while allowing the solar centre to have the greater influence.

Now let us take for our example Sun in Aries, Moon in Gemini. In this polarity the intellectual tendencies are increased and a quick-witted or clever expression of the mentality is denoted. In the first case we find the triplicities concerned are Fire and Earth, Aries and Taurus, and in the second case Fire and Air, Aries and Gemini. Throughout the whole circle there is a blending of different characteristics, a synthesis of the energies that manifest through life and form, consciousness and vehicle.

These blendings may be either harmonious or inharmonious; in the case of the Sun in Aries and the Moon in Cancer there is not complete harmony owing to the disagreement of fire and water, as well as because of the fact that the square aspect is never harmonious. There is, however, a partial agreement because the polarity is formed in Cardinal signs, so that some affinity is denoted along the line of activity. The inharmonious tendencies would arise from too much mental activity, which would cause worry, peevishness and hyper-sensitiveness. Astrologically we should find possibilities of transmutation through the Sun's dignity by exaltation and the Moon's strengthened position in her own sign Cancer. The imagination could be trained and sympathy encouraged until a unification of the polarity was made; each one thus affording some opportunity for additional experience necessary for the growth of the Ego.

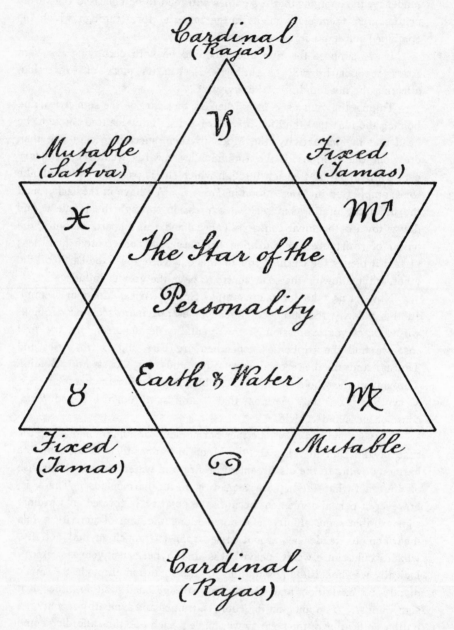

DIAGRAM XI

The Sun in Aries and the Moon in Leo would be a good blend, but might easily produce an over stimulation of the intellect through the fiery triplicity, which is that under which the separate mind is evolved, but because it is a combination of the cardinal and fixed influences it would be beneficial, the restlessness and activity of Aries being made capable of more concentration and steadfastness through the fixed and reserved Leo. We should judge the polarity as mentally impulsive with a tendency toward extremes of mind and feeling. A judicious blending of many factors is obtainable by a careful synthesis of the luminaries in the signs.

The Sun in Aries and the Moon in Virgo is a polarity in which some repetition of the Sun in Aries and the Moon in Taurus appears. It may not seem harmonious because fire and earth do not blend easily, but it brings discrimination out of the critical nature of Virgo and the intellectual nature of Aries.

The Sun in Aries and the Moon in Libra is probably the ideal polarity. It turns all the intellectual and mental qualities of Aries into abstract thought and feeling, and may, by a careful use, produce clairvoyance and intuitive faculties.

The Sun in Aries and Moon in Scorpio would be rather an unfavourable blend, as fire and water are by no means favourable mixtures, but here again judgement would be necessary to give a correct synthesis, because Aries and Scorpio are the positive and negative signs of Mars, their ruling planet. This polarity would therefore accentuate the martial tendences in an immature Ego, but give powers to an exceptionally evolved individual.

The Sun in Aries and the Moon in Sagittarius would be an excellent blend. It would accentuate the fiery and intellectual tendency, but considerably modify the magnetic or attractive influence, and might cause a positive and somewhat hard nature. The possibilities of expression would be very great.

The Sun in Aries and the Moon in Capricorn does not appear to be a particularly good blend, Mars and Saturn ruling these signs, and therefore producing some tendency toward extremes and hardness of character.

The Sun in Aries and the Moon in Aquarius is another blend of the same kind, but is improved by the combination of the fiery and airy triplicity.

The Sun in Aries and the Moon in Pisces is a contrary combination,

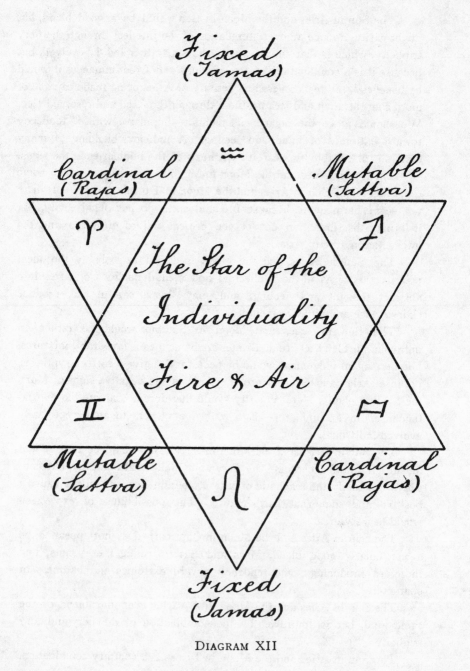

DIAGRAM XII

blending fire and water, cardinal and mutable conditions, and is liable to produce contradictory elements of character.

The principles upon which these combinations are based, are sufficiently illustrated by the above brief descriptions, and may be elaborated by those who wish to carry the ideas further.

The Sun in the negative signs denotes that the permanent, vital and individual characteristics are less positive and also less abstract, and that there is a distinct inclination towards the more practical and concrete side of existence. In these cases the Moon in positive signs will tend to give a rather positive type of personality which may become somewhat unmanageable for the solar self behind it.

Some Problems

The consideration of these polarities gives rise to many problems that we are not yet in a position to settle very definitely. Questions are sure to occur such as—Do we follow the signs in succession through successive lives? Are we born with the Sun always in the same sign? and so on.

Answers obviously cannot be given until horoscopes for successive incarnations have been accumulated and examined, and up to the present this has only been done in one or two cases, too few to justify generalisation ; such as they are, however, they seem to indicate that both the above questions are to be answered in the negative. What little information is available from occult investigations into past lives, such as those that have been published in *The Theosophist*, also seem to agree with this in so far as they show that the Ego sometimes chooses to put quite different aspects of himself down into incarnation, or else is obliged to do so by Karmic law.

In spite of this, however, we appear justified in believing that in the majority of cases the Sun's position represents that aspect of the individual Ego which is found within the sphere of the personal self. But a distinction has to be drawn here between an immature unevolved soul and one that is highly progressed and in the front rank of evolution. In the former case the Sun, and in the latter Uranus, has the greater significance in connection with the degree of awakened self-consciousness of the Ego in its own world. It seems probable also that something similar holds true of the Moon, Neptune, and the Personality ; that when immature and swept about by the tides of feeling, with very little control

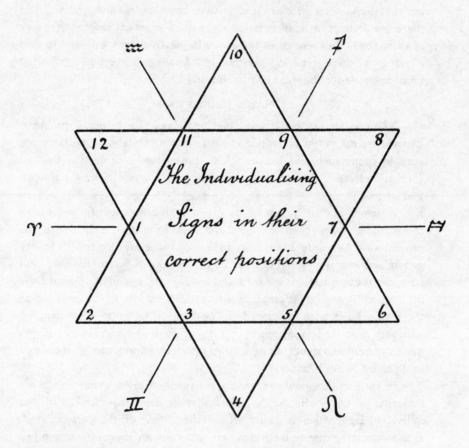

DIAGRAM XIII

established within, it is mainly subject to the Moon; but that when strong and harmoniously accordant with the Ego, Neptune is its symbol. But neither of these can be said to be known definitely, and we await further information.

THE RELATION OF THE ASCENDANT TO THE POLARITY

The polarities of the luminaries do not by any means exhaust the the whole subject of polarisation ; for manifestation is by ternaries, so that when there are two extremes there is always a mean between them to supply the third factor and complete the triangle. We have to take into account not only the relation of the Sun to the Moon but that of both these to the Ascendant.

Of these three we seem justified in concluding that the Sun signifies the Individuality, or, in another sense, so much of this as is expressed within the limits of the Personality. The amount of this and the extent of its influence apparently varies considerably in different cases. In the physical man the Sun governs the vital energies and has much significance in connection with the father and the positive side of the nature generally.

The Moon signifies the Personality and gathers up all the planetary forces that are active therein. In the physical man it governs the physique, the matter rather than the force side of body, the material basis of life rather than life itself. It has relation with the mother and the negative, receptive, plastic side of the nature.

The Ascendant signifies the separate sense of Self in the child apart from its parents although in close relation with both. It may be more closely identified either with the Individuality or the Personality according to circumstances, or may vary and fluctuate. It may be more positive and vital or more negative and receptive according to the sign rising and the state of the horoscope.

DIGNITIES AND DEBILITIES

The task of analysing and classifying the various modes of these three is far too great to attempt at present, but it will require attention if Esoteric Astrology is to be made more efficient than it is in this direction at present. In conjunction with the polarities a careful consideration of the planets' dignities and debilities will have to be undertaken by the esoteric student.

The zodiac is an abstract representation of all the grades and types

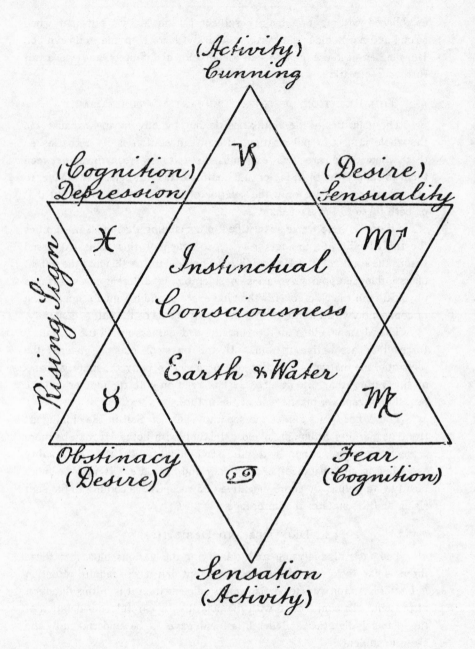

DIAGRAM XIV

of matter that are manifested or manifesting in the world in which we live, and the planets are the centres of spheres of influence representing the changes of consciousness as affected by the various types of matter when translated in terms of the zodiac.

Planets have their zodiacal affinities and antipathies or signs in which their influences are strong or weak, as described previously.

Taking the signs to represent the matter or vehicles through which consciousness is expressing itself, Jupiter, the planet of growth and expansion, will expand the feelings and sympathies when in Cancer.

The Sun, the giver of life, will illuminate the brain in Aries. Saturn, the planet of depth and meditation, will give balance and intuition when fully expressed in the sign Libra. Mars, the planet of energy and action, will give skill in action when fully expressed in Capricorn.

In this way the signs and planets act and react. Changes in form produce changes in consciousness and *vice-versâ*. The debilities are, in a general sense, depressions ; the forms of consciousness expressed by the planets do not find the lines of least resistance in these signs. The detriments are indifferent expressions and usually denote inharmony between the life and the form.

AN EXAMPLE

The polarities of the Sun and Moon, especially when taken in conjunction with the ascending sign, are generally an index to the whole life-plan of the current incarnation. For example Mrs. Annie Besant has the Sun in Libra (positive cardinal-air), the Moon in Cancer (negative cardinal-water), and the Ascendant in Aries (positive cardinal-fire).

Here the polarity is CARDINAL Air-Water-Fire, a combination directly related to the three planes of consciousness, the intuitional, emotional, mental. The expressions of the consciousness represented by the Moon, Jupiter, and Venus are all on the lines of least resistance.

The polarity in this case forms a Cardinal Cross, the apex of that Cross having no planets, but ruled by Saturn. The polarity is a remarkably strong one, bringing the life into intense activity. Around this well-polarised Cross are grouped the majority of the planets. The Sun is closely associated with Venus and Mercury, the Moon with Jupiter, and the ascendant with Uranus. The luminaries bring the benefics into the polarity, and the ascendant is nicely poised between the so-called malefics, absorbing them into the personality for the purpose of transmutation.

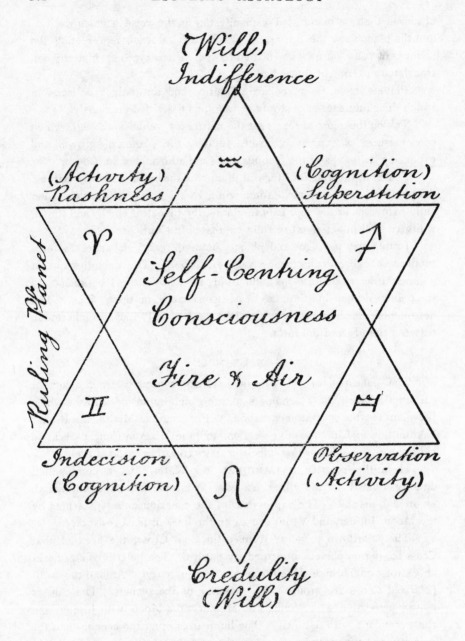

DIAGRAM XV

CHAPTER XVI

The Star of the Personality

THE Star under which a human entity is born, says the occult teaching, will remain for ever its star throughout the series of its incarnations in one life cycle. But this is not his *astrological* star. *That* is concerned and connected with the personality, the former with the individuality. *Secret Doctrine.*

THE Individual, or as it is sometimes called the *individualised* self, as it starts into existence is a white spark of Divine Light enclosed in a colourless film of matter. *Studies in the Bhagavad Gita.*

BOTH the above statements imply an individual influence that is distinct from the personal, and it would appear that while Exoteric Astrology is concerned with the personality it cannot in any way deal with the individual or discover its star.

That the individuality is born under a star is admitted, also that it remains forever under this influence. It might also be assumed that there is an occult astrology by means of which the occult teachers are acquainted with the name and influence of that Star.

Now Esoteric Astrology may be said to come between Exoteric and Occult Astrology; and while it does not directly concern itself with the MYSTERIES, or Occult Astrology, it does indirectly afford a clue to those mysteries which are unrevealed to the ordinary student of Exoteric Astrology.

Exoteric Astrology has established the truth that the astrological star under which a man is born is that which describes his personality, and that this is the ruling planet, or lord, of the ascending sign at birth; and it also goes further and summarises the personality under the influence of the Moon and the sign it occupies.

The Occult teaching of the Secret Doctrine deals with man in his three aspects of Spirit, Soul and Body, which have their reflections in the physical world through the physical body, the emotions, and the intellect. The lower three of the personality are mortal until they are changed or transmuted into the Higher mind, the Spiritual soul, and the Spirit; these three constituting the Individuality, or as it is commonly called the Ego. Esoteric Astrology, going further than the Exoteric

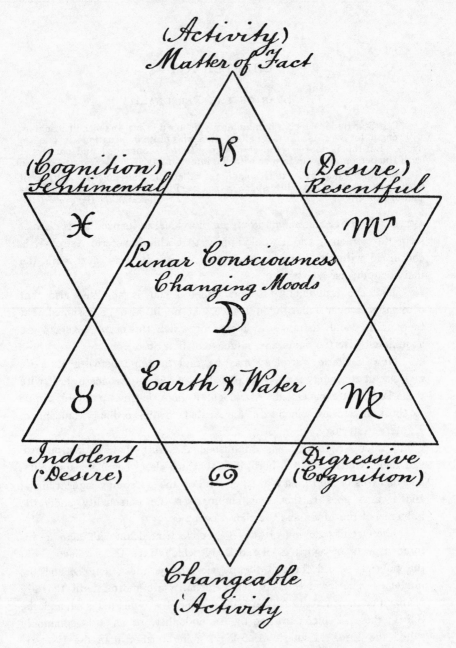

DIAGRAM XVI

study, finds the Individuality in each horoscope through its reflection in the personality. Using the terminology of Spirit, Spiritual-Soul and Human Soul or Manas to describe the Individuality, we find this triad reflected in the image, or personality, as Lower Manas or the brain mind, the astral desires, and the activities of the physical body.

Now by a perfectly legitimate system of correspondences, according to the idea of " as above, so below," the ascending sign, or, to be more exact, the ruling planet, represents the lower manas or the personality as focussed in the brain ; the Moon represents the astral, or body of feeling ; and the Sun the Prana or life of the physical body. It is an occult teaching that the Spirit is reflected into the Physical body, the Wisdom aspect in the astral or Desire body, and the Manasic or mental activity aspect in the lower Manas, represented by the brain.

REVERSING OUR SPHERES

When a man has reversed his spheres, as it is termed, or transferred the attitude or attention of the self from the personality to the individuality, he does not dispense with his horoscope or cease to come under its influence ; he simply rules his stars and changes their vibrations from objective to subjective influences ; and when he has effectually identified himself with the new order of things he also changes the rulers.

As an illustration we may take the life of an ordinary man whose consciousness is almost wholly turned outwards towards the objective world. His brain and the mind-substance passing through it, will be coloured by the rising sign and ruling planet ; his feelings and changing moods of emotion will be under the influence of the Moon ; and his actions and moral attitude will be energised by the position of the Sun. The Sun, therefore, will be the representative of his Individuality and the Moon of the Personality. For many lives the solar influence will become stronger and stronger until it gives him a fairly good moral view of life, and more or less dominates his lunar fluctuations of moods and feelings. It may even dominate his ruling planet.

As the ordinary man becomes more and more self-consciously individualised, the solar aspect will impart more and more colouring to his individuality. From the Mars colouring he will pass to Saturn, which will establish his *self*-conscious individuality ; then to Jupiter for expansion, and finally to Uranus, full individualisation.

The Sun's positions, aspects and influence will now dominate his

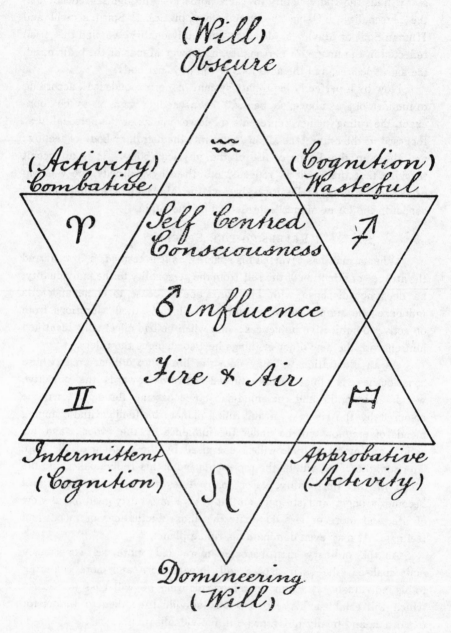

DIAGRAM XVII

horoscope and he will no longer be classed as an ordinary man, but as a progressive individual.

The occult teaching states that the Sun and Moon are substitutes for two other planets; and while it is admitted that Uranus is the planet for which the Sun is substituted, it is more than probable that Neptune is the other; and therefore our progressive individual is preparing to live the Uranian life of the houseless or signless wanderer, whose individuality is ready to become more than *self*-conscious, *i.e.*, Super-Conscious.

AN ILLUSTRATION

To take a particular example of this idea of transmutation or individual representation, let us take the horoscope of the most progressive individual of our time—Mrs. Annie Besant. (p. 132.)

This famous orator was born under the sign Aries, and Mars must be taken as the ruling planet of the Personality. Mars is placed in the sign Taurus, the sign of its detriment. Mrs. Besant has stated that for half of her life her consciousness was darkened, but it awoke under exceptional circumstances, by hearing a voice. Taurus is the sign of the voice or spoken word. The Personality is also denoted by the Moon in Cancer, conjunction Jupiter, showing great expansion of personal feeling and emotion. The Sun, ruler of the normal individual consciousness was in opposition or complementary to Uranus.

Mrs. Besant reversed her spheres when she came into contact with the occult teaching through the *Secret Doctrine*, and she changed the lower mind into the higher through Venus, the ruler of Taurus and the planet of the human Soul or higher Manas. Her feelings were transmuted into the Buddhic or Wisdom aspect of consciousness through Moon conjunction Jupiter, trine Neptune.

By the fierce conflicts of Uranus opposition Sun, she established he Will and came under the individual star Uranus; and by a response to the Uranian vibration playing upon her ascendant, she came under the influence of her Master and has lived individually ever since.

THE INDIVIDUAL STAR

The above statement may be taken to represent the particular view of the esoteric astrologer looking at the subject from below. If, however, it is viewed from the standpoint of the Principles, it may be said to fit in with the occult teaching regarding the Individual Star.

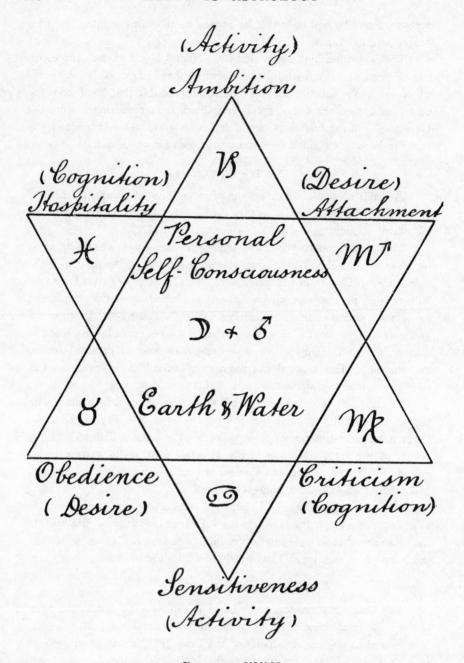

DIAGRAM XVIII

Taking the zodiac as a representation of the Causal body of the earth, corresponding to the horoscope of a human being, we may think of the planets as above that circle of necessity, and as external expressions of the Sons of Mind, Who colour the Causal body of each "Divine Fragment." This faint colouring of the Spiritual Intelligence is refracted through the signs of the zodiac, and interpreted symbolically through the planets in each nativity; and the Seven Individual Stars appear to be lost in the maze of compounded matter comprising the various vehicles of consciousness, and represented by the signs of the zodiac. In the lower worlds the ruling planet now becomes the representative ray of the individual and as such appears to be a sub-influence of the primary colouring. In each life the man works from this centre, his ruling planet, his representative throughout the current life; and the sign in which this planet was placed at birth represents the *guna* or quality of matter through which he is working; and not until he has outgrown the limitations of the Causal body, *i.e.*, the whole circle of the zodiac, can he afford to part with the characteristics of this ray.

Now the environment of each individual for the time being, that is until he has absorbed their rays or vibrations into himself, is represented by the six planets outside his ruling planet; and the signs they are in, together with their aspects, denote the relationship between the man and his environment. From this interplay of the colourings coming from the other planets the melody of his life is composed, and according to the relationships of the ruler with the other planets we may predict the lines of least resistance for any individual. From this we may trace the diversity of the many from a primary unity, and through that diversity back to unity again; for although there are said to be seven individual stars and seven ruling planets, each of the seven may have seven hundred and seventy-seven combinations, or more, with the others.

We may surmise that whatever the primary colouring may be in the causal body, all that colouring which is abstracted in the lower worlds is stored in the man's aura, and those finer colourings which have affinity with the *original* colour in the causal body go to swell out that colouring, and give it a richer and more transcendent hue. In other words the more *self-conscious* the consciousness becomes in the higher vehicles, the more effectually does the lower man respond to the higher; and the more in tune the man becomes with the individual ray, star, or colouring, the more free is the man of his vehicles; or to put it in another way, the more

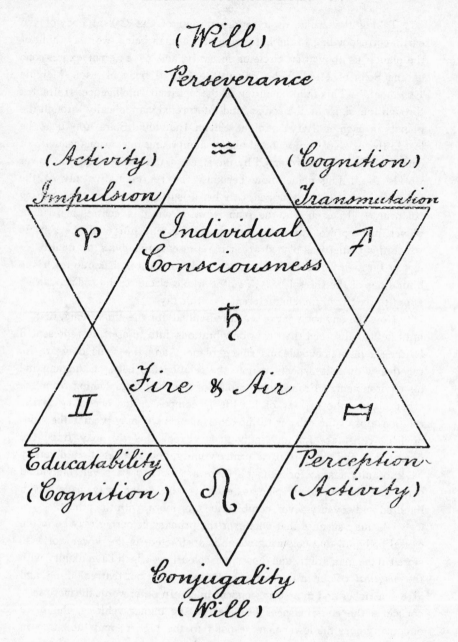

DIAGRAM XIX

stable the individual centre becomes the greater become the possibilities of expansion.

With this brief sketch we may seek for the reason of the difference in the astrologer's statement that the Individuality is seen in the horoscope, and that of the occult teaching which states that the individual star is not the Astrological star.

We may illustrate these ideas by using the word Star in its fullest sense, which literally means to sprinkle forth, or shine, like the stars in heaven.

Each man is a star, radiating from himself (through the form he is wearing) an influence which is either personal, that is, limited to his physical consciousness, or individual, that is, of the spirit or inner character. In this sense man is truly related to the stars.

" Paracelsus regarded the starry host as the condensed portion of the Astral Light which fell down into generation and matter, but whose magnetic or spiritual emanations kept constantly a never ceasing communication between themselves and the parent fount of all—the Astral Light. 'The STARS attract from us to themselves, and we again from them to us,' he says. Life is fire, which comes like the Light from the stars and from heaven. Everything pertaining to the Spiritual World must come to us through the Stars, and if we are in friendship with them, we may obtain the greatest magical effects. As fire passes through an iron stove, so do the stars pass through MAN with all their properties and go into him as rain into the earth. The human body is subjected, as well as the earth, the planets, and the stars, to a double law; it attracts and it repels, for it is saturated through with double magnetism, the influx of the Astral Light." (*Isis Unveiled.*)

The Stars of the Personality and of the Individuality

It is this Astral Light which forms the basis of our material universe, and every human being is a star in the Astral Light. The Stars of the Personality and the Individuality, taking into consideration the forms through which they are expressed, are not any particular planets, although the planets are associated occultly with the stars and denote their especial quality and colouring. In the personal star the signs of the zodiac play the most prominent part, since they yield geometrical figures describing the peculiar form of each star, and also denote he personal colouring by the arrangement they take in each particular case. Every soul is there-

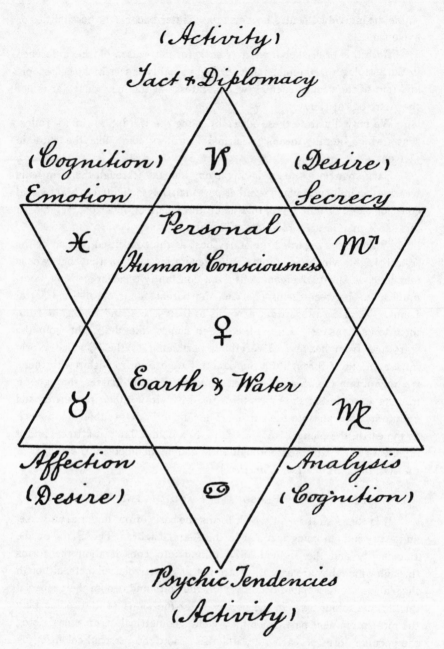

(Activity)

Tact & Diplomacy

(Cognition)　(Desire)
Emotion　Secrecy

♑

Personal

Human Consciousness

♈

♀

Earth & Water

♓　♍

♉

Affection　Analysis
(Desire)　(Cognition)

♋

Psychic Tendencies

(Activity)

DIAGRAM XX

fore connected with the star of its individuality, but before it can be self-consciously aware of that star, it must have transcended the star of the Personality which for the majority may be symbolised by the half circle, the symbol of the Moon, or geometrically (for the more advanced) by the Pentagon.

The Moon is ruler over the earthy and watery signs of the zodiac, these two triplicities forming interlaced triangles and representing, figuratively speaking, the true star of the personality. This " Star " is connected with the purely physical conditions of existence, or all that is concrete and definite in form ; also with the sensations which culminate in the passions, and with the fluidic part of nature, or the selfishness of the solid and concrete life of the lower planes ; in order to express itself finally in a complete and separate personality.

Before we deal with the star of the Personality in any definite way we must consider its complement, the star of the Individuality ; which is also a pair of interlaced triangles, and also capable of being changed into a Pentagon or Five Pointed Star.

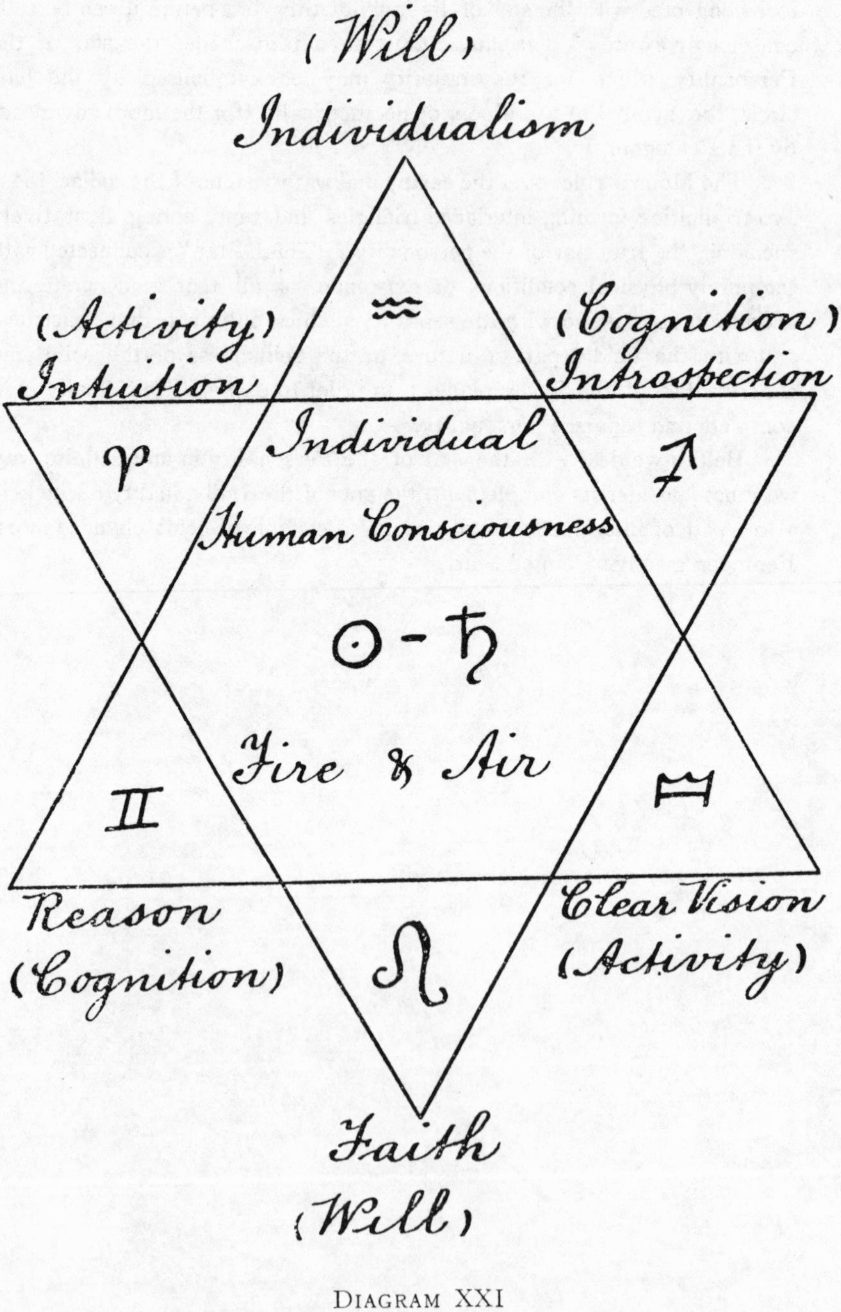

(Will)
Individualism

(Activity)   ♒   *(Cognition)*
Intuition   *Introspection*

♈   *Individual*   ♐

Human Consciousness

☉ - ♄

Fire & Air

♊   ♅

Reason   *Clear Vision*
(Cognition)   *(Activity)*

♌

Faith
(Will)

DIAGRAM XXI

CHAPTER XVII

THE STAR OF THE INDIVIDUALITY

A NOUMENON can become a phenomenon on any plane of existence only by manifesting on that plane through an appropriate basis or vehicle . . . the Hierarchy of spiritual Beings through which the Universal Mind comes into action, is like an army by means of which the fighting power of a nation manifests itself, and which is composed of army-corps, divisions, brigades, regiments, and so forth, each with its separate individuality or life, and its limited freedom of action and limited responsibilities; each contained in a larger individuality, to which its own interests are subservient, and each containing lesser individualities in itself.   *Secret Doctrine.*

THE Star of the Individuality belongs to the triplicities of fire and air, and as these triplicities are not confined to the concrete and purely material mode of expression, but are more subjective and connected with the internal activities of consciousness, the symbols of fire and air signs need not necessarily be placed at the apex and base of two fresh triangles, as in Diagram XII; they can be intersected between the other two, as in Diagram XIII, thus forming a complementary condition of fire and air without being so strongly marked or divided as is the case with the signs connected with the personal triangles.

These Star Maps are illustrated in the series of diagrams accompanying these chapters, and when the two stars are placed together it will be seen that the whole twelve signs of the zodiac fall into their natural order in the circle.   But as the circle is divided into two groups of positive and negative signs, so the two stars of the Personality and the Individuality may be said to represent these positive and negative halves of the circle, or the objective and the subjective. Now at each point in the six-pointed star certain planets are placed which are rulers over the signs belonging to those points, and they are the same for Personality as for Individuality—with the exception of the Sun and the Moon.   These hexagons therefore are really pentagons, the Moon being ruler of the whole star in the case of the Personality and the Sun in that of the Individuality.   The planets ruling the signs of both stars have entirely different meanings when studied esoterically, and we will take the meanings of the rulers of the Personal star first, in order to show how the same planet has two different expressions in connection with these stars.

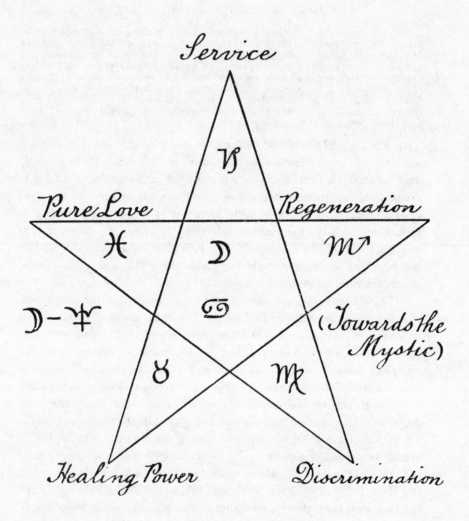

DIAGRAM XXII

THE NEGATIVE SIGNS

We will first deal with the Star of the Personality. At the apex of this triangle Capricorn is placed, and Saturn is therefore the ruling planet. The influence of Saturn in connection with the Personality, without any subjective or new interpretation, represents the lower or concrete side of that planet; and those under its dominion from the personal standpoint are subject to varying moods, much self-centredness, a great deal of worry and anxiety, impatience, miserliness, and a tendency towards selfishness and everything that panders to the personality. But good is extracted from this apparent evil, and the true purpose of this self-centred influence is that the personality may be less fluidic and more solid and concrete. In fact, its influence may be summed up as that of solidarity, concreteness and limitation, to produce a stronger centre of self; and, as the apex of the star, it may be said to be the king or crown of the Personality.

At the left hand base of this triangle Taurus is found, and Venus is the ruling planet. The influence of this planet is more concerned with the acquisition of possessions, and this storing of personal possessions explains the meaning of the saying of Jesus, when the young man came to Him and asked Him what he should do to be saved. The Master replied, "Sell all thou hast and follow Me"; but it is said that the young man turned away sorrowful as he had great possessions. But the word possessions here does not wholly signify worldly goods, it includes all powers and faculties regarded as owned by or limited to the Personality, such as intellectual pride, obstinacy and aloofness, Venusian qualities particularly connected with the sign Taurus; and it may be marked in parenthesis that the Moon, ruler of the Personality, is exalted in Taurus, showing chiefly the bondage to these possessions that are wholly connected with the personal and separated self.

Virgo belongs to the right hand base of the triangle, and Mercury is the ruling planet; its influence from a personal standpoint is indifference to others, over-absorption in personal interests, particularly with regard to study and mental acquirements, and it reacts upon the physical body when strained beyond the normal point—worry, ill-health and affections of the nervous system being the result.

The triangle with its apex downward is governed principally by the Moon, Cancer being at the apex, and as the sum total of the personality

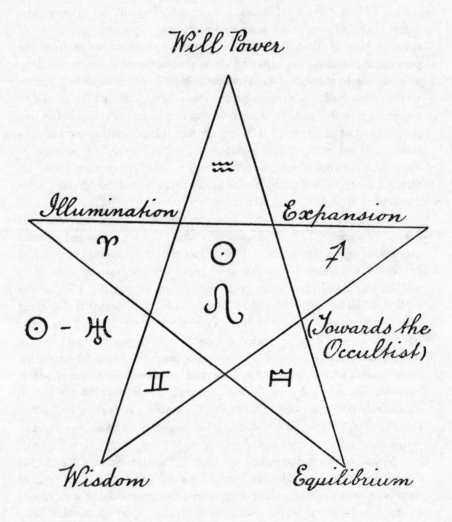

DIAGRAM XXIII

we have from the lunar influence that carping or harsh criticism, arrogance and narrowness of view which regards all things from the personal outlook, and which shows indifference to all other considerations than those of the personal self.

At the left hand base of this triangle is the sign Pisces, governed by Jupiter; and its personal influence is concerned with formalism, narrowness, superficial judgment, bigotry, all those limiting conditions that are usually associated with very sectarian religions, and out of which *enemies* are made, unreasoning prejudices that arise out of personal bias, and sometimes pride and hypocrisy.

At the right hand base of this triangle we have Scorpio, over which Mars is ruler, and its influence in connection with the personality is to bring selfish love, jealousy, aggressiveness, partiality, and a tendency to lean on others through over-attachment; out of which arise tragedies associated with personal loves and hates, sometimes including violence, murder, quarrels and all those separations.

The whole is summed up under the Moon as ruler of this star, in the interblending of earth and water, which, as was once caustically remarked by a student of astrology many years ago, is apt to produce mud!

THE POSITIVE SIGNS

The distinction between the two stars will be brought out more clearly if attention is now turned to the positive one, the Star of the Individuality, consisting of the fiery and airy triangles, intersecting the former at the eastern and western points, on the right and left hand of the figure. Here is the sign Aries on the left, governed by Mars, and the positive interpretation of this influence is strength, individualisation, self-sacrifice, love of purity and truth, and a fearless determination to accomplish right for right's sake only; for Aries gives us a higher and more refined interpretation of the martial influence, which in ordinary astrology is closely connected with the head and brain, and in fact represents the ray of consciousness in manifestation in the physical body.

On the opposite point in the western angle, or at the right hand side of our figure, we have the sign Libra, ruled by Venus in its positive aspect, denoting sympathy, toleration and devotion, the complementary influence of all that is denoted by the planet Mars; for as Mars tends to externalise or make manifest in the objective world, being represented

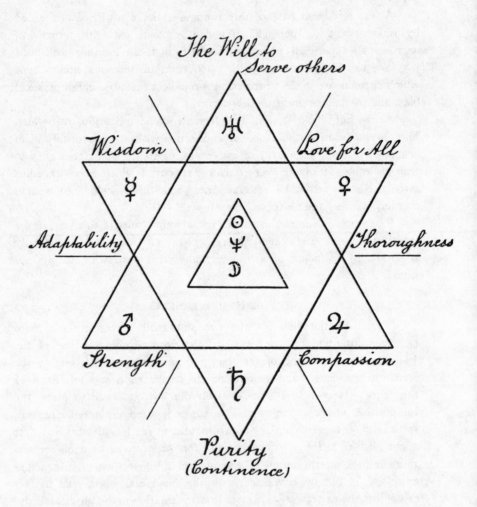

DIAGRAM XXIV

symbolically as the cross over the circle, so on the opposite side the circle has surmounted the cross and completion is accomplished of all that which began as strength and energy under Mars, to be transmuted through Venus into sympathy, tolerance and devotion.   In fact, these two influences are paired in mind and intuition, in strength and beauty, in energy and grace; and from the individual standpoint they become complementary influences instead of polarities, the whole gathered up into the individuality, coming out of the base of the triangle.

In the lower portion of the left hand side of the figure, we have Gemini, ruled by Mercury in its positive aspect, denoting clear insight, discrimination, and a mental compassion which embraces humanity in the external or exoteric rendering. This position is connected with relatives and the intellect generally, but from an individual standpoint it is connected with all men as brothers, and the whole of humanity as relatives; and from the higher standpoint of Mercury we have that clear vision and discrimination which enables the individuality to distinguish the real from the unreal.

At the bottom of the figure we have Leo, governed by the Sun, which is now the ruler of the whole of the Star of the Individuality, all the influence connected with this triangle being merged into the individuality itself; therefore it has no particular influence, excepting as synthesised in the Individuality; the Sun, so to speak, being the symbol of the Individual in formation.

On the right at the upper side of the figure, we have Sagittarius, governed by Jupiter in its positive or individual aspect, denoting the fulness of the true realisation of the inner sympathy which alone can be connected with the Individuality.   Here we have all the expansion connected with the mind, a widening out that embraces all religions, and in fact all Truth with which associations and groups of souls are connected.

At the top of the figure we have Aquarius, governed by Saturn in its positive and highest aspect, denoting confidence in one's own inner nature, a realisation of purity, self-control and serenity, indicating all those virtues connected with meditation and contemplation.

At the head of this figure might be placed the symbol of Uranus, which is the symbol of the perfected Individuality, for this planet synthesises the whole of the other influences and brings an entirely new interpretation into the reading of nativities.

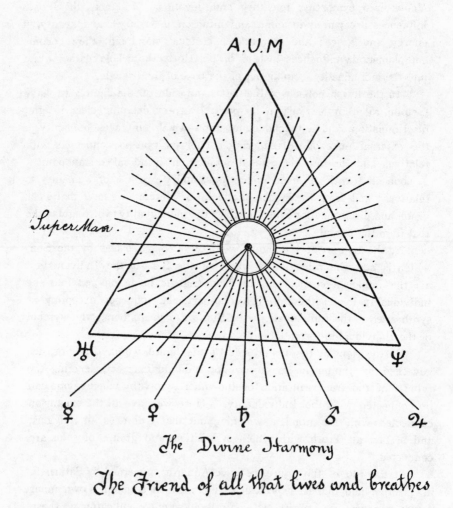

DIAGRAM XXV

PLANETS IN SIGNS

Now in the same way that Exoteric Astrology deals with the planets in the various signs, giving strength to those that are in their own houses, an added strength to those in signs of exaltation, and diminishing the influence of planets in signs of detriment or fall, so does Esoteric Astrology give a different interpretation to planets occupying different signs in either of the triangles connected with the Personality and the Individuality; but the interpretation is a more psychological one, being concerned with the subjective picture of things, operating behind the plane of the outer actions. It therefore lays stress on all planets connected with cardinal signs, and on those in the houses or signs connected with the cardinal cross, which are Cancer and Capricorn in the Personal triangles and Aries and Libra in the Individual. Therefore planets in Cancer and Capricorn affect the Personality considerably, while those in Aries and Libra have more connection with the Individuality. This is true at any rate so far as the signs are concerned but it is not quite so applicable to the houses, although it might be safe to say that the individual character is much strengthened by planets rising or setting, and that events or occurrences in the life are more concerned with the midheaven and nadir.

A few illustrations may be given of the application of this idea to planets in signs from an esoteric standpoint in order that a general rule may be established for the benefit of those who are making a special study of this subject. We will take for instance Jupiter, ruler of Sagittarius in the Individual triangle and of Pisces in the Personal; placing Jupiter in Cancer, the sign of its exaltation and the apex of the Personal triangle. Here we should expect to find the Personality enriched by the social virtues, the moral principles connected with the domestic life, and the family associations, as to make it exceedingly receptive to the higher vibrations connected with the spiritual or individual life; so that there would be an interaction of influence between the personal and individual through this exaltation in Cancer. Or again, we may take Mars, the planet having power of a different kind in both triangles, and find in its exaltation in Capricorn a blending of the personal and individual characteristics, bringing into operation through the Personality and physical body self-control in all outgoing energies, purity of life so far as the

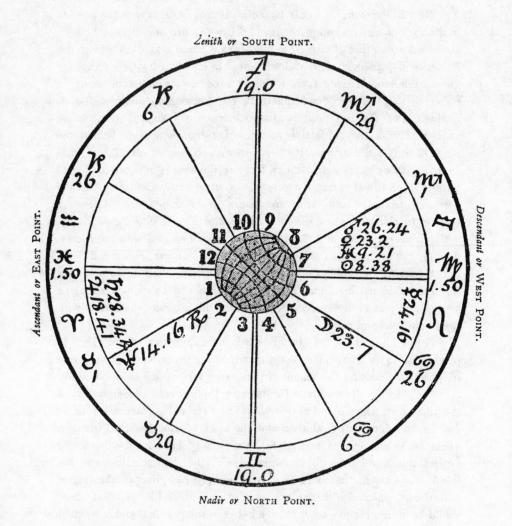

Zenith or SOUTH POINT.

Ascendant or EAST POINT.

Descendant or WEST POINT.

Nadir or NORTH POINT.

QUEEN WILHELMINA OF HOLLAND

passions and senses are concerned, a strong personal self-confidence in right action, and eventually a calming of the senses, bringing them into line with the saturnine vibrations.

We may again apply this method of dealing with the exaltations to the individual triangle. Saturn, ruler of the apex of the personal is exalted in Libra, where it is balanced in tolerance, impartiality, and justice, and is the bridge between the Personality and Individuality, because the latter finds its line of least resistance in the sign of the balance, where two triangles are balanced in a moving equilibrium. Then again, we find in the individual triangle that the Sun has its exaltation in Aries; the brain is illuminated and the whole of the Individuality is brought into line with the Personality through the brain, and definite steps are taken towards the perfecting of the man.

It will be noticed that in the individual triangle there are only these two exaltations, the Sun and Saturn; Saturn bringing the Personality to a state of mergence into the Individuality and becoming balanced in Libra; while the Sun, ruler of the Individuality, reaches its exaltation in Aries, the sign of the head.

With regard to the two exaltations not mentioned connected with the personal triangle, Venus in Pisces and the Moon in Taurus, we find that the true exaltation of the Personality comes through reverence, obedience and respect for law and order, a tendency towards accuracy and carefulness which we find those with the Moon in Taurus living up to and exhibiting in a very marked degree. Here the Personality may be said to be brought to the condition wherein it becomes astrologically obedient and accurate. The exaltation of Venus in Pisces denotes a wide sympathy for suffering and the devotion of the personality to the needs and requirements of others; so that here we find a far more satisfactory reason than can be accounted for in the ordinary exoteric astrology. We shall, however, apply these rules in a general sense to the various horoscopes that we have taken for examples in succeeding pages, and which are delineated more fully further on.

In the study of a nativity from an exoteric standpoint the whole aim is an endeavour to harmonise the vehicles with the consciousness playing through them, and this is why we have planets in harmony with various signs; and while it is true that the more planets we find placed in their own houses the more harmonious is the working of consciousness, yet we have always to consider how far these signs compare with the

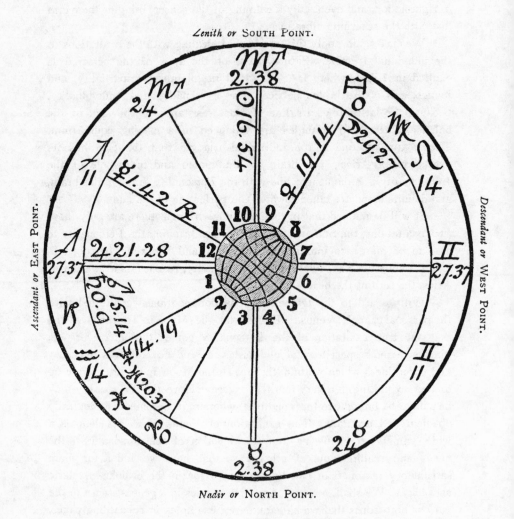

Zenith or SOUTH POINT.

Ascendant or EAST POINT.

Descendant or WEST POINT.

Nadir or NORTH POINT.

KING EDWARD VII

houses ; for, with the three factors of houses, signs, and planets, there is always a tendency for such complex interactions to disturb the harmony.

In a general sense we may correlate houses, signs, and planets. But while planets strengthen and accentuate all that is denoted by the houses, unless the ideals connected with the planets are fully realised in the life there is apt to be discord and disharmony, until the three factors, of house, sign and planet, are brought into line with each other. For illustration we may take some horoscope that will show how changes of environment produce changes in the life and consciousness of the native. A very good illustration of this would probably be that of King Edward VII., who, on coming to the throne, was stated to have passed through an entire change in every direction, this being so marked as to be noted by all who had been in contact with him. On examining the horoscope, it will be seen that the rising of Jupiter and the elevation of the Sun allowed the life to flow very evenly until the death of his mother Queen Victoria, when this influence had to give way to the rising of Saturn and Mars in Capricorn in the first house. This brought out the influence of the intercepted sign Capricorn by diminishing to a great extent the Jupiterian influence and bringing the sudden realisation of responsibility, and the inner determination of the soul to adapt itself to the important conditions into which the Personality was placed.

In this influence we can trace Uranus in square to Jupiter between the personal and individual triangles, breaking up old and existing conditions and bringing into prominence those of Saturn and Mars. In his personal life, Mars ruling the midheaven, events moulded and shaped the consciousness through the position of the planet in the ascendant, bringing out all the power of its exaltation in Capricorn. It will be noted that the Moon was just on the point of leaving Virgo and entering Libra, and although this horoscope reveals many interesting phases of consciousness from an esoteric standpoint, it is more interesting to the student of Esoteric Astrology to notice that on the change of environment there was a corresponding change of consciousness, giving opportunity for the expression of much that had hitherto been latent. In this nativity many examples of a similar nature might be taken, but the above is sufficient to illustrate the idea.

Let us take the horoscope of the young man who was born into a remarkably good environment but who was deprived of the faculties of hearing, seeing, and speaking, being born deaf, dumb and blind, with the

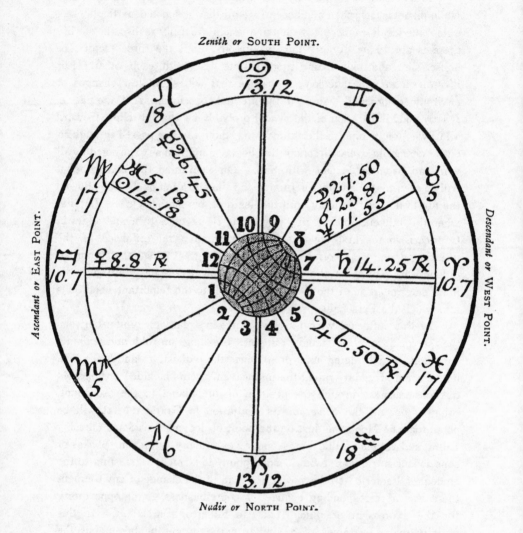

THE EARL OF ARUNDEL AND SURREY

mental faculties undeveloped.   Looking at this horoscope (p. 168) from an inner point of view we see that Taurus held the Moon conjunction Mars, destroying some of those worldly possessions which, if rightly used, would have been exceedingly valuable.   The Sun in conjunction with Uranus and in opposition with Jupiter was also destructive and inimical to personal expression.   No less than six planets were concerned with the Star of the Personality ; and those that related to the Individuality, Venus and Saturn, were in opposition and tending in every way to limit the consciousness in its normal expression.

A careful study of horoscopes like these will reveal much that is not seen in the ordinary Exoteric Astrology and may lead the intuitive student to the cause of those limitations.   If the horoscope of Lady Burton is compared with that of Georges Sand, some very important characteristics will be seen from an esoteric standpoint ; again, the horoscopes of Robespierre and Prince Bismarck, and that of Gladstone and Churchill are marked contrasts ; but sufficient has been said to indicate the way in which these ideas may be followed out.

This method of interpretation was adopted by a certain school of Rosicrucian astrologers, who blended the personal and individual influences in a famous symbol of unity.

THE STAR MAP DIAGRAMS

Although likely to prove very suggestive to an intuitive student, the star map diagrams given on pages 140 to 162, may for the more practical and less intuitive students require some further elucidation.

All desires are more or less personal, therefore the Star maps representing the personality will show the desire nature in various forms of manifestation.

In these star maps an attempt has been made to show that the " pairs of opposites " are ever at work through the opposing signs of the same quadruplicity ; thus Taurus, the house of Venus, is opposed by Scorpio, the house or station of the planet Mars, and so on throughout the circle of the zodiac.   The planetary influences are refracted here, and the sense of true proportion is lost through the activity of the desire nature and the bondage of the mind that is enslaved by the desire forms.

In the individual Star maps there are represented higher mental states in which the intellect is withdrawing from desire, and the desire is changing into will ; neither desire nor intellect is so much subject to the

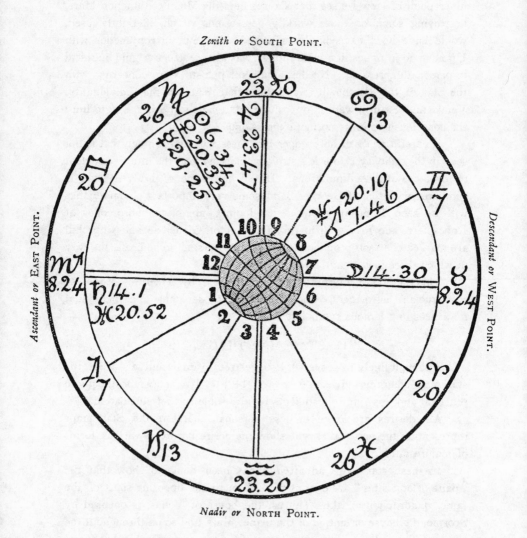

MALE, DIED OF WATER ON THE BRAIN 27/1/'97

forms as is the case with the personal or negative signs, for the individual is now beginning to know himself as individual and is not so much the creature of moods and changes.

In Diagram XIV, which may be termed the star of the indefinite Personality, the instinctual consciousness is the most active, the natural promptings are mainly influenced through negative signs, such as hunger and appetite—Taurus; the search for food—Virgo, and the search for employment—Capricorn. The feelings will be also aroused through the tendency of Cancer to produce sensitiveness say to the craving for food, etc. The passional nature may be stimulated by Scorpio and the reaction of elation may result in depression or fear, etc.

In Diagram XV, which may be said to relate to the star of the Individuality, the indefinite individuality may be self-centring, and beginning to strengthen the "I"-notion, either through the rashness of Aries or the observation of Libra; or it may be through superstition by the influence of Sagittarius, or the indecision of Gemini. The Will of Leo and Aquarius, in all probability, will be latent, and credulity or an easiness of belief will take the place of Will; in other words the individual will be submerged and the personal tendencies will have first claim.

With the personal, the rising sign may show the most pronounced influence, and the other signs (so far as character is concerned) will be latent. The rising sign however will find its polarity in the Moon, the seat of the lunar or instinctual consciousness. The Individuality will be more or less represented by the ruling planet.

Diagram XVI is intended to show an advance in the expression of the signs. The lunar consciousness is more established and the personality more definitely formed. In Diagram XVII, the individuality also is shown as forming; the planet Mars influences the nativity in addition to the separative influence of the rising sign, ruling planet, etc. The Will of Aquarius is obscure and latent, and when manifested through Leo it is domineering and assertive. The consciousness is becoming more self-centred and combative.

Diagram XVIII is intended to represent the personal self-conscious stage. The Moon and the planet Mars are marked in their influence; sensitiveness, through the sign Cancer, and attachment through the sign Scorpio are more and more pronounced as the personality develops. The crowning state of consciousness is ambition. The developing Indivi-

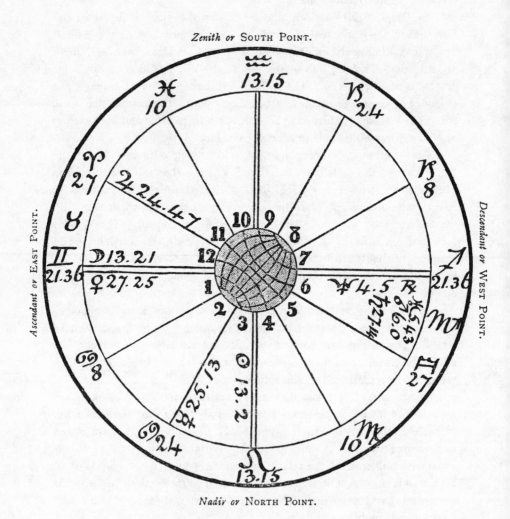

Zenith or SOUTH POINT.

Ascendant or EAST POINT.

Descendant or WEST POINT.

Nadir or NORTH POINT.

LORD TENNYSON, POET LAUREATE

duality represented by Diagram XIX shows a more active influence of each of the positive signs. The will is beginning to act through conjugality and perseverance, and the individual consciousness is seen to awaken through the growing influence of Saturn in addition to the influence of the ruling planet, the ;Moon, and Mars, etc. The activities are still governed by impulsion, although educatability and perception are also beginning to influence them to some extent.

In Diagram XX we have a representation of the developed personality in which the influence of Venus in a concrete sense is becoming very active through affection, and cognition takes the form of analysis which is eventually to lead to discrimination. The crowning activity is expressed in tact or taste, and in diplomacy or more skill in action.

This devolopment marks the stage of the personal human consciousness.

In Diagram XXI we have represented the conditions of a developed Individuality. The Sun and Saturn share in influencing the nativity, making faith as well as individualism the forms in which the Will is most likely to be expressed. The individual human consciousness is awakening through intuition and a clearer vision. Reason and introspection are becoming active. The individual is expressing himself as a higher octave of the personality. Desire is giving way to Will, and the cognitions are more abstract and refined. The activities are duties, and moved by a better understanding as to the value of responsibility.

The stars are now changing from the six- to the five-pointed star, or Pentagon.

In the Pentagon one of the signs is indrawn, the pairs of opposites are ceasing to exist, polarity is giving way to one-pointedness. It may be the sign Cancer, or any other sign that is withdrawn, but each in turn is gathered into the Centre and its qualities handed on to the polar sign, until finally there are but three operative in the personal side of the Pentagon.

It is the same with the individual aspect; one after another of the signs is indrawn; it may be Leo that begins the synthesis, or Aries or Sagittarius; in any case only three signs finally remain to form the triangle of the true Human Monad.

This transmutation of the signs, however, is not affected until the

Zenith or SOUTH POINT.

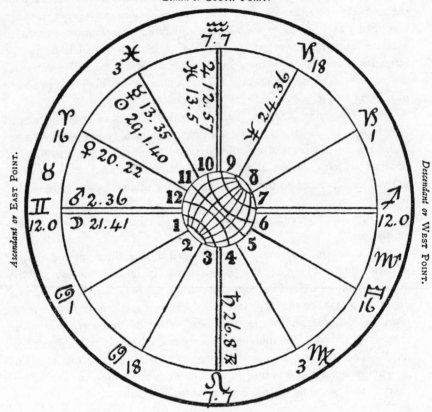

Ascendant or EAST POINT.

Descendant or WEST POINT.

Nadir or NORTH POINT.

PLANET	LAT	DECL.	ASPECTS.								
			☉	☽	☿	♀	♂	♃	♄	♅	♆
SUN	✕ ✕	0 S 23	☉	□			✶	∠		∠	✶
MOON	4 S 52	18 N 20		☽	□	✶		△.P.	✶	△.P.	
MERCURY	2 S 16	8 S 32			☿	P		∠		∠	
VENUS	0 S 39	7 N 22				♀		∠		△		□
MARS	1 N 15	21 N 55					♂			□	
JUPITER	0 S 31	17 S 26						♃		♂.P	
SATURN	1 N 40	14 N 23							♄		
URANUS	0 S 38	17 S 32								♅	
NEPTUNE	0 N 30	20 S 44									♆

NAME *Lady Isabel Burton*

Consciousness of the Ego has risen above the changes in the body, for the physical body has then become the perfect instrument for use; and instead of conflicting desires, and the constant shifting of view arising from the personal equation, the Ego has become harmonised with his vehicles.   In this sense the sign Scorpio becomes the sign of non-attachment, and the generative force of that sign is transmuted in the creative power of Taurus. As shown in Diagram XXII Cancer is indrawn and, no longer exhibited as the changing sensitiveness of the personal feelings, is transmuted into the real service hidden in the sign Capricorn and now expressed as the highest activity.   Pisces and Virgo take up the polarity of earth and water and decide the Pathway that shall be trodden by the personality, until discrimination becomes knowledge, and emotion devotion, either of which is to be absorbed by the Individual Ego.

Individually, as illustrated in Diagram XXIII, the Faith of the sign Leo becomes the Will of Aquarius, the "I-" notion of the sign Aries is expanded through the wider perception of the sign Libra, and the introspection of the sign Sagittarius absorbed in the pure reason of Gemini unfolded.

When the triangle is complete the unity of the One Life may intuitively be seen by those who are seeking to tread the Path of liberation, and the three influences merged into the one planetary vibration which connects the liberated soul with the Father Star in Heaven. (XXIV, XXV.)

SOME QUESTIONS, WITH THEIR ANSWERS

Those who seek for further light regarding the symbols, and inner workings of Esoteric Astrology, should consider the following questions and answers:

What are the abstract conceptions of the house divisions of a horoscope?

Answer: *Limitations in Space.*

What are the abstract conceptions of the twelve signs of the zodiac?

Answer: *Limitations in Time.*

What is the meaning of Planetary Influence?

Answer: *Causality.*

How do we begin to transcend these three great illusions?

Answer: *By Meditation; definite abstract thinking or abstract feeling.*

Zenith or SOUTH POINT.

Ascendant or EAST POINT.

Descendant or WEST POINT.

Nadir or NORTH POINT.

PLANET	LAT	DECL.	ASPECTS.									
			☉	☽	☿	♀	♂	♃	♄	♅	♆
SUN		23 N 6	☉				∠			□	⊼
MOON		14 N 57	☽		✶	△	⊻	☌	⊼		⊼
MERCURY		19 N 47	☿			✶	⊻	△	□	△	□
VENUS		15 N 20	♀	P			□			✶	□
MARS		17 N 56	♂		P			⊼	△		☌
JUPITER		8 S 54	♃						⊻		⊻
SATURN		3 N 4	♄								✶
URANUS		4 S 23	♅								∠
NEPTUNE		17 S 4	♆	P			P				

NAME Georges Sand

Of whom may it be said that they *rule* their Stars ?

Answer: *Those who are no longer subject to the three great illusions of time, space and causality.*

Who are they ?

Answer: *Those who live in the Eternal.*

For those who do not concern themselves with abstract conceptions but prefer the practical demonstration of symbolism, we shall now take into consideration a few nativities of well-known persons including the interpretation of an interesting Human Document.

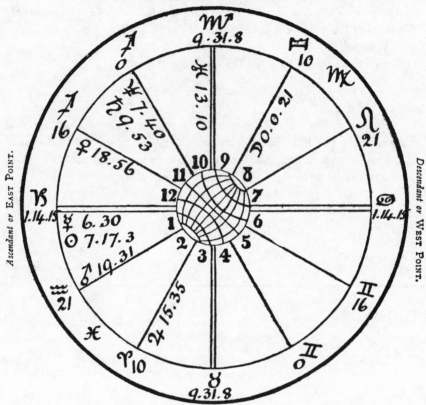

Zenith or SOUTH POINT.

Ascendant or EAST POINT.

Descendant or WEST POINT.

Nadir or NORTH POINT.

	ASPECTS.									LAT	DECL.
	☉	☽	☿	♀	♂	♃	♄	♅	♆		
☉		□	☌		∟		⊻		⊻	X X	23 ♋ 16
☽			□		⊡			∟		1 S 46	1 ♋ 37
☿	P			18°	∟				⊻	1 S. 42	24 ♋ 56
♀	P				✳	△	☌		☌	0 N 34	22 ♋ 27
♂					✳		□	⊡		1 S 9	16 ♋ 3
♃							△		△	1 S 19	4 N 55
♄									☌	1 N 38	20 ♋ 21
♅					P					0 N 24	15 ♋ 25
♆							P			1 N 33	20 ♋ 5

NAME W. E. Gladstone

CHAPTER XVIII

EXAMPLES OF ESOTERIC ASTROLOGY

SPIRIT is the root of individuality of every kind and grade, sub-human, super-human—for there is individuality apart from that which we recognise as individuality in man. A Self is an individual, and the root of I-ness abides in the Unit of Consciousness, even though that " I " has not flowered into Self-recognition in its vehicles. *An Introduction to the Science of Peace.*

ESOTERIC CONTRASTS: (pp 132, 164)

THERE is a strange similarity between the horoscope of Mrs. Annie Besant, and that of Queen Wilhelmina of Holland. The former has the Star of the Individuality strongly marked; in the latter the star of the Personality is the stronger, though both accentuate the horizontal line, that of the Individuality.

In temperament, however, there is a marked difference. In Mrs. Besant's case, the Cardinal-Air influence predominates; in that of Queen Wilhelmina the Mutable-Earth is the stronger, with a powerful secondary influence through the angular planets, although the signs on the angles are mutable.

In one case the Teacher is by caste a Ruler, in the other the Ruler is zodiacally a Teacher.

The position of Uranus rising, in Mrs. Besant's horoscope, has its correspondence in the young Queen's Sun conjunction Uranus angular. Both have the Moon, ruler of the Personal Star, in the sign Cancer, but in Mrs. Besant's case the Moon is conjunction Jupiter while in the Queen's map it is in square aspect to Jupiter and Saturn.

The one has temporal power, the other spiritual power. The psychic tendencies differ in the two cases, so far as their application is concerned, but in both it is active ; in one physical, in the other mental.

In the Queen's horoscope the ruler of the M.C. is rising in the angle of the first house, in the Cardinal sign Aries. In Mrs. Besant's horoscope the ruler of worldly fame and distinction is in the Cadent twelfth house and sign Pisces.

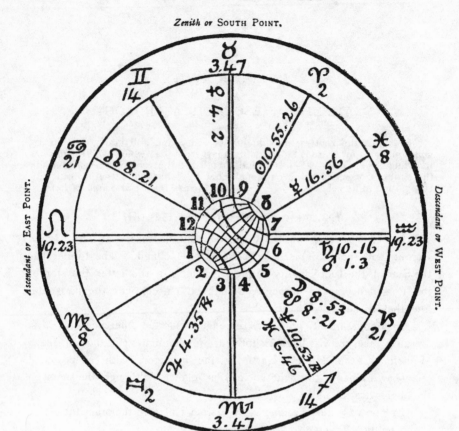

Zenith or SOUTH POINT.

Ascendant or EAST POINT.

Descendant or WEST POINT.

Nadir or NORTH POINT.

		ASPECTS.								LAT.	DECL.
	☉	☽	☿	♀	♂	♃	♄	♅	♆		
☉		□				☌	✳	△		⚹ ⚹	4 N 20
☽			△			□	⊻	⊻		0 5 4	23 S 13
☿				∠		36°		□		0 S 18	5 S 27
♀					□	⊼	□	⚼		0 S 13	12 N 41
♂			P			△	☌	✳	∠	1 S 0	20 S 55
♃							△	✳		1 N 37	0 S 21
♄								✳		0 S 33	18 S 13
♅			P	P					☌	0 N 7	21 S 21
♆			P	P				P		1 N 23	21 42

NAME .... Prince Bismarck

The positive and negative signs ruling in the same houses in these horoscopes, with their rulers reversed, in positive and negative signs, is also significant.

The strongest sign in each case, shows the influence of the ruler, again reversed. In the Queen's horoscope Virgo is the strongest sign, a mutable-earth sign; its ruler Mercury is in the fixed and royal sign Leo, but in a cadent house, and therefore considerably limited. In Mrs. Besant's horoscope Libra is the strongest sign, Venus its ruler is angular in the cardinal-air sign, and therefore in a sense free from limitation.

If we could accurately read the influence of the Personal star in the Queen's horoscope we should find Mercury the predominating influence, and the active representative of the gateway through which individual self-consciousness could be reached in the present life. Personally the Star is Jupiter; Individually it is Mercury.

Students of Esoteric Astrology desiring to know how changes may be made, from one vibration to another, or, from one mode of development to another, will note in the Queen's map that the mutable-earth influence may be changed, by the angular positions, into Cardinal-earth, or the line of practical activity, instead of mental activity. Those who study the history of nations will see how applicable is this horoscope to the destinies of the land over which Queen Wilhelmina rules.

Personally she is full of sensitiveness, knows the true value of obedience, and lives in a world of analysis that will culminate in faith and discrimination.

In Mrs. Besant's map we also find sensitiveness, allied to compassion, a true obedience, and the purification of emotions culminating in a clear perception.

CHANGING STARS: (p. 166)

The change from the personal to the individual star is clearly marked in the horoscope of King Edward VII. Upon coming to the throne the personal star blazed into a great light, and the responsibility of state was apparently keenly felt, causing the pronounced Capricorn element to rise to the apex of the nativity, entirely replacing the Sun in Scorpio, which caused the influence of Saturn and Mars to work out to the full their rising destiny.

The link between the personal and the individual came through

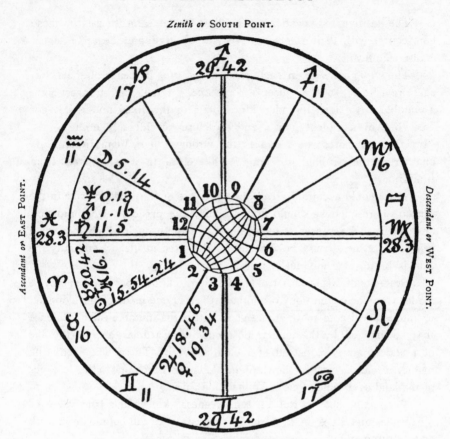

Zenith or SOUTH POINT.

Ascendant or EAST POINT.

Descendant or WEST POINT.

Nadir or NORTH POINT.

	ASPECTS.								LAT.	DECL.
	☉	☽	☿	♀	♂	♃	♄	♅	♆		
☉							✱	⊼			16.36.41 N
☽				⊓		⊓	36'	Q		5 N 0	14.6.28 S
☿				✱		✱		☌		2 S 59	5.19.29 N
♀					☌		✱			1 N 34	24.35.56 N
♂						☌	L	☌		1 S 44	12.39.24 S
♃							✱			0 S 16	22.42.36 N
♄								☌		1 S 39	8.56.15 S
♅			P						L	0 S 38	5.43.17 N
♆				P						0 S 33	11.55 S

NAME......*Earl Rosebery*

Venus square Mars, and sextile Jupiter. As Prince the whole of the personal effects of the square aspect were expended, as King the whole of the sextile influence came into operation and earned for King Edward the title of Peacemaker.

The square aspect of Uranus and Jupiter was a great problem to many students, who sought to penetrate beneath the superficial influence of this important square; those who can obtain a fuller reading of the horoscope will, however, blend Sun trine Uranus with Jupiter square Uranus; both occurring from Pisces as centre of the influence.

The Moon was just leaving the personal sign Virgo, and entering the individual sign Libra, the sign of the inner perception and balance, a very significant position. The position of the Moon in Virgo on the cusp of the ninth house, the house of the higher mind, was a critical position as it separated from the opposition of Uranus and the square of Jupiter, *and met the sextile of Mercury in the ninth sign Sagittarius*.

The earthy triplicity was completed by Saturn, Mars and the Moon in the three decanates as follows: ♄, ♑, ♂ ♑-♉, ☽♍-♉.

The King apparently learnt more during his ten years of temporal and responsible power than during the whole of his previous life. The rising decanate of Sagittarius accentuated the Leo decanate of that sign, the merging sign of the individual. The ideal of duty was *lived* by the King as King.

A SOUL IN BONDAGE : (p. 168)

It is so very rare to find the senses of a human being completely paralysed that this nativity from the personal and individual standpoint must become fascinating to the seeker after the causes of events. The Earl of Arundel and Surrey was unfortunately born deaf, dumb, and blind, with his mental faculties undeveloped. With the exception of Neptune, the transcendental planet, there is not a single good aspect in the nativity.

If the personal star of this nativity is studied, the physical causes may be symbolically seen. The Star is reversed, Capricorn being at the North point, and the influence of the luminaries converge therein, with Mars between, in the Taurus- and Virgo-Capricorn decanates. Saturn, the apex personal star or bridge, was setting in its fall, retrograde and *opposing Venus ruler of the nativity*. Venus is the true planet of the mind, or intellectual principle, in man. Here Venus was retrograde, and formed no connecting link with any planet. Its influence was completely

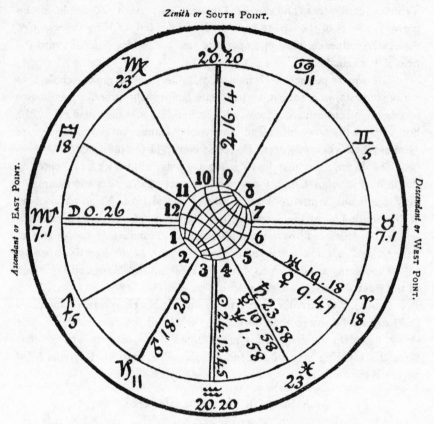

Zenith or SOUTH POINT.

Ascendant or EAST POINT.

Descendant or WEST POINT.

Nadir or NORTH POINT.

PLANET	LAT.	DECL.	ASPECTS.								
			☉	☽	☿	♀	♂	♃	♄	♅	♆
SUN	✕ ✕	13. 27. 16 S	☉			∠	36"	☌	⊻	✳	
MOON	3 N 56	7 57. 4 S	☽								△
MERCURY	1 N 57	5 32. 37 S	☿		⊻						☌
VENUS	0 N 40	4. 29. 8 N	♀	P				△		☌	
MARS	0 S 45	22. 56. 48 S	♂					✳	□	∠	
JUPITER	1 N 0	16. 49. 8 N	♃							△	
SATURN	2 S 4	4. 17. 56 S	♄		P						
URANUS	0 S 36	7. 0. 36 N	♅	P							∠
NEPTUNE	0 S 39	11 25 S	♆								

NAME Lord Randolph Churchill.

paralysed by the parallel of Uranus from the discriminative sign Virgo, and Jupiter in sesquiquadrate aspect with Mars and the Moon.   Jupiter also was retrograde in Pisces, and in opposition with the Sun and Uranus, from the sign of discernment Virgo.   Beside the many other afflictions the Sun was in complete quincunx aspect with Saturn setting in the decanate of Aries-Leo.   The *water* sign of this horoscope did not blend well with the earthy signs.

The affinity between the fire and air signs was also severely disturbed by Mercury, in the Aries decanate of Leo, being in sesquiquadrate aspect with Saturn setting.

In this horoscope the disharmony between the individual and the personal is somewhat extreme.   The Self within could not function harmoniously through the mental sheath.

A SIMILAR CASE : (p. 170)

Another case, somewhat similar to that of the Earl of Arundel, although differing in effect, may be useful to those who prefer the practical to the metaphysical.

In this case death came through water on the brain.   Here we find Saturn reversed, it is rising and not setting.   Its position on the ascendant is exactly opposite to the Moon setting.

The afflictions are nothing like so severe, but the positions are equally disharmonious.   Uranus is in square aspect to Jupiter from the important first and tenth angles.   The ruler Mars is in quincunx aspect to the ascendant, it is also in square aspect to the Sun, and parallel the Moon.

The map is wholly personal, the individualising influences being extremely weak.   It is the horoscope of a young ego in whom forbearance had not begun to germinate and the past was probably devoid of much virtue.   There is no link with the Capricorn element of the earthy signs, Taurus and Virgo alone being represented by either sign or decanate of the earthy triplicity.

In this case, also, the watery and the earthy elements did not make a satisfactory blend.   The astral and the physical bodies were not in tune.

Here, again, the apex sign of the Star map is at the north angle. The inversion of the apex sign of either the personal or individual maps, may account for the difficult lives those born under Libra and Scorpio often have to live.

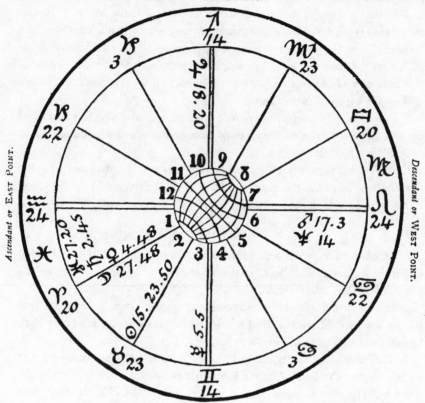

Zenith or SOUTH POINT.

Ascendant or EAST POINT.

Descendant or WEST POINT.

Nadir or NORTH POINT.

PLANET	LAT	DECL	ASPECTS.									
			☉	☽	☿	♀	♂	♃	♄	♅	♆
SUN		16.28	☉	18ᵈ			□		Q	∠	□
MOON		10.40	☽					△		⊻	
MERCURY		23.26	☿			✶	Q		□		
VENUS		2.23	♀				⊡		⊻		
MARS		17.34	♂	P				△			♂
JUPITER		22.16	♃		P						△
SATURN		11.48	♄		P						
URANUS		1.45	♅			P					⊡
NEPTUNE		17.0	♆	P			P				

NAME......*Robespierre*

It is the adjustment of Venus and Mars that may be at fault in some of these cases.

The child was born 11.10 a.m., 29th August, 1896, Lat. 52°49′ N. and Long. 2° W. and died 27/1/′97. It therefore lived only five months; just sufficient time for the Moon by secondary motion to arrive at the opposition of the rising Uranus.

THE AIRY TRIPLICITY MADE MANIFEST: (p. 172)

At Lord Tennyson's birth the sign Gemini was rising, and the third decanate, Gemini-Aquarius, was accentuated by the position of Venus. The Moon was in the second decanate, Gemini-Libra, the house of Venus ; therefore through the rising sign Gemini, the Moon in the second and Venus in the third decanate the whole of the triplicity was able to manifest.

The Poet Laureate gave full expression to the mutable influence of his individual star, and his nativity denotes harmony between the inner and the outer nature.

The ruling planet Mercury gave the necessary activity, through its position in the cardinal sign Cancer, to express his ability in action, and the third house gave especial facilities for expression in writing.

The personality was psychic and sensitive enough to respond to the individual life, and the environment was a satisfactory one, in which both personal and individual characteristics were in harmony.

The triangle of this horoscope should be drawn from Aquarius on the cusp of the M.C. to the ascendant Gemini and the fifth house mainly occupied by the sign Libra.

It is then interlaced by the fiery triplicity, from Leo on the cusp of the fourth to the seventh and eleventh houses, embracing the Sun, Neptune and Jupiter.

Drawing the Sun into the centre with the sign Leo, the pentagon is formed of mutable air.

The intuitive student by meditating upon the symbolism of this horoscope will discover its interpretation as—the ideal of a Universal Life.

LOVE, AFFECTION, AND SENSATION: (pp. 174, 176)

The individual characteristics were well marked in Lady Isabel Burton's nativity, and this apparently enabled what might otherwise have

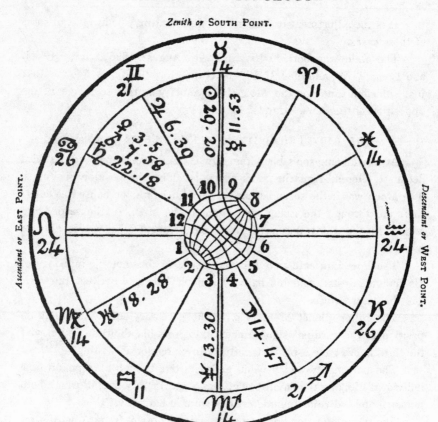

Zenith or SOUTH POINT.

Ascendant or EAST POINT.

Descendant or WEST POINT.

Nadir or NORTH POINT.

PLANET	DECL.	ASPECTS.									
			☉	☽	☿	♀	♂	♃	♄	♅	♆
SUN	20.1	☉							✶		
MOON	22.35	☽					☍			□	⊻
MERCURY	12.23	☿				✶		Q	△	☍	
VENUS	25.11	♀					☌				
MARS	24.28	♂			P		⊻			Q	△
JUPITER	20.53	♃	P						⊡		
SATURN	21.50	♄	P	P			P		✶		
URANUS	5.17	♅									✶
NEPTUNE	15.0	♆									

NAME....*Balzac*....

been the selfish limitations of the personality to be overcome through love and devotion to another.

The Watery and Earthy conditions of the personal star are ever seeking to bind and hold the soul in form, while the Fiery and Airy conditions of the individual star seek to burn the dross from the nature, and dissolve the crystalizations of the lower forms.

As a study of the emotion of love this nativity affords much fruitful result. The personality through the astral body, is one of deep emotion, in which sensitiveness and attachment bring a rich harvest for the expansion of the individual centre. Here we find every circumstance favourable for the expansion of the Causal body by the conjunction of Uranus and Jupiter in the midheaven, and at the apex of the Individual triangle of air.

The whole of the airy triangle is magnificently coloured by four powerful influences. The apex of the individual star, expanded by Jupiter and Uranus is carried into the sign Gemini by the ascendant and there strengthened by Mars.

The influence of Gemini rising is carried on to Libra (second decanate of Gemini), and the Moon completes the triangular influence through the Aquarian decanate of the rising sign Gemini.

This is nearly a perfect expression of the airy triplicity through its connection with the midheaven, and the ascendant of the personal horoscope. It is, esoterically rendered, a union of the individual with the personal through Mercury ruler of the nativity in Pisces, which strikes the chord of devotion through the mutable signs.

This horoscope would seem to merge the Star maps XXI and XXII into one.

Comparing the above with the horoscope of Georges Sand, we can see that the position of Sun and Uranus in the latter map disturbs the harmony of the individuality, by accentuating the personal element. This horoscope is a strange mixture, in which the fate shown by the personal horoscope seems to be the result of internal disharmony. In the end the Mercurial influence serves as a link between Gemini and Libra, and somewhat restores the equilibrium between the personal and individual conditions.

The square aspect of Mars and Venus from the negative sign Taurus to the positive sign Leo, denotes the friction between the two planes of consciousness, which the Moon in Aries in opposition to Jupiter

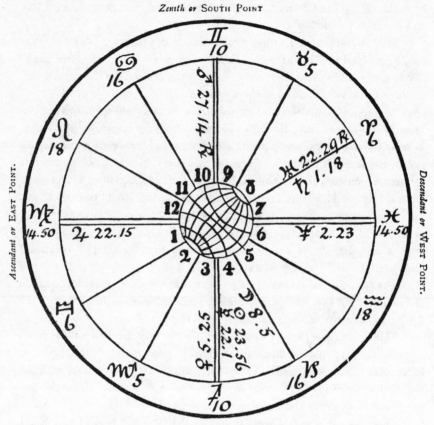

Zenith or SOUTH POINT

Ascendant or EAST POINT.

Descendant or WEST POINT.

Nadir or NORTH POINT.

PLANET	LAT	DECL.	ASPECTS.								
			☉	☽	☿	♀	♂	♃	♄	♅	♆
SUN	✕ ✕	23 S 19	☉		☌	18°	☌	□		△	
MOON	3 N 43	19 S 23		☽					□		⁎
MERCURY	1 S 9	24 S 22	P		☿		☌	□		△	
VENUS	0 N 54	20 S 20		P		♀		Q	△	⊡	□
MARS	2 N 59	26 N 25					♂		□	□	⁎
JUPITER	1 N 12	4 N 10						♃		⊼	
SATURN	2 S 27	1 S 44							♄		⋎
URANUS	0 S 36	8 N 12								♅	
NEPTUNE	0 S 42	11 S 19									♆

NAME   *Viscount Hinton*

the ruler of the mid-heaven supported. In the inconjunct aspect of Saturn to the ascending degree we find the linking influence between the Personality and Individuality.

Through marriage and partners the seventh house of Georges Sand's nativity denotes enough karma or fate to awaken to the full the signs Virgo and Libra occupying the seventh. Saturn brought out the analytical and discerning qualities of Virgo, and through Mercury upon the cusp of the fourth, and the sign Gemini, finally brought discrimination which Uranus in the sign Libra helped to produce through the constant disturbance of the square aspect to the Sun.

The square aspects of Mars and Venus, and the Sun and Uranus, produced all the variations of sensation which caused the attachment to the artificial sense of the physical Ego.

Physical unions produce realisations that are food for the soul who is developing individually. From the lowest attachments to the highest, they are tuned to strengthen either the personal or the individual life. Happy are they who find true union with family, partner or friends, but more happy are they who find union with the higher Self.

A COMPARISON IN STATESMANSHIP: (pp. 178, 180)

Mr. W. E. Gladstone was admittedly a great and useful statesman, who devoted much of his life to service for the nation he represented. The personal star in his horoscope shows the way in which this service was wrought into his life.

At the apex of the personal triangle ruled by Capricorn the Sun and Mercury were placed, bringing into activity the whole of the earthy triangle, first through the Sun in the second decanate of Capricorn-Taurus; and secondly, Virgo through Mercury rising in an earthy sign. Esoterically interpreted we find adaptability and individual effort prominent.

He probably learnt a valuable lesson in secrecy through Uranus culminating in Scorpio; and the failure of the Home Rule Bill, which he sought to have sanctioned, must have brought some remarkable realisations to his personal consciousness. His ruling planet Saturn evidently gave him many opportunities during an active public life to transmute his personal experiences into individual quality.

We may assume astrologically through the position of the Moon in Libra that he needed, and probably acquired during his public career, a

Zenith or SOUTH POINT.

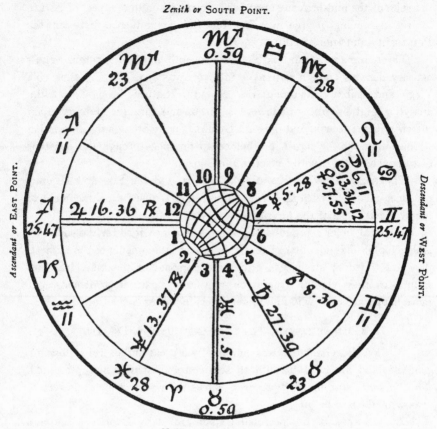

Nadir or NORTH POINT.

PLANET	LAT	DECL	ASPECTS.								
			☉	☽	☿	♀	♂	♃	♄	♅	♆
SUN	♓ ♓	22.45.57 N	☉		☌					∠	✱	△
MOON	1 N 31	24 49.10 N	☽			⊻		⊻			✱	△
MERCURY	1. N 25	20 18.58 N	☿				✱	□		□	
VENUS	1 N 19	21.52 48 N	♀	P			□	✱		□
MARS	0 S 5	21.40 15 N	♂	P			P	☌		□.
JUPITER	0 N 28	22.19.52 S	♃	P			P	P		□
SATURN	2 S 0	17.45.8 N	♄							
URANUS	0 S 26	14 59.57 N	♅							✱
NEPTUNE	0 S 57	7. 19.29 S	♆							

NAME....*Cecil Rhodes*

true sense of proportion or a clear perception of human nature as expressed in national affairs.

The horoscope of Mr. Gladstone whilst denoting a great deal of individualism shows that it was mainly used in *Service* and apparently for the nation's welfare.

The culmination and disappointment of this individualism, and the breaking of hopes and attachments, are clearly marked by the square aspect of Mars from Aquarius, the apex sign of the individual star, to Uranus in Scorpio.

"Home Rule" would appear to have taught both Mr. Gladstone and the nation an important lesson, irrespective of the merits or demerits of the Bill.   He was apparently just the man fitted to undertake the particular task of drawing the line between socialism and individualism.

Nations may learn through the failure of statesmen, especially when these do not read the handwriting on the wall of heaven.   Esoteric Astrology is not so much concerned with the results as the causes behind events.   Prince Bismarck, however, struck a much more definite note of individualism than Mr. Gladstone.   He had both Mars and Saturn in Aquarius, and he had his realisation through a greater power than his own, that of his master the Emperor Wilhelm I., who is represented by Venus in Taurus culminating.   Although a very strong man he had to give allegiance and render obedience to a superior.

The Man of Blood and Iron had the power to carry his individualism beyond the imagination of ordinary mortals; but his service was more personal than Gladstone's, although he apparently achieved more for his nation; for the Moon in Capricorn is the sign of personal service, while the Sun in that sign lifts it into the higher realm of the individuality.   We must not, however, cast reflections on either, for each serves its purpose in the evolution of the soul.

Gladstone had his opportunity, through the transmuting influence of Saturn in Sagittarius, to rise individually by his temporal fall; for we all learn most through our failures and mistakes.   He was assisted, by his own inherent strength, individually and personally, by his love of service, and by his strong attachments, to realise the causes of his own self-undoing, shown by Venus in Sagittarius in the twelfth house.

In the horoscopes at birth the planets are rising in Mr. Gladstone's nativity and setting in that of Prince Bismarck; and this includes Saturn,

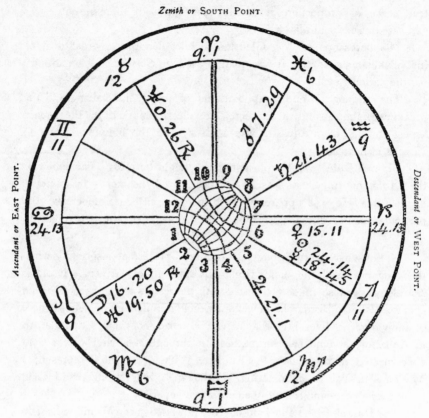

AN ADVANCED SOUL

PLANET	LAT	DECL.		ASPECTS.								
				☉	☽	☿	♀	♂	♃	♄	♅	♆
SUN		23 S 20	☉		△	⚹				⚹	△	△
MOON		19 N 31	☽			△	⚹		□	☍		
MERCURY		23 N 46	☿	P				P		⚹	△	⚹
VENUS		23 S 57	♀	P		P			⚹	☍		
MARS		19 S 39	♂	P								⚹
JUPITER		17 S 8	♃							□	□	
SATURN		15 S 32	♄								☍	
URANUS		15 N 34	♅							P		
NEPTUNE		9 N 57	♆									

the planet of human destiny. It is significant that a nation ruled by Taurus, the sign upon the cusp of the fourth, should be the cause of Gladstone's downfall especially as its ruler is in the twelfth house; also that Venus ruling the tenth house in the horoscope of Prince Bismarck should be stronger by sign and position than the Sun in exaltation. They are both related to star maps XX and XXI.

Mr. W. E. Gladstone was born at 7.59 a.m. (rectified time) 29/12/1809, at Liverpool. Prince Bismarck was born at 1.30 p.m., 1/4/1815, Schonhausen, Germany.

The horoscopes of these great statesmen are full of instruction for the student.

Esoterically we can see fathoms deeper into any horoscope than by the ordinary exoteric analysis.

CONTRASTS OF AFFINITIES : (pp. 182, 184)

We will now compare the maps of a high grade of individuals whose lives are fairly well known, in order that the difference between the personal and individual expression of life may be more clearly seen.

Comparing the maps of Earl Rosebery and Lord Randolph Churchill we find much in common. Individual power is strongly marked in both cases, in one case by the Moon in Aquarius, and in the other by the Sun in the same sign.

Lord Randolph Churchill's career seems to have suffered in the same way as Mr. W. E. Gladstone's through the square aspect of Mars and Uranus. They both fought for a principle, although the particulars with which it was concerned were different. The whole of the individual triangles are in evidence through the primary and sub-influences in the nativity of Earl Rosebery, but the personality does not appear to be equally strong for it is only affected by four of the earthy and watery signs.

The elements in this nativity are :—

5 planets in Mutable Signs ♅ ♂ ♄ ♃ ♀
2   ,,   ,, Fixed   ,,   ☽ ☉
2   ,,   ,, Cardinal ,,   ☿ ♅
3   ,,   ,, Airy   ,,   ☽ ♃ ♀
2   ,,   ,, Fiery   ,,   ☿ ♅
3   ,,   ,, Watery   ,,   ♅ ♂ ♄
1   ,,   ,, Earthy   ,,   ☉

Combination Mutable-Air.

The polarity of the watery and earthy signs, ruling the eastern and western angles, is harmonised by the sextile aspect of their respective rulers, Jupiter and Mercury. This is also reflected in the sextile aspect of the Sun and Saturn. The Mutable-Air influence is the most pronounced, owing to the Moon being in Aquarius and the benefics in Gemini in the third house.

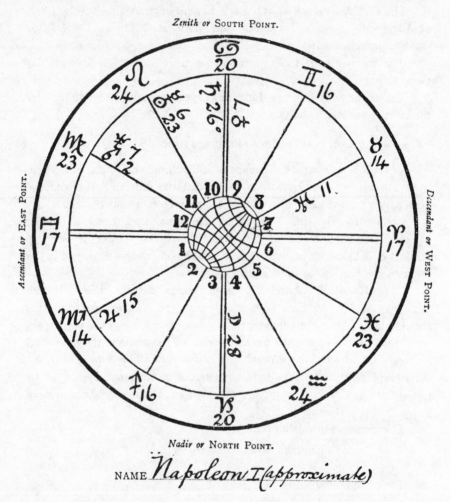

Zenith or SOUTH POINT.

Nadir or NORTH POINT.

NAME *Napoleon I (approximate)*

Lord Randolph Churchill had also three planets in the sign Pisces, and one of the luminaries in Aquarius, but in other respects the maps are not similar; yet both sought to blend knowledge with power. Lord Randolph failed through the disturbing influence of Mars square Uranus from cardinal signs which disturbed the trine aspect of Uranus and Jupiter in the fiery triplicity. The personality of the map was in conflict with the karma, resulting in an attempt to introduce reform in high places.

The personality is here shown to be an effective agent for individual realisations of a reforming character. The elements in this horoscope were:

3 planets in Mutable signs ♄ ☿ ♅
3 planets in Fixed signs ☉ ♃ ☽
3 planets in Cardinal signs ♀ ♂ ♅

1 planet in Airy signs ☉
3 planets in Fiery signs ♃ ♀ ♅
4 planets in Watery signs ♄ ♆ ☿ ☽
1 planet in Earthy sign ♂

The balance of the Gunas is here disturbed by the Watery element, and also through the Fiery signs, denoting that the mind mixed with feeling was moved to activity through the ruler of the personality being exalted in the Cardinal or active sign; but that activity was rendered extreme action through Mars being square to Uranus. The Individual and Personal characteristics were not in harmony.

This inharmony is shown by the polarity of the Sun and the Moon as described in *Astrology for All*, page 143. The whole horoscope is a useful study, and the student who seeks for the causes of individual action will do well to study each portion of the horoscope in its bearing upon the actual life.

Is it not true that we see the world as a reflection of ourselves, and find in it the conditions suitable to restore or disturb the harmony?

THE INDIVIDUAL AND PERSONAL: (pp. 186, 188)

Robespierre and Balzac were born under the same degrees of opposite signs, Aquarius and Leo. Both men came prominently before the French public, and played important parts in history. Robespierre was an idealist, Balzac was a mental medium. If the contrast may be allowed the latter was possessed by ideas, the former possessed ideas, they did not possess him.

Robespierre obtained his touch of individual reality through the violence which he suffered at the hands of his enemies, and that terminated his physical life. The square aspect of Saturn and Mercury was the cause of his downfall ; Saturn robbed Mercury of the intuition it should have given at the critical period of his life, and caused him to have fear and sentiment, instead of courage and strength. It is a strange fact that a mundane square aspect, of Mars to Jupiter, waited to fulfil a fateful destiny should he fail to realise the value of the zodiacal trine aspect between the same planets. His test was concealed in the square of Mercury and Saturn from the mutable signs of air and water. The mutable fire influence was too weak to override the two important squares, the one mundane, and the other zodiacal. The mundane aspect coincided with the square aspect of Saturn and Mercury. Taking the period, and the part played by Robespierre at that time, the horoscope is very significant. A fuller judgment is given in *The Art of Synthesis*, page 241.

The horoscope of Balzac is a personal one, in which the brain is shown to be very receptive, and the feelings peculiarly mixed with the mind. Had there been more individual character and less mediumship or psychic imagination, Balzac would have led a happier life; the majority of his experiences were externally physical and astral, the only touch with the individual being through the Moon in Sagittarius opposed to Jupiter in Gemini. The position of Mercury in opposition to Neptune caused him to have weird tendencies, and the trine aspect to Uranus gave a sort of genius for mental and literary affairs.

The watery element prevailed over all the others, the earthy coming next, these two triplicities absorbing no less than seven planetary influences. This gave great receptivity to surroundings, and combined with the Leo ascendant, the power to imitate and reproduce within his brain all the sensations of the sign Cancer with its three important planets therein.

The imagination of Cancer is a remarkable factor where mind and feeling are mixed, as is always the case when planets are in this sign. The successful novelist builds his images in mental matter and moves them about as he pleases, so that the plot he has pictured in his mind is literally acted out before his mental vision. Now these mental images when formed through the influence of the earthy or watery signs may become quite objective, and will sometimes take tangible form.

Some novelists find that the characters they have created become very real and actually persist in taking a part in the moulding of the fiction with which they are connected. This has been explained in various ways, such as a dead novelist on the other side influencing the writers, or by nature spirits ensouling the thought forms created by them.

Balzac was a medium for such entities. In this respect he differed from Robespierre, who was often a medium for those living on this side of the phenomenal universe. Robespierre was the more individual and Balzac the more personal. The former tried to live for the nation, the latter mainly to serve himself; but both were right according to their stage in evolution.

EXTREME CASES: (pp. 190, 192)

"Viscount Hinton" and Cecil Rhodes were both born with Jupiter rising, the former however was born with this planet in the sign of its detriment and the latter with the planet strong in its own sign. The horoscope of "Viscount Hinton" is full of discordant vibrations. It forms a cross of the mutable signs on the angles of the nativity, the planet Mars at the top of the perpendicular line opposes the Sun and Mercury. Jupiter from the ascendant is in square aspect to Mars in the M.C. and Sun and Mercury from the nadir; and to complete the cross aspects Saturn is in square aspect with the Moon from Aries to Capricorn. In this case the personal element is absorbed in Jupiter rising, causing the life to be wasted in the persistent claiming of personal rights and worldly possessions. His life practically ended on the physical plane when his case was taken to the House of Lords, and judgment was given against him. In this climax he obtained the experience that he was fated to receive through Uranus in the eighth house and the sign Aries.

In common with all who have the Moon in Capricorn at birth, he had to realise through personal failure of ambition the transitory value of personal desires.

The particulars of this horoscope have been given in *The Art of Synthesis*.

Cecil Rhodes had apparently a much more fateful and personal horoscope, for the figures regarding the planetary influences affecting positive and negative signs were reversed, and yet Cecil Rhodes made better use of the minority than did "Viscount Hinton."

Circumstances took Cecil Rhodes into the country where the

personal element was powerfully exercised, and the individual influence
used to the best advantage for the welfare of the personality.   Here we
have the use, and abuse, of planetary influences.   In the one case the
inharmony between the personal and individual characteristics is accentuated, through the detriment of the Moon, ruler of the personal
tendencies, and in the other case the Moon is well placed, in the western
angle and its own sign in harmony with the other planets, and the ruler
of the personal horoscope is placed in an individual sign linking by parallel
the influence of the Sun Venus and Mars.   There is no conflict of ideals
or desires in the case of Cecil Rhodes, but in that of " Viscount Hinton "
the whole of the horoscope shows a conflict between the individual and
personal self.

Every soul has to pass through the pairs of opposites, or the
experience of duality, to know itself ; but in the case of " Viscount
Hinton " this duality is accentuated to a marked degree.   The ruler
of the personal horoscope is not only very weak, in its fall and opposed
by Mars, but is in conflict with the rising Jupiter in the personal,
and in this case critical, sign Virgo.

With the ruling planet as index and a correct knowledge of the
individual and personal tendencies it can readily be seen how important
is the statement that character is destiny, also how the terms may
become interchangeable.   For if character is destiny, then surely destiny
reacts upon character, making the life harmonious or otherwise.

An Advanced Soul : (p. 194)

We shall now consider the nativity of an advanced soul.   This
nativity will also serve to illustrate the value of the sub-influences in a
horoscope and the importance of carefully considering the decanates
of signs.

The rising sign is seen to be Cancer in the third decanate—Cancer-
Pisces.   This sub-influence brings into the Ascendant a ninth house
influence, Pisces occupying the ninth house.   Jupiter is, therefore, as the
ruler of the sign Pisces, part ruler of the horoscope, with the Moon the
natural ruler.   The Moon was in conjunction with Uranus in the second
decanate of the sign Leo, Leo-Sagittarius ; and this gives to the natural
ruler another Jupiterian sub-influence.

Jupiter was placed in the sign Scorpio, and in the third decanate of
that sign, Scorpio-Cancer ; so that Cancer has through this decanate of

Scorpio another Jupiterian influence.   The Sun was placed in Sagittarius, a Jupiterian sign, and a Leo decanate of that sign, strengthening considerably the trine aspect of Sun and Moon.   Mercury was in Sagittarius, a Jupiterian influence, and in the second decanate, linking up the Midheaven to which the Moon and Mercury formed a trine aspect.   Venus was in the second decanate of Capricorn, a Taurus decanate, belonging to Venus.

Saturn was in the third decanate of its own sign Aquarius, thus producing a sub-influence of Libra in which Saturn is exalted.

Mars was in Pisces in the ninth house wholly representing the Jupiterian influence.   Neptune, the most elevated planet, was nearly free of aspects save a sextile to Mars and a trine to the Sun.   The influence of Jupiter through the various sub-influences of the horoscope is therefore the strongest in this nativity and Jupiter is in trine aspect to the ascendant.   The student who probes deeply into a judgment of nativities will have no difficulty in seeing great strength in the ☽ ☌ ♅ rising, and the ☉ ☌ ☿ in the house of service.   He may, however, find some difficulty in reconciling the positions of Mars, Saturn and Jupiter with adeptship.

If viewed from the standpoint of the law of compensation we shall find the compensating positions so well balanced as to bring out all the essential qualities of each.

The ☽ ☌ ♅ rising is equal if not of greater value than Uranus rising alone upon the ascendant.   Uranus and Neptune practically govern the whole of the eastern portion of the nativity, and make them part rulers of the horoscope.

The ☽ ☌ ♅ absorbs ♃, ☉, ☿, and ♄.   It transforms the influence of those four planets into a powerful Uranian vibration.   With the exception of ☽ ♅ and ♆, all the planets represent the karma to be worked off in the present life.

The position of Saturn is harmless and supplements the Moon and Uranus.   It is also sextile the Sun and Mercury.   Saturn and Jupiter are in the decanates of exaltation, and necessarily in square.   Now note the power of the fixed cross.   Saturn is at the western angle ruling the fixed-air sign, Aquarius—the Man, and governing the mind, giving it the steady and permanent quality of meditation and contemplation.   On the eastern angle we find ☽ ☌ ♅ in the fixed-fire sign, Leo—the Lion.   The heart and passions are regenerated by the faith established in this sign through the working of the higher principles; the will and the mental unit being one. Jupiter is at the foot of the cross in Scorpio, the sign of regeneration and attachment to principles, and also, through the decanate (Pisces), the germinating of the seeds of compassion.

At the apex of the cross is the mystic sign Taurus, containing Neptune. On the cardinal cross we find Venus alone, setting, and its influence in the sign Capricorn is read as the transmutation of activities, denoted by this planet of the creative mind, into service. On the mutable cross, that of Sattva and wisdom, the fiery Mars yields its outgoing energies to the refinement of love. Pisces, the exaltation of Venus and the sign of the universal solvent, has changed the passion of Mars and the senses into the passion of devotion. Note the exchange of exaltations; Venus in Capricorn, Mars in Pisces. The whole of this horoscope is full of intuitive suggestions to those who study on esoteric lines.

All horoscopes in which one of the crosses is pronounced, have some special meaning for good or ill. Taking this particular horoscope, which reveals so much to the intuitive student by illustrating the concealed sub-influences, the key to every horoscope, we note the scattered positions of the planets throughout the heavens—which denotes versatility. The fixed cross gives stability amid the versatility; so that there are present both flexibility and stability.

Now by relating the fixed cross to the decanates of the planets therein, Saturn in Libra decanate, Jupiter in Cancer decanate, we have two arms of the cardinal cross out of the fixed cross; and Venus the ruler of Taurus in the fixed cross, being in Capricorn makes the third arm of the cardinal cross, and with Aries on the M.C. the cardinal cross is complete.

Will power and the creative activities, or love in action, are denoted by these important crosses, by primary positions and decanates, or sub-influences.

A COMPARISON : (p. 132)

To make the ideas regarding Esoteric Astrology clearer, we may refer to the horoscope of Mrs. Annie Besant, which is mainly on the cardinal cross, showing the creative, active, and building influences to a pronounced degree. Examining the decanates of this cardinal cross we find ♅ in the second decanate of ♈, ♈-♌; the ☽ ☌ ♃ in the second decanate of ♋, ♋-♏; and ☿ ☌ ♀ in the second decanate of ♎, ♎-♒.

To complete the fixed cross, Mars, the planet exalted in Capricorn, the apex of Mrs. Besant's cardinal cross, is in Taurus, so that in her case we have the order reversed.

In our example horoscope it is Fixed-Cardinal, but in Mrs. Besant's case it is Cardinal-Fixed.

In the example horoscope the fiery and watery triplicities are completely represented.

In Mrs. Besant's case the airy and the watery triplicities are complete.

A STRONG PERSONALITY : (p. 196)

Lest by any chance it should happen that an undue censure be passed on maps that seem too personal and therefore weak, it will be well to take the horoscope of an exceedingly strong personality, that of Napoleon I., in whose nativity no less than seven planets illuminated the Personal Star.

Napoleon had all the tenacity of mind which Venus in Cancer denotes, he had also all the personal ambition which Saturn upon the Midheaven in this sign indicates.

The Sun well placed in the sign Leo is the only direct indication of the Strength of the Individuality. The ruling planet, the benefic Venus, in Cancer, supported by Saturn, and the Sun its own sign, supported by Mercury, were indications of a character in which the elements of personal power were strongly marked.

The psychic side of the personality was singularly efficient in securing the temporal power he obtained over a nation governed by Leo.

In the early part of Napoleon's remarkable career the positions of the planets were highly favourable, especially his ruler Venus, in the ninth house, in sextile aspect with Mars, and *trine to Jupiter;* but it is evident that the personal craving for power carried him to a height that he could not individually maintain, and he over-reached himself by pushing the personal side of his nature beyond its limits of success or endurance.

The rising Jupiter and the culminating Venus were indeed lucky stars, but their glory was refracted in the watery signs of tenacity and attachment. The sensations of Cancer were vivid enough while the opportunity to gratify the lust of power was achieved, and the resistance of Scorpio was sufficient while it held the influence of Jupiter in sextile aspect to Mars ; the crisis came however when the personal triangle of the watery or astral element was expended. Napoleon changed in himself, and his fortunes changed with the change that followed his defeat in a project upon which he had set his heart. He was never the same man again ; it was then that the Moon in Capricorn in opposition to Saturn began its work. Napoleon knew that his benefic and culminating star, Venus, would set. He was truly a man of destiny, with all the personal and physical ambitions a worldly man can have, and while he had opportunity he made the most of it ; but the story has been told of how he met a man whose star had not set and who was individually his superior. Psychologists alone can explain the mystery of Napoleon.

CONCLUDING REMARKS

A little abstract thinking upon horoscopes on these lines quickly demonstrates the difference between Esoteric and Exoteric or Horary Astrology.

If these examples have been followed carefully, the difference between primary positions and their sub-influences will have been ascertained from the judgment of those given.

Esoteric Astrology is quite practical in teaching us that each triplicity of signs is a perfect representation of the plane with which it is concerned ; and also that each triplicity has a sub-influence, through the quadruplicities, relating it to a power or special quality of vehicle or sheath through which the consciousness, represented by the planets, may be expressed.

Each sign of the zodiac gives forth certain vibrations which establish forms, and the vibrations of the planets representing self-conscious life either respond to the forms and harmonise with them, or clash and produce inharmony.

A fortunate destiny or good karma is the result of the harmonious blending of planet and sign ; bad fate or evil karma in the result of an inharmonious blending. We cannot judge of the reality or the Monad behind the manifestation, for that is always the unmanifest ; but we may know the qualities of the forms through which the Ego is manifesting. A young Ego has just the horoscope that would deceive many who sought to judge the growth of the soul or the character of the Ego apart from the karma attached to that particular personality.

All students of the esoteric or deeper side of astrology should look upon this from the experimental point of view so far as the Ego is concerned, until the intuition is sufficiently active to see clearly.

It it the same with all other departments of occultism where abstract thought and feeling are concerned.   The psychic is examining the hidden laws of Nature in the same way, and will often make serious mistakes until the lower vibrations are wholly subject to the higher.

Our next Chapter deals with a particular horoscope, giving a more detailed account of the life and a fuller rendering of the esoteric interpretation.

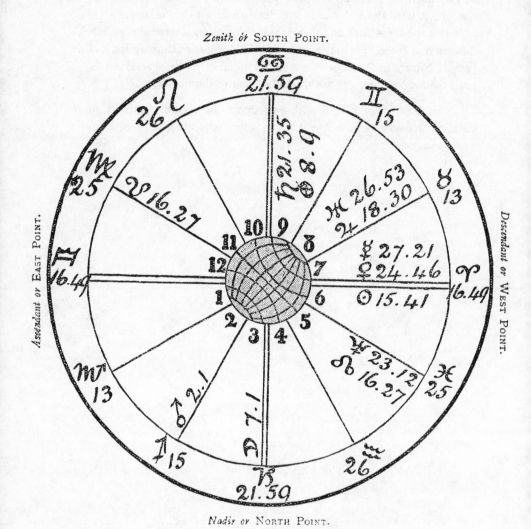

A HUMAN DOCUMENT

CHAPTER XIX

A REMARKABLE HUMAN DOCUMENT

Nor is the individuality—nor even the *essence* of the personality if any be left behind—lost, because reabsorbed. For however limitless, from a human standpoint, the Nirvanic state may be, it has yet a limit in Eternity. This limit once reached, the monad will re-emerge therefrom as a still higher being on a far higher plane, to recommence its cycle of activity.　*Secret Doctrine.*

THE following life history is that of a person whose horoscope faces this page. For the sake of those interested in directional astrology the Speculum is appended here. An esoteric interpretation of the nativity is given later.

SPECULUM

	Right Ascension.		Meridian Distance.		Semi-Arc.		Mundane Position.			
	°	′	°	′	°	′	°	′		
☉	14	26	80	41	82	18	1	37	under	7 cusp
☽	277	57	15	48	131	35	28	4	from	3 ,,
☿	25	8	88	37	104	7	15	30	,,	7 ,,
♀	23	16	90	29	101	1	10	32	,,	7 ,,
♂	240	7	53	38	116	13	23	51	,,	2 ,,
♃	46	16	67	29	111	39	6	57	,,	8 ,,
♄	113	23	0	22	119	58	0	22	outside	10 ,,
♅	54	37	59	8	115	42	18	0	from	8 ,,
♆	354	13	60	28	94	39	2	38	outside	6 ,,

THE STORY OF MY LIFE

Born of old parents, my mother being 42 and my father 52, I was an only child, precocious and difficult to rear. I started by being a healthy baby, but vicissitude and troubles speedily fell upon me. First I was very nearly starved, for my mother, who could not nurse me herself, provided as substitute a wet nurse, and also fed me with pap, which would have been all right but for the fact that at the time my mother had in her employ a young servant who being particularly fond of nice things, ate most of it and put in a little milk to thin out the remainder; this my mother discovered when she was able to attend to her domestic duties again, much to my benefit.

At the age of 2 weeks the monthly nurse who attended my mother in her accouchement managed by accident to push me out of bed; fortunately I fell on a soft rug and thus sustained little injury, though my mother, awakened by my cries, leaped from her bed, and flew to my assistance, fearing it was my death-warrant, for in those days beds were very high and it was disastrous for a baby to fall so far; however, there must have been some protection round about me, for I do not seem to have received any injury.

The next calamity arose at the age of 3 months, when my mother could not understand why I continually cried and became wasted almost to a skeleton; at last she sought the aid of the doctor, who discovered that the wet nurse, a young buxom woman who fed her own babe as well as myself, had suddenly become a dry nurse, the fount of nature's nourishment having dried up.

She was a poor woman, and needed the wage my mother paid her and so said nothing whatsoever about it; thus had it not been for my three daily meals of pap prepared by my mother herself I should have been starved to death : however my mother at once procured another wet nurse and all things went on smoothly.

At the age of 2 when toddling after my mother I missed my footing at the top of the staircase, and commenced to roll rapidly down it; my mother threw herself half over the well of the staircase, and reaching downward as far as she possibly could, just managed to grasp one foot and so drew me up backwards, and thus probably saved my life.

Karma, however, being cheated in one direction, had to be paid in another; so shortly afterwards, just before I was 3, I fell ill of a slow malarial fever, lasting for over two months, became wasted to a skeleton, and was unable to walk for weakness and for three months was wheeled out reclining on a little bed, made up in a perambulator. No one thought at the time I should recover, but eventually I did. Between 5 and 6 years of age I sickened with scarlet fever and one night both my parents watched to see the last breath disappear ; my parents were passionately attached to me, for I was their only child, and my mother's age precluded her having any more ; I can dimly remember my mother's tears falling like rain, as, sitting by my bedside, she held my little hand, and I half consciously wondered *why* she cried : the doctor said he feared I could not live through the night, and I have heard my mother declare that I lay as one dead for several hours, and at last as she could discover no breath stirring, she took a mirror and laid it against my lips, and as she saw it slightly clouded she knew I had not yet departed. That night was the crisis, I slept at last for several hours, and finally recovered; but that was a three months' illness, and I had to be taken to the sea, which gave me great delight, and where I grew quite strong again.

I had more vitality and became much stronger after seven years of age, but until that period was passed I was several times near the gateway of death.

The Period of Mercury

I learnt to read very readily, practically taught myself, and at 7 years of age could read and write well; indeed, my mother's sisters, maiden aunts, thought my letters wonderful for so young a child; they sent me a bright new sovereign in a little box for each, which my mother immediately banked for me, much to my childish sorrow, as I liked to play with shining things.

I was a queer, weird child; I had practically no physical plane playfellows, but used to construct dream children and play with them, and was always trying to fly. I would stand on a high chair and stretch out my arms and try to fly, only of course to come ignominiously to the ground.

My chief delight in childhood was, and is to-day, BOOKS; at that early age I revelled in fairy tales; that was the world I lived in. I was Red Riding Hood, Cinderella, and all the rest, living in a world of my own, following my own fancies, among practical business people who did not understand the finer nature of a child, or believe in anything beyond physical plane realities.

I was always looking for fairies, and frightened of goblins, and when the curtain of night fell and shut out the light I would scream if my mother left me alone in the dark. For I saw or imagined things (which, even now I cannot say), queer little figures, humped-back little people would flit about me and I would get terribly frightened. My mother sought in vain to hide the books, but I always discovered where she had hidden them; she would emphatically declare that there were no fairies and no goblins, and that all these things were only put in books to sell them, and that I ought to learn to sew and do some useful work, and not imagine all sorts of nonsense which had no foundation. Ghosts, fairies and hobgoblins were all lies, had no existence, but I knew better;

did I not see real children flit about me and sit on the chairs I placed for them ? But she would never believe that I could see anything.

My mother loved me dearly, and was very proud of my childish beauty, and spent hours curling my hair, which fell to my waist, and designing beautiful dresses for me ; but my mind and soul were alien and strange to her perception. I was like none of the family, such a curious child, almost like a changeling ; what had she ever done that God could afflict her with such a child, with her head always buried in a book and imagining all sorts of impossible things ?

My mother declared when she was my age she could hem and sew and embroider, dust rooms and was very useful to her mother, while I loathed needlework and if she gave me a handkerchief to hem managed to lose it on the way to school !

I used to learn poetry and recite it to an imaginary audience if not a real one, and in my childish fashion was always trying to teach. I had a large family of dolls, about twenty in all, I think (for my mother's business being a large toy emporium, I could have toys, dolls, and children's books *ad lib.*). I used to place these dolls in rows on the stairs and teach them, tell them stories and set them lessons; it was a real school to me, who was verily the dolls' teacher, meting out rewards and punishments ; and looking back it is clear that I lived a vividly imaginative life, an inner life rather than an external one.

I always slept with a book under my pillow, childhood and early youth alike, and waking in the early dawn, would at once proceed to delve into its pages ; generally fairy books or childish tales of heroism were my delight.

At 8 years of age I had whooping cough very severely, and later on measles ; and at 10, a bad eye, which lasted for three months ; yet withal my health was steadily improving, and my education going rapidly forward, though the schools I attended were not versed in the principles of tuition, and the children were left much to their own devices.

I learnt music very readily, and I was fond of drawing and painting, for which I showed marked aptitude, but my parents being chiefly concerned with business matters, gave me but little attention ; there was no one to see to my home lessons or take any interest in my education, consequently I never became really educated in the proper sense of the term, or a real student.

Superficiality took the place of thoroughness; my parents were

told that I must practise at least two hours a day, and so they forced me
to do it, but as they were never there to superintend, I generally
practised my scales with a story-book for the music. As a matter of fact
I really taught myself, and what came easy was accomplished and that
which was difficult remained undone.

GROWING UP

Had I only been given a capable governess who loved and understood me, what a difference it would have made to the whole of
my future life.   At the age of 12 I left girlhood behind me and
remember packing up two or three of my most loved dolls, toys, etc.,
into a big box, and writing on the cover : " Finished with all childish
things ; I am a woman now and must take life seriously," and after
that I never played again with toys or dolls.   I chose for my birthday a
volume of Longfellow's poems and for the next two years practically
lived with him ; sleeping with the volume under my pillow.   I loved
poetry at this period better than anything else in the world, and from 12
to 20 revelled in all the standard poets I could lay my hands upon.   I
went to a school of art and studied painting and drawing, and took a
certificate and medal for both.   My music master declared I had great
aptitude but no perseverance, so as I could now play the piano fairly
well my father said it was no use wasting any more money upon my
musical education.   I played well enough to amuse him.

But as the School of Art was inexpensive I continued there.
When I was about ten my parents had given up business and retired,
living in another house with a nice garden ; my father had through
investment and speculation become a very rich man, though he lived as
if he had a small income, because his nature was a miserly one, and he
hated to spend one unnecessary penny.

In my twelfth year I was sent to a boarding school at Kilburn.
My feelings and emotions at being separated from home and my parents
made me sick for a week with sheer grief ; the head mistress of that
school was both hard and unkind, and all the girls feared her, myself
among the number.   It may be I tried her patience somewhat, for while
I readily apprehended most subjects there was one I could never succeed
in understanding, and that was arithmetic ; I never have been able to
master figures, and no amount of effort on my part or my former teachers
could make me an arithmetician.   Mrs. Dunn, the head mistress,

declared it was sheer obstinacy, and said she would teach me herself, but it ended in her boxing my ears at last in anger and impatience at my stupidity. After that episode I wrote home privately and declared that if my mother did not come for me I should run away, so she came and brought me home. At the end of two months another school was found for me and once again I suffered the pangs of separation and cried myself ill, but this school was in the country and of a different type.

The ladies at the head of it were both kind and sympathetic, and they tried to make each girl's life happy; it was a country school, and while such subjects as ethics, religion, and morality were well sustained, it was not a first-class school, and with the exception of arithmetic I found lessons there very easy. I received a medal for recitation and a silver one for essays on original subjects, and just before my fifteenth birthday my parents declared that I had received quite enough schooling for a girl and that I should study music and drawing at home, so after a year and three months at boarding school, chosen rather for its low rate of fees than for the excellence of its teaching, I came home for good.

DOMESTIC DISHARMONY

At the age of 16 my parents, whose relationship had for some time been strained, started domestic differences, and disharmony became the state of the home atmosphere; finally a separation took place between them; my father left my mother and moved to another town, taking me with him. My father was Hebrew and my mother Christian, so that I was brought up in each faith, though as it was a cathedral city in which I was born, and there was no synagogue there, Sunday was more to me than Saturday; but after our removal to a town with a large synagogue, the Jewish minister, a learned doctor, taught me Hebrew thoroughly and inculcated into me the mysteries of the Hebrew faith.

I now went regularly to the synagogue and used to wonder which religion was true, my father's or my mother's, or if either of them were. My mother remained behind in that quiet cathedral city, and I used to visit her sometimes; she was a most unselfish woman and actually sent me from her (though she loved me better than her own life), to live permanently with my father. She considered that as my father was wealthy he would be able to do much more for me than she could ever accomplish, so at the age of 16 I was managing my father's house, with servants to supervise, and cooking to attend to, and what I suffered with all these domestic details to superintend, and no woman to advise me it would be impossible to depict; for I was left motherless, practically, at just the age a girl most needs a mother. Occasionally when things grew too hard for me and my father's tongue had given me a terrible lashing, I fled back to her for a few days ; but she would not let me remain, she ever sent me back again, impressing on both mind and heart that I must never leave my father, no matter what happened ; declaring she had made a supreme sacrifice, and given me up to him, and it would break her heart entirely if I ever left him; she loved us both with a great power of attachment, unselfishness and fidelity.

My father was a man of strong will and most selfish disposition, but he had his good points, and one of them was a passionate love for children ; and as long as I remained a child and obeyed him implicitly seldom spoke harshly to me, but kissed and fondled me. Alas! from 16 onwards practically every bit of this fondness changed in character; he now expected me to take charge of his house, cook, manage and economise in every possible way, and though he could then have lived at the rate of £5,000 a year he lived at the rate of two hundred, for his ruling passion was avarice. He was very unreasonable as he expected me entirely without training to be an experienced housewife and manager, just as experienced and careful as my mother was; but I had never been trained in any method of domestication, so a war of words ensued, tears and recrimination became the order of the day, and life became a scene of misery for me. For a period of about fifteen years I rarely spent one day without, at some period or the other of it, shedding bitter tears, nor did I ever eat one meal in peace.

RESTRICTIONS

My father loved me in his fashion, but he loved money better than anything in the world, the money possessed him rather than he the money ; he clothed me extravagantly, but gave me no pocket-money, and had not my mother sent me some my life would have been still harder ; out of the small sum she sent me I used to supply all the breakages and everything that got worn out in the house ; as to tell him of a breakage was to invite a most furious fit of passion.

I made several girl friends, girls of my own age and older women, but as I could rarely ask them to the house and was seldom allowed out unless I was with my father, I used to have to pay visits by stealth ; they were sorry for me, and one man, my father's doctor, tried to urge upon him that I should sometimes go to concerts, and have a little pleasure, that a life suitable for a man of seventy and upwards was scarcely the atmosphere that a young girl could be happy in, and as my father had great respect for him (he was a very clever physician, and a good man), at his instigation I had a few rare pleasures which I should not otherwise have obtained.

My father's idea was that there was only one person in the world to study and that was himself, that no one else mattered, that I must live for him alone, so for many years I lived somewhat in the position of a nun, going to bed each night at nine, each evening playing the piano and reading for many hours to my father, occasionally being allowed a young friend to tea. One girl friend I loved dearly, and one night she met with an accident and sent for me ; my father declared I should not go, saying if I did I should never enter his doors again ; I spent that night in bitterest pain, writing and explaining why I could not come. My father completely dominated my life, and when occasionally I used to remonstrate with him said he would break my spirit or break my heart, and he had such furious fits of passion that he did not hesitate to strike me if I in any way annoyed him, and even after I was twenty would think nothing of slapping my face in his anger. Yet curiously enough, in spite of all this I loved him ; whether it was because I was of an affectionate disposition, or whether it was the tie of blood, I cannot say, but I was devoted to his best interests ; nursing him in sickness and trying in every possible way to please him.

A Double Event

At 21 a dual event happened. I had two months' foreign travel with my father, and became a Jewess, —much to my mother's pain ; but my father wished it, and some of the inner teachings of Judaism, particularly the belief in the unity of the One life, and the daily prayer, " Hear, O Israel, the Lord our God is One," greatly attracted me ; I thought it would do as well as any other religion, for at that time I had no religion at all. I was seeking for the truth and called myself to my own intimate friends a truth-seeker.

My father spent a hundred pounds in attaching me to the Jewish faith, and as his greatest love in the world was money, it impressed me very much.

At that time I was a very fair Hebrew scholar, and as I knew all the dogmas of the Hebrew faith and had kept most of the feasts and fasts of the Jewish church for several years, there was little difficulty, and I was baptised at the hands of Dr. Adler and given a certificate.

Looking backwards I see ceremony, forms, and religion all meant nothing to me; I think my father's mind somewhat dominated mine and I did it chiefly to please him; I do not think my father meant to be cruel, but he certainly was the most selfish human being I have ever met, and I had to live his life and do just as he wished, or he would by sheer force make me do it; thus my life was a very unhappy one—books were my one and only joy! My mother lived in another town, and though I saw her sometimes and loved her always she was helpless to alter my conditions, indeed she was more frightened of my father than I was and never crossed his will, and in her brief visits to us both could only counsel patience, saying that some day he would surely die (being a very old man then) and then I could do as I liked, as I would be very rich; anyway she was helpless where my father was concerned. My father would rarely let me out of his sight and yet spoilt my life, as well as his own, by continual fault-finding, grumbling and upbraiding.

MY MOTHER'S DEATH

So things went on, month after month. At the age of 25, practically on my twenty-fifth birthday, I lost my mother; she had a fall while out walking and died of concussion of the brain after only one week's illness; my father came over to see us, and in that hour was very kind, but as he disliked seeing either sickness, death or sorrow, spent but one hour with us; it was my first touch of mortal pain, for I loved my mother deeply. How I suffered, what anguish I endured! I nursed her day and night until she died, and felt as if half my life had gone with her. At her death I had a curious psychic vision, I saw her standing all in white near the door, and heard her voice faintly declare it was well with her and beg me not to grieve; and once later, during a severe illness, I saw her sitting opposite to me in the easy chair, looking towards me with eyes of compassion and of love; many times in my life I have had curious dreams and visions, and strange psychic happenings have occurred to me, while all my life my intuitions have been my sheet anchor.

After selling up the home I returned to my father's house having lost my best friend on earth, my dear mother. Soon after this period I met by chance a book on phrenology and this I studied hard for several months, and then I found another dealing with physiognomy and later on one on palmistry and graphology.

Self-Help

The study of human nature I loved, and required no compulsion to drive me towards it ; for three years I studied these subjects thoroughly, getting every book on the subject I could procure. My father one day in one of his curious fits of passion taunted me with the fact that I had never made a penny in my life, and his usual remark as to what could I do, and if it were not for him where should I be, etc., etc., called out for once an answering spark from within me, and I plucked up my courage and declared " I can make a good living as a phrenologist and can be quite independent of you if you will only let me do it." He laughed in derision, but I said " Will you let me try, give your consent," and he answered " Yes," never thinking for a moment that I meant to act. So I took my diploma from Fowler's and put my name on a brass plate at the door as professor of Phrenology, Graphology and Palmistry. Almost immediately clients called on me ; at first I charged the modest sum of 5s. for a reading of their characters, but afterwards as I grew successful a guinea, and for a full written delineation even two.

When I had saved about £40 in gold, I took it into the dining-room, poured it out on the table and said to my father "There, that is my money, I have made it, you neither gave it to me nor lent it to me." For the first time he treated me with respect ; I had now become clever according to his idea of cleverness, for I could make money, something on his own lines. Up to that day he had always thought me a fool, and always nick-named me in derision the Good Samaritan, because he declared I ran after beggars and nursed all the sick people ; he never gave to any beggars and avoided any sickness for fear he should take the complaint. His one idea of me was that " God had never endowed me with any common-sense, for anyone could tell *me* a sorrowful story, and get anything out of me." His maxim was—what does the world do for you ? always think of yourself first, number one should be your maxim, and he declared with great regret that after all his teachings I was just as foolish as ever.

So any good I could do or any help I could give had to be done in secret, for if he discovered that anything had been given away, he was furious and made my life miserable.

We were entirely opposite, my father and I, yet in his way he loved me, and I devoted my life to him; it never once occurred to me that it was a great sacrifice, and only now, on looking backwards, do I realise I could not live those years again. Death would be preferable. Constant disharmony, jangle and jar—my faults all recited to any visiting friends, or even casual strangers who happened to visit the house, and yet in spite of much bitter pain I remained and bore my daily cross, for my dead mother's prayer, " Child, never leave your father, remember the sacrifice I have made ; stay with him to the end," kept me beside him. For at this time I had a profession, was dependent on none, and could easily have made my own way in life. However, things grew somewhat easier as my father found there were many persons coming to consult me, who praised my skill, and declared that my delineations were wonderfully accurate.

COMPARATIVE FREEDOM

Thus I gained more and more freedom, and in time the old man even occasionally allowed me to go out into the world and lecture on phrenology, palmistry and kindred subjects, being particularly delighted on receipt of a cheque sent to me for five guineas for an evening's lecture and examinations. Thus my absence from his side took on another character, for this as he said was work, not pleasure ; I received remuneration instead of spending money for concerts, theatres, etc. So from my 28th year onwards I became a speaker and lecturer on the science of human nature, often travelling and giving examinations daily. My time was now very fully occupied with scarcely a moment to spare, so that by reason of my profession I had now to spend hours writing, and seeing clients in another room apart from my father ; but then he gave his consent, for the fact of my earning money was to him a very great thing.

Strange anomaly of human nature : at this time my parent was worth about £80,000, but this made no difference whatever in his dealings with me, as I only had what money I could earn. At this period, my 28th year, I lost by death an old and valued friend, the doctor I have previously alluded to, who in my early girlhood and until the day of his death always sought to help me, and did his best to induce my father to give me a little pleasure and change from time to time. This was a great grief to me and even drew from my father some expressions of regret, for this estimable gentleman was the only man my father, to my knowledge, ever trusted—except later on my husband.

I was now a member of the professional classes and came into touch

with others of a similar occupation, and hence I met a man who speedily
became very attracted towards me, and finally proposed to me, but I did
not care for him ; he urged me to marry him but I refused, partly because
I did not love him and partly because I knew my father would never
permit the union, because as he was a Christian it would be against my
father's religion.   So matters stood for a long time : his sister, my great
friend, together with her husband kept a large hydropathic establishment by
the sea, so when I stayed there for my summer holiday we came in touch ;
we also occasionally corresponded.   Meanwhile several Jewish suitors had
asked my hand in marriage according to Jewish custom ; one in particular
my father favoured because he was a wealthy man, and my father, to induce
me to take him, said he would give me £10,000 on my wedding day.   But
I did not want to marry, I preferred a celibate life, and had strong views
of a platonic life, built up of pure love and to live within wedlock as
friends for companionship alone.

My father said I was crazy in thinking such a thing possible, my
mother in her lifetime said she thought such a thing was not possible for
human men and women, yet that was my ideal ; if I took a mate it
would be for the purposes of help and companionship.   So I refused
to marry the man my father had found for me, and in that one
particular he did not seek to coerce my will, as he said jokingly I had
saved him £10,000.

A Religious Crisis

At this period I was about 30 years of age ; I gained greater liberty
now I had a profession and I came in touch with many people, heard
many sad histories and am thankful to say was able to help and console
many sorrowful hearts.

My mind was now turned in the direction of God and religion ; vainly
I sought for some faith I could accept, for at this period I was almost
a materialist ; it was true I went to the synagogue, but it was simply to
please my father, to me it was all external form with the spirit lacking, and
the problem always pressing on me for solution was, Is there an all-
powerful God, with all this misery in the world ; if so and He is a God of
Love, why does He allow it ; why do some suffer so much and others have
nothing but enjoyment ; life is a riddle ; would I could solve it !   But I
could find no answer to my problem.   I procured a book from the town
library with all the religions of the world set down therein to see if I

could find one to suit me, but none explained the cause of human misery and human pain.

I attended lectures on religious subjects, Unitarian, Christian, Hebrew, but found no comfort from any. After two years of searching for the light, it suddenly came to me in the shape of a book.

A book sent from the East to a soul in the West, and as this was the most potent event in my life I can record every incident in connection with it. On the November previous to my 33rd birthday a book called *Esoteric Buddhism* fell into my hands; its coming was strange and the events connected with it stranger. Some two or three years earlier I had met an old man about 70 who became interested in me and the subjects which I taught; his name I will call Bentley. He was poor, somewhat decrepit, his garments tattered and disreputable, but he was well educated and had had an eventful career, living for many years in the East, and together with myself had a great desire to understand the problems of life. I had introduced him to my father, but the latter would hold out no hand of friendship, for poverty in his eyes was a crime.

I was very sorry for the old man, because he lived alone and had so little money and no friends, so I used sometimes to go for a walk with him, and we would discuss life, death and immortality; he lived quite by himself in a tiny cottage, a mile or two out of town, and did all his own work; I used occasionally to give him a little help in putting his small place straight and cooking for him. I discovered that he had two sons in Adyar, who sometimes wrote to him; he occasionally showed me their letters, they seemed to be about to join some society of which they spoke with great enthusiasm. Well, one particular day Mr. Bentley wrote me a line asking me to meet him, as he had some news for me. How well I remember that day, a Saturday morning in November, but fine and bright. As we met he smiled and said: "I have something here you will like, a book after your own heart, for it tells you how to put your feet on the chimney corner and go out into space; I do not understand it at all myself, but I have read it to please my sons, who told me I must, as they feared I might not live long and were anxious that I should have the knowledge of the Truth as they call it; but at any rate you will, I know, be delighted with it; I think it is just what you want." I thanked him warmly and he gave me his son's letter to read, which had come with the book; looking back I am inclined to imagine that those sons must have been psychic, with a prevision of what was going to happen! I did not know what it all meant at the moment but I took the book and asked him how long I could keep it. "Keep it altogether if you like," he said, "I do not want it again."

As I said good-bye I noticed he was not looking well and he said his heart had been troubling him lately; I remember feeling very grateful to him for his thought of me and the gift of the book, and so returned home.

THE BOOK!

I knew I should have no chance of reading quietly until my father had retired for the night, but as he generally went upstairs at 8.30, his great age making rest a necessity, I eagerly waited for that time to come. After seeing him safely tucked up under the bed clothes I myself retired for the night. I locked my door, turned up the gas, sat down by the fire and opened the book, and read on and on steadily throughout the night, except for intervals when tears literally rained from my eyes and I could no longer see the print. I pressed the book to my bosom as a well-loved friend, crying: "I have found the truth, I have found the truth; Oh God, I thank Thee for the light." When the maid brought my tea in on the Sunday morning I was a Theosophist, and after twenty-four years in the Theosophical Society am not a firmer believer in the doctrines than I became in that hour. It was a conversion for me, out of the darkness of ignorance the light flashed forth, and I who had been blind, saw. I was indeed happy, for I had been so hungry and the bread of wisdom was so good. I had thirsted for the truth and had at last found the living water and knew I should never thirst again. That night I became as one re-born; now I understood the ways of God to man, Karma and re-incarnation explained to me the inequalities of the human race and that there was a great law working and that at the heart of all things was the love of God for humanity. I locked up my treasure, *Esoteric Buddhism*, most carefully, but the thoughts filled both heart and brain. On Monday, as we were having dinner, my father said, "Who do you think is dead?" I said I did not know. "Why, your old friend, Mr. Bentley; they say he was found dead in his arm chair with his feet on the mantelpiece; one of the neighbours discovering milk and bread lying outside his door wondered if he were ill, and went to see and there found him dead."

My old friend! how truly my friend! how many times have I blessed him since for giving me that book. On the Saturday he gave me *Esoteric Buddhism* and on Monday he was dead. This made a great impression on my consciousness. One month later Annie Besant came and gave two lectures on Theosophy, one on Karma and Re-incarnation and the other on the Law of Evolution; needless to say I attended, and at the close of the lecture asked her several questions which she took great pains to answer. I felt my heart go out to her in admiration and worship, for she was indeed a most wonderful speaker, and wished I knew her personally—when a little voice that I have often heard interiorly said quietly, "You will know her very well later on." All my life I have been conscious, at critical periods, of an inner voice which seems to speak and guide me, and I have several times been saved from danger, both physical and otherwise, through its influence. A month later I discovered there was a Theosophic Lodge at Bournemouth, and became a member of it; this was about my 33rd birthday.

RIDICULE AND CRITICISM

I tried to make my friends around me understand some of the truths which were all the world to me, and wondered why the truth which appealed to me so strongly should incur ridicule from those around me; but I found in my enthusiastic presentment of it that ridicule and criticism were often the result, and I was told that Madame Blavatsky was a charlatan while Mrs. Annie Besant was associated with that atheist Bradlaugh: in vain I tried to explain that Madame Blavatsky was one of the greatest teachers of modern days, and that Mrs. Besant was endeavouring to spread the truths she had presented to the world in *Isis Unveiled* and the *Secret Doctrine;* in time I realised that there were few able to apprehend the truths of the Wisdom Religion. I tried vainly to give a little of the Theosophic teaching to my father, an orthodox Jew, but he begged me not to tell anyone of these ideas but himself, or they might put me under restraint as a lunatic. At last I found one person who listened at any rate, and appeared to believe some of the teachings; it was my friend's brother, who now implored me to become his wife; he was staying in our town for a month's work and a month's lectures.

I told him I had never yet cared for any man in that way, and repeated what I had said a year or two back, that my marriage to a Christian was impossible, that I could not grieve my father who had become very aged, and might not live long. One day to my great surprise he said: " I will become a member of the Hebrew faith for your sake, and shall call on your father and tell him so." I tried to point out the physical danger he would incur and that it would be a great ordeal, but it was of no avail; I also told him I did not care for him save as a friend, and put forth my ideals of a platonic life. He declared they were his ideals also, and that companionship was all that he desired in the marital relation. It never once occurred to me that as my father was then a very wealthy man I should be considered a good match from that standpoint. He further pleaded that as we were both phrenologists I could help him at his own profession, which was also mine, that we would work together and in time should build up a competence ; he further said he would become a Fellow of the Theosophical Society and that though he had no money he was a hard worker, and that together we should do very well financially. I pleaded for six months' delay in which to think the matter over, and during this period I applied for membership to the inner school of the Theosophical Society, and apart from my work was busy studying *Isis Unveiled* and the *Secret Doctrine.*

Finally I gave my consent to become engaged if my father gave his.

MARRIAGE

Now my father had by this time begun to think I should never marry at all, and from the Jewish standpoint marriage is incumbent upon every woman ; curiously enough he took a fancy to this young man for his courage in wishing to become a Jew, and said if he went through the ceremony he would give him his daughter, but that he would not give him any money. If I chose to marry a poor man that was my own look out. A month later he entered into the Covenant of Israel, and the following spring we were married according to the rites of the Jewish Church.

ASTROLOGY

Meanwhile I had been at Andermouth attending meetings, giving papers and helping the T.S. Lodge of which I was a member. One day the subject of Astrology came up, and I declared I had not much faith in it, for my nativity had been cast by two or three professors, and that none of it was true. "Who did it," said one of the group, "was it Alan Leo?" "No," I said, "Who may he be?" and then I was told he was an astrologer and the Editor of an astrological magazine, and that if I became a subscriber to its pages he would give me a written reading of my map. I said "Very good, so I will," but I remarked to our Secretary, "You send my birth data so that the astrologer can judge nothing by the handwriting,"—for I knew that a great deal could be learnt from that. So the Secretary of the Lodge sent up particulars of my birth, and later on the magazine and my horoscope came, and he sent them on to me.

It was a very short one, scarcely two pages, but every word was true. "Now," I said, "Here is something I must study for myself," so I sat down and said how pleased I was with my delineation, that its accuracy surprised me, and I asked the writer if ever he came to the town in which I lived would he call on me, as I wished to become his pupil; and one day he came. I don't think I was in the least attracted towards his personality, but the stars fascinated me, and I at once wanted to become his pupil by letter. So after this meeting he gave me teaching by correspondence, and as we were both deep students of the Eastern wisdom we had a good deal in common. He loved Astrology, but though I grew quite fascinated with it, it did not present itself to me from any religious aspect; it was to me only a science, but deeper and fuller than any I had studied before.

I believed in it but I could not understand its rationale ; it was only later on when in a dream I was told that the sun was the outward body of the God of the solar system, and that the stars were planetary spirits whose outer covering was the star, that I realised the spiritual and religious side of Astrology.

DIVORCE

On my return to England from America we met again at Andermouth, and my husband, who thought there was some money to be made out of it, thereupon took up the study of Astrology. I used to spend each week-end with my father, but had an office for business purposes and a reception room where I saw people, and worked often from 10 a.m. until midnight, examining heads, lecturing, speaking. Much knowledge of human nature came to me through my profession, and also the realisation that my marriage was a mistake, for I was very unhappy. I discovered I had not been wedded for love and companion-

ship as I imagined but for the fortune I was likely some day to receive ;
I had the whole responsibility of the business on my shoulders, and did
most of the work, although I handed the money to my husband, so that
while I worked day in and day out I never had any money. To add to my
troubles I discovered that my husband's ideals were quite foreign to mine,
and that like my father he was very fond of money, and to my mind far
too economical,—money being to me a means to an end, rather than an end
in itself.

He never really became a Theosophist, and our relations grew very
strained. Finally, after only six months of married life I received through
the law courts an annulment of my marriage with the power to take my
maiden name again.

If ever a marriage was peculiarly karmic this one certainly was,
many things in connection with it being of a most peculiar and private
nature, and much deception had been practised the result of which
could only be a rupture of the relationship.

In my father's house I again took up my work, supplementing it
now by studying Astrology. About two years later on I married my
present husband, whom I deeply love, for the purpose of work together.

A SECOND MARRIAGE

My second marriage was kept secret for a few years, as I feared
that if my father discovered I had married out of the Jewish faith he
would never forgive me, and probably turn me out of the house. So I
had to live a dual life, spending part of it with my father and part of it
with my husband ; prior to this I had been travelling and lecturing for
several years, so it was possible for me to keep the old man in ignorance.
I did this chiefly for his own sake, as he was now nearly 90 and I
feared if he got into a furious passion it might make him seriously
ill, if not kill him, and also I did not want to make him unhappy.

However, someone seeing my husband and myself often together
told my father if I was not married I certainly ought to be, so on
my return from one of my visits to my husband, he said to me
suddenly, "Tell me the truth, are you privately married ?" I
knew in that moment all that would happen, but I could not tell the
old man a lie, so I said "Yes," and as he looked at my marriage
certificate he said, "You have pleased yourself, and now I shall please
myself ; I will only leave you enough to keep you from starvation, and I

will never forgive you for having deceived me." So thereupon I returned to my husband's house and remained there. Afterwards when he grew feebler and his health declined, he wrote and asked me to come and look after him, but I must come alone ; later on, he asked me to bring my husband.

From that time onward he became very fond of my husband, trusting him and leaning upon him ; and one day he told me that he considered the man I had married was neither a rogue nor a fool but a good man.

After a long illness, through which I nursed him day and night, he made a new will wherein he left me all his worldly possessions, which had now considerably dwindled and decreased ; for at 90 a man's brain is not able to cope with the intricacies of the Stock Exchange, and as a matter of fact he had been steadily losing money for years, though as he said he could not give it up ; he knew he was a gambler, but still he must go on to the end. And indeed he speculated until four or five years before his death, when he had a serious illness and the doctor warned him that any excitement would prove fatal. Then and only then did he quit all business, when we made the discovery that there was only about seven or eight thousand left from all his fortune !

GOOD AND BAD FORTUNE STRANGELY BLENDED

With my second marriage began quite the happiest period of my life. We had drawn many around us whom we could teach and help ; we loved each other dearly, and life became fuller and happier year by year.

My father who gradually grew feebler and feebler died of sheer old age at 102, just about the date of my fiftieth birthday. Previous to that event I had a very serious illness, bronchitis and slight pneumonia, which confined me to my bed for six weeks, and left me very feeble for a month afterwards. Two years later I was involved in a law suit which was decided in my favour, and since then have had by good Karma the inestimable privilege of visiting Adyar. Surely out of some good Karma of the past has destiny guided me to the feet of so great a soul as Mrs. Annie Besant, whose life and teachings have been my inspiration, who has kept my ideals living in tangible form, and to whom I owe so deep a debt of gratitude for all the help she has given me that nothing I can do will in any way repay it.

During the past five years my health, which had never hitherto failed me, has more or less broken down, and stands in the way of the work I would do.   If exertion be stronger than destiny I place it on record that I have tried by every means in my power to restore my vitality, as one needs a strong physical vehicle for service in the outer world.   What the future holds is at present on the knees of the gods.

I have only one desire and that is for good health, so that I can work better for that great cause of Theosophy and Brotherhood I love so well,—from a grateful heart to pass on in fuller measure to others the light that has been given to me.   But if my past Karma be too heavy and my physical vehicle rendered unfit for activity, which with so many planets in cardinal signs is the vital necessity of my being, may I at least remember, that "they also serve who only stand and wait."

ESOTERIC INTERPRETATION OF THE NATIVITY

The foregoing human document, taken as a study for students of Esoteric Astrology, gives the facts as they actually occurred in a life which may be considered one of peculiar realisations in which the Karma, or the fate accumulated throughout the previous lives, had to be dissolved in the present existence, in order that greater progress might be made towards spiritual unfoldment.

In the ordinary judgment of the nativity each event may be accounted for by the positions in the nativity, which, however, would only show the events and the extraordinary happenings, the student having to judge the internal experiences likely to arise out of the happenings.   We may briefly run over the exoteric judgment of the nativity to account for the events before dealing with the judgment from an esoteric standpoint.

THE EXOTERIC JUDGMENT

The native was the only child of elderly parents, the mother being 42 and the father 52 years of age; the mother is signified by the Moon in Capricorn in the third house, and the father by Saturn in Cancer, in the midheaven; she was reared with difficulty, the Moon in Capricorn applying to the square of the Sun, and the Sun being in square aspect with Saturn.

She was born healthy, Venus the ruler in an angle and the Sun in Aries.   The events during infancy can all be accounted for by the Sun in

opposition to the ascendant, Saturn elevated in square to the Sun—
Saturn governing falls; then again, Saturn in Cancer in square to Venus
accounted for the events indicated with the wet nurse, and the fact that
she was nearly starved to death. At the age of 2 she missed her footing
at the top of a staircase, but was saved by her mother; this is again
accounted for by Saturn, and the Sun in sesquiquadrate to Mars: also
feverish ailments emanate from these two influences.

The native was quick to learn, Mercury in the seventh in Aries in
conjunction with Venus.

Serious domestic difficulties occurred at the age of 16; separation of
the parents took place; the progression of the Moon to the parallel of
Uranus now brought a crisis, the mundane opposition of Mars and Saturn
rulers of the fourth and tenth (Mars being in parallel to Uranus at the same
time) denoting a breaking-up of youthful and irresponsible conditions.

The mother was a Christian and the father a Jew; note the double
signs on the cusps of the third and ninth houses.

TRAVEL AND RELIGION

Now from an esoteric standpoint there is one important event that
is worthy of careful notice; at the age of 21 the native became a Jewess
to please her father, and was rewarded by two months of foreign travel.
It will be noted that Mars was placed in Sagittarius, the ninth sign,
governing religion, and it is stated that the native had always been
between two faiths; was closely drawn towards Christianity, indicated by
Mars, through her mother, but definitely became a Jewess when the
Moon was passing over her ascendant through the sign Libra. It is said
that she had doubt upon all religious matters, Mercury ruling the ninth in
square aspect to Saturn.

Mars soon after birth became retrograde, it passed out of Sagittarius
into Scorpio, moving to the trine of Saturn; Saturn was the most elevated
planet in the nativity, closely concerned with the father, and being in
square aspect to Mercury, ruler of the ninth, the esoteric cause for the
two faiths can easily be discerned.

There is one vital thing in a nativity from an esoteric standpoint,
the effect that events in the life have upon the consciousness. Here we
also see the events that external changes produce, as well as the internal
changes of consciousness, for out of these two faiths influencing the

earlier portion of the life the native finally came into Theosophy which has no particular creed, but yet is based upon the idea that Truth underlies all religion.

From the progressed horoscope we can see that the planetary positions had so changed from birth as to bring the opportunity for new light to dawn upon her consciousness, which came at the age of 33, when Mercury arrived at the conjunction of Jupiter and formed a sextile aspect to Saturn; the Sun was then applying to a conjunction with Jupiter, which has to do with all religious thought and internal changes in consciousness.

MARKED DUALITY

The dual influences in this horoscope are very strongly marked, so strong are they that they produce duality in nearly all the events of a vital character which affected the life. The native was brought up in two faiths of a decidedly opposite character, with the possibility of blending the two into one had she chosen to do so; then again, she had two homes during the major portion of her life, and two peculiar love affairs; she also had two law suits; the first dissolving marriage, while the second dissolved all her relationship with the Jewish parentage, severed her from everything concerning her father, and, as her mother died without relatives, left her practically alone without further ties in this respect.

Now from an esoteric standpoint we should have to seek the blending of the two faiths into one producing her strong attachment to Theosophy, in the breaking-up of all her ties a realisation of a state of consciousness freed from these encumbrances, and in her attachments a union that brought satisfaction, and realisation of some of her ideals; all of which can be connected by an esoteric rendering of the nativity.

From an exoteric standpoint none of these experiences are clearly shown, and only indications of them can be given by an ordinary interpretation of the horoscope. But upon throwing the searchlight of esoteric knowledge upon this nativity we can see the underlying influences which affect consciousness as well as the form, and we can follow the interplay of life and form throughout the whole of the life. There is of course a psychological interpretation to every nativity as well as a scientific rendering, but without a knowledge of Esoteric Astrology it is exceedingly difficult to harmonise the psychological interpretation with the scientific.

Mars, Saturn, and Uranus

The duality of the whole horoscope is so very marked as to give the clue to the idea that the outgoing energies are to cease in the present life and a return to be made toward the inner and more subtle phases of existence.   For instance her father was an old man, exceedingly worldly and external, living the normal life of a materially minded man, who influenced the form side of her life considerably ; but note how another old man comes into her life, gives her a book which unlocks the whole of her spiritual nature and enables her to see the light through the teachings contained therein.   The responsiveness of the nature made it possible to experience the three distinct religious phases of her life ; Mars rising, the Christian religion ; Saturn elevated, the Jewish ; and Uranus, the Theosophist, which was unfolded through Jupiter, a religious planet, being in conjunction with Uranus.

A very singular experience which cannot be explained from an exoteric standpoint, is that although twice married the native remained a virgin, a unique experience difficult to trace in the horoscope from the ordinary rules of judgment.   At birth the second decanate of Libra rising is connected with the sign that rules the fifth house of the nativity, which enabled the square aspect of Venus and Saturn to change its influence into a transmutation of the affections from the physical and material into the spiritual ; in fact the whole horoscope is a peculiar revelation of the transmutation of influences from lower into higher.   And with so many planets setting, the life is shown to be fated, events occurring over which the native had little or no control, so that the transmutation of the ordinary indications into the spiritual conditions is very plainly marked.

The Progressed Horoscope v. Primary Directions

Another very peculiar position in this nativity requires an esoteric rendering and that is the progress of Mercury to the exact conjunction with Jupiter, and then its return to its place at birth, owing to its being retrograde directly it arrived at the conjunction.

It will be understood that in all esoteric renderings of a nativity the progression of the planets is of much more importance than the mundane aspects or primary directions, which have to deal with externals only.

EXOTERIC AND ESOTERIC: ANALYSIS AND SYNTHESIS

We will, however, take the horoscope from an exoteric standpoint into which the esoteric renderings will be blended in order to elucidate a little further the above remarks.

We will first examine the horoscope in the light of the various methods of synthesis. Analysis separates a horoscope into its component parts of house-position, sign-position, aspects, triplicity, quadruplicity, dignity, debility, and so on. Synthesis employs some of these same groupings as methods of bringing together otherwise separate influences and considering them under a few general heads so as to simplify the study of the horoscope. For instance in this map Mars and Venus are in no aspect to each other, but both are in fiery signs; the Moon and Saturn are in no aspect, but both are in cardinal signs; the Moon and Neptune are not in aspect to each other, but both are in cadent houses.

When dealing with groups like these, we bring together in one class influences that otherwise would very often remain separate, and much light is thrown upon the problem of the particular type or order to which the horoscope belongs.

Beginning with the houses, it will be seen that there are four planets in angular houses, three in succedent and two in cadent.

Angular houses are therefore the most strongly occupied, and will dominate the horoscope, so far as this system of classification is concerned. The seventh and tenth are the two houses concerned, and the Sun, Venus, Mercury, and Saturn are the bodies occupying them. Angular houses bring the native prominently before the public in some way; whether pleasant or unpleasant depends upon the nature of the combination; it gives her many friends and acquaintances, and ensures that she will be widely known. Marriage and association with others outside the home life are seen to be the chief agencies for accomplishing this in the present case, because the seventh house is the most strongly occupied. If the Sun, Venus, and Mercury could be considered quite alone, the result would be pleasant and congenial, ensuring popularity, goodwill, success, and happiness; and these are indicated to some extent in any case, because although there are drawbacks which will make themselves felt they cannot wholly neutralise such strong seventh-house positions. The adverse influences come partly from Mars ☉ ⯒ ♂—involving money, disagreements about money, loss of money, a law suit about money—but largely from Saturn in square to the seventh from the tenth and ruling the fourth; which shows trouble in the home life, parental inharmony, the conflicting influences of the father and marriage, sorrow and gloom through the father, and danger of hostile criticism and of being brought before the public in some unpleasant manner. Saturn, however, also gives some degree of power and authority, which is strongly supported by the angular Sun in its exaltation, and the squares do not contradict this.

If we turn now to sign-position, there are five planets in cardinal signs, two in fixed, and two in common. This gives a considerable excess to the cardinal, and the fact that a sign of this quadruplicity rises makes the indication stronger still. Speaking generally, cardinal signs correspond to angles, and afford somewhat similar indications; but sign-position has to do with the inner impulses springing from character, whereas house-position is more concerned with what seems to the ordinary man like fate or the stress of unavoidable circumstances in life. The two coincide in this case; for, with the exception of the Moon, those bodies that are in cardinal signs are also angular. Cardinal signs indicate an active, energetic character, enterprising, self-reliant, fond of change, developing in many directions, with many interests, coming in contact with many different people and forming a variety of associations with quite unlike types of persons. This conduces to the acquirement of many friends (or enemies if the aspects are evil) and to coming in some way before the public prominently; but whereas a person with strong cardinal signs will bring this about through his own actions, more or less deliberately and even of set purpose, one who has planets angular but few or none in cardinal signs may seem to have prominence, power, fame, or notoriety, whichever it is, thrust upon him by circumstances, and may either not wish very much to live up to it or not succeed in doing so. Lord Tennyson had Moon, Venus, and the Sun angular, but only two planets in a cardinal sign, and a common sign (Gemini) rising; he obtained great fame, which he appreciated quietly, but he was very reserved and disliked personal prominence or publicity. Lord Byron also had three planets angular, Mars, Saturn, and Venus, but he had five in cardinal signs and a cardinal sign rising, and he fully appreciated popularity and was fond of attracting the attention of the public.

Of the various factors that support or contradict the indications

afforded by sign-position and other groupings, the ascendant is of course
the most important because it signifies the owner of the horoscope
in the most direct manner, and is the key to the whole situation.   In this
horoscope and also in Lord Byron's the rising sign being cardinal,
belongs to the same group as that which contains the majority of the
planets, and this fact gives much additional strength and importance to
the cardinal indications.   In Tennyson's horoscope, on the contrary, the
common sign Gemini rising has very little sympathy with angular
houses or cardinal signs and therefore not only detracts somewhat from
their significance but makes their influence more indirect.   Several
different combinations of sign-position and house-position are obviously
possible in this way.

THE STRONGEST PLANETS

If tested by the strongest planets, we find that Saturn is exalted over
all the other heavenly bodies and therefore has the greatest mundane
strength, and that the Sun is exalted in Aries and has the greatest
zodiacal strength.   These are both cardinal and angular and they
support all the indications that have been referred to as being given by
these groups.

SUN, MOON, AND ASCENDANT

If the method be adopted of examining the three chief points in the
horoscope, the Sun, the Moon, and the Ascendant, they are found here to
be all in cardinal signs; so that once again the importance of this group
is emphasised.   The classification according to these three is given in
full in the *Art of Synthesis* (Third Edition).   The union of all three in
signs belonging to the same quadruplicity, all cardinal, all fixed, or all
mutable, concentrates them and brings them sharply to a point, so to
speak, so that the whole nature is acting in one direction; all the various
energies, cognition, desire, and action, are co-operating towards the same
end; the character is rendered more clear-cut and falls more definitely
into its class than do those horoscopes in which greater difference is
seen.   Other well-known persons who have Sun, Moon, and Ascendant
all in cardinal signs are—Mrs. Besant, Gladstone, Sir Isaac Newton,
Sir Isaac Pitman, L. N. Fowler, " Carmen Sylva," Swami Vivekananda,
Mr. A. P. Sinnett, Bhagavan Das.   However much these people may
differ in other respects, they all belong obviously to the cardinal group;

they have come very prominently before the world ; they are persons of much activity and enterprise, mentally or physically or both; most of them have exercised power of some sort, or have held some official position ; they have discovered or have quickly responded to new ideas ; and they have shown in one respect or another a reforming and pioneering spirit.

POSITIVE OR NEGATIVE ?

If we turn to the question of whether the horoscope is more positive or negative only four planets are in odd signs as against five in even ones and if this were all we should have to consider it relatively negative ; but there are other factors to be taken into account.   A positive sign is rising ; the Sun is much stronger than the Moon, which is relatively obscure and weak ; if we include the Sun on the cusp of the seventh house, there are six planets above the earth and only three below in the negative half of the map, and these six include the ruler of the ascendant ; two heavenly bodies are on the cusps of angles, the strongest positions in any horoscope, and these are the Sun and Saturn—both positive. These facts are sufficient to give considerable predominance to the positive temperament. This bestows strength of will, energy, determination, ability to shape one's own destiny and to control both persons and circumstances, strength of feeling, decision of character and self-reliance ; but these act to a large extent through the Mars and Venus elements in the nature which can co-operate with the negative factors to give some degree of receptivity and adaptability.

PLANETARY SIGN-GROUPING

If we examine the way in which the planets are distributed through the signs classified by the rulers the result is :—planets in martial signs, three; in Venusian signs, two and the ascendant ; in Mercurial signs, none; Solar none; Lunar, one; in signs ruled by Jupiter, two ; by Saturn, one. This brings us to the same con-clusion that has been stated more than once previously, that signs of Venus and Mars dominate this horoscope and that the native's outlook on life is largely coloured by the feelings and swayed by motives that are based upon feeling. The emotions are very strong in her, both positively in the sense that they urge her to action in the world, that they largely shape the course of her life and determine her attitude to other people, and negatively in the sense that she can adapt herself to the feelings of other people, can share their joys and sorrows almost as if they were her own, and can respond easily to an emotional appeal from without.

These two planets, Mars and Venus, are complementaries, are a pair of opposites; of which Mars is more active, energetic, outgoing, impetuous, ardent, enthusiastic, and rash, and Venus is more affectional, loving, kindly, tender, compassionate, sympathetic, and companionable. On the plane of the mind we have a similar pair in Mercury and Jupiter. The perfected man will balance such opposites as these, utilising both and controlling both from within, and not allowing himself to be swayed too much either in one direction or in the other. Between each pair of opposites sits the Self, and it is his duty to learn to keep the balance; and when it is impossible to avoid the rise and fall of changing thoughts, feelings and experiences, he must adapt these to his ends, utilise them for bringing about the necessary changes required by life. A harmonious balance of Mars and Venus emotionally and of Mercury and Jupiter intellectually will bring mankind very near to perfection; but in each case it is Saturn that is required to enable the balance to be adjusted and harmony attained, whether in feeling or in thought.

TRIPLICITY AND QUADRUPLICITY

If we test the horoscope by the distribution of the heavenly bodies among the four triplicities, the result is:—air, ascendant only; fire, four, including the Sun and the ruling planet; water two; earth, three. This gives the majority to fire, that rather mysterious element which both creates and destroys. It creates by supplying the energy which animates body and soul, emotions and mind, being one manifestation of the will-to-be which makes all things live; and it destroys by tearing asunder forms of all kinds and setting free their component parts to enter into new combinations. Aries, the only fiery sign here, is separative and individualising; it corresponds to the ascendant, the separate self of the horoscope, of which all the other houses and signs are so many different aspects and powers. Aries is self-reliant, separative, courageous, independent, active, positive, ardent, enthusiastic, and changeable. The bodily form is Libra and Venus, but the life that animates it is from Aries and Mars and belongs to the state of fire. If this pair could be brought to a balance, the result would be a splendid physique and an active energetic soul; but the preponderance of fire, taken with the many cross aspects and the debilities of the Moon, Saturn, and Venus, show an energy that wears out its physical vehicle, and a body that cannot respond quickly enough to the great demands that are made upon it.

The combination of the fiery triplicity and the cardinal quadruplicity has been commented upon in the previous chapters and need not be repeated here.

A BRIEF SUMMARY

All these are so many different methods of weighing or testing a horoscope, so many different points of view from which it can be examined in order to determine to which order, class, genus, and species it belongs. In this case most of the methods come to much the same conclusion, and we may classify the horoscope as follows:—rising sign, Libra; ruler in the seventh house in Aries; strongest triplicity, fire; strongest quadruplicity, cardinal; strongest planet zodiacally, the Sun; strongest planet by mundane position, Saturn; strongest sign, Aries; strongest house, the seventh; more positive than negative; strongest quadrant, the south western; twice as many planets above the earth as below; number of houses occupied, six; planets in dignity, the Sun by exaltation; planets in debility, Moon, Venus, and Saturn by detriment; planets angular, Sun, Venus, Mercury and Saturn.

The horoscope therefore denotes a Venus-Mars type of character, showing that the major events and characteristics of the life will be coloured by Venusian feelings, and Martial impulses, ever tempered with Saturnian chastity. Quick perception, followed by quick impressions and swift judgment, mark the ability to observe keenly all things relating to form. The perception denoted by Libra, and the interest in human nature shown by the Aquarian decanate of Libra rising, will give all the incentive necessary to express the main features of the ruler setting between the Sun and Mercury in Aries in the seventh house. There is an interplay of Libra and Aries, or Venus and Mars, on the personal ray, or horizontal line, of the first and seventh houses, showing the personality to be strongly coloured, clearly defined, and polarised toward the head and brain. The intuition of Aries and the perception of Libra accentuate the activities of the brain, and make it the centre from which the whole of life is viewed. The exaltation of the Sun and the conjunction of

Venus and Mercury in the sign Aries cause the brain to be very sensitive, the life and nerve force being easily drawn to that centre. Connected with the planets setting in Aries, denoting public approval and appreciation, is the sign Taurus, linked to it by ☉⚹♃ and ☿⚹♅, giving the gift of speech, and the desire of expression. From this combination we may easily judge the native to be a keen observer, quick to receive impressions, well able to express herself through speech, and with a good flow of language.

This fitted her for the profession she naturally chose, and the study to which she was able to give her whole attention, making her a successful phrenologist, palmist, graphologist, and general reader of character, always in her element when before the public addressing them upon any subject dealing with the study of character and character reading.

REMARKABLE PSYCHIC GIFT

In connection with this ability to read character successfully there are positions and aspects from which the skilful and intuitive astrologer may draw further conclusions. Neptune in this horoscope is well placed in Pisces on the cusp of the 6th house, and brilliantly aspected by ⚹♀ and ☿, ⚹ ♃ and ♅, and △ ♄ without a single affliction.

This has endowed the native with a peculiar and remarkable psychic gift. It has given her a strange power of prevision, a prescience which acts in what may be termed a clairaudient and clairvoyant method, in which knowledge comes to the native of events that have happened in the lives of those in whom she is deeply interested; these events pass before her brain as pictures, which she describes easily and readily without knowing the method by which they are seen. It also endows her with an intense sympathy for all things of a psychic and occult nature. It has also given the native remarkable dreams, and what appear to be vivid astral experiences.

GENERAL SYNTHESIS: WESTERN SIDE

We may synthesise the influence of the three signs, Aries, Taurus and Pisces, containing the majority of the planets, both in terms of the houses they occupy and the nature of these signs. It will be noticed on reference to the map that the positive sign Aries is in an angular position between the negative signs Pisces and Taurus. Normally the positive, assertive and outgoing energies are most in evidence, and thus Aries in this case denotes the line of least resistance, the life forces being polarised and all the impressions expressed through the head and brain. There is, however, the ebb as well as the flow of this life force, which in this case finding no outlet through the generative system is regenerated or transformed into psychic force, giving the soul those intermittent flashes of intuition and pictures of past occurrences. In a sub-normal state this negative influence brings a crowd of sorrowful entities around the native who delight to dwell in her sympathetic aura, and bathe in the warm light of this regenerative force. This is explained by the position of Saturn in Cancer, which is square to Venus while it is in trine to Neptune and sextile Jupiter. This position of Saturn denotes a very sympathetic and receptive emotional nature, placed thus in the beginning of the Pisces decanate, the sign of deep and profound emotions. A servant (sixth house influence) in trouble, or an inferior who is helpless, beggars, and those who are sick or ill, will at once awaken the whole of the sympathies and draw out the affections to an abnormal extent, and this is often the cause of what appears to be foolish action and wasted sympathy.

In this train of synthetical reasoning, we have come to a series of conclusions embracing the influence of no less than seven planets, which almost exhausts the major influence of the horoscope ; but it is the method by which all successful deductions are made in the complete reading of horoscopes.

GENERAL SYNTHESIS: EASTERN SIDE

All that now remains is to bring in the influence of the Moon and the planet Mars on the eastern side of the nativity. Mars rising in Sagittarius re-affirms the prevision already noted. The sign is a prophetic one, expressive, straightforward, and direct. Alone in this sign it is harmless although enthusiastic, impulsive and over-independent. The evils arising out of it are carelessness, impulsive speech, and intolerance. The aspect to ☉, ♉, arouses anger, a tendency to extremes and irritability. Checking this the Moon in Capricorn gives caution and conserving tendencies.

These two positions of the Moon and Mars shew the failings of the horoscope from an ethical standpoint. Mars in Sagittarius supported by planets in Aries denotes impulse, a tendency to go to extremes in

certain directions, some extravagance, exaggeration, and a peculiar independence and love of freedom of thought and action. The Moon pulls
away from this very considerably and will cause the native at times to
express two natures. The Moon in Capricorn denotes the desire to acquire
possessions, carefulness over small and insignificant matters, saving of
pence and economical tendencies. This is well elaborated by the polarity
of the Sun in Aries and Moon in Capricorn. It strikes the personal note
in the nativity, and inclines to a love of self-indulgence, and the accentua-
tion of the self-protective instincts. It has its complement in the elevation
of Saturn in its detriment and the square to Venus. It shows the
native to be strangely assertive at times as the result of a selfish
heredity and environment; thus we have exhibited extremes of selfishness
and unselfishness, economy and liberality, exactitude and sympathy.
From an esoteric standpoint the native has gone out to the furthest
extent during the present life, and the return from matter to spirit is
assured through the progression of the horoscope.

PLANETS IN DEBILITY

We may now conclude this summary with what (from an esoteric
standpoint) is a most important consideration; the position of no less
than three angular planets in their detriment, ☽ ♑, ♄ ♋, ♀ ♈; with only
one planet in exaltation. When a planet is in its detriment or fall its
influence is, from all standpoints, weak, having little power to express
its particular qualities. The three planets in this case represent the
father, Saturn; the mother, Moon; and the native, Venus.

The parents, the environment, and the native's relation to it, are all
exquisitely expressed by these three planets in their detriment in this
nativity. The marriage partner is represented by the Sun exalted in
Aries, and through marriage the environment changed and happiness
resulted. Note here that the Sun first applies to ☌ ♂; first partner,
legal separation, ♂ ♐. Sun next applies ⚹ ♃, second partner.

The study of this nativity has been gone into very fully because it
furnishes a useful example of the method of applying the teachings of
Esoteric Astrology to the many details that may be gleaned from the
ordinary exoteric reading of a horoscope, and it is hoped that the practical
insight into the working out of these ideas thus gained will enable the
reader better to appreciate the importance of the Chapters which follow.

ESOTERIC ASTROLOGY

THIRD PART

THE DIVISIONS OF THE ZODIAC

AN ESOTERIC GLOSSARY

Many terms in common use in Exoteric Astrology are employed in Esoteric Astrology in what may almost be termed a new sense, and therefore a Chapter has been included in which the explanation of these terms from an esoteric standpoint is given. (Ch. XXIII.)

ESOTERIC ASTROLOGY

Third Part

CHAPTER XX

THE THREEFOLD AND FOURFOLD DIVISIONS

DARKNESS radiates Light, and Light drops one solitary Ray into the Waters, into the Mother-Deep. The Ray shoots through the Virgin Egg, the Ray causes the Eternal Egg to thrill, and drop the non-eternal Germ, which condenses into the World-Egg. The Three fall into the Four. . . . .

Stanzas of Dzyan.

AN attempt has been made in this work to lead up to ONE principal thought, difficult to express in words, but nevertheless important to understand, for it is the basis of all ideas connected with Esoteric Astrology.

Why are we born into this world? Why do we live to suffer and enjoy? Why do we die when we are just beginning to learn how to live? And why are there so many inequalities in the human race?

From an astrological standpoint there is only one hypothesis by means of which we may expect to answer these questions :—

Every human being is a "Divine Fragment," a centre within the universal divine consciousness, inseparably united with every other centre, and all blended in one ultimately by the universal Life and Consciousness in which they are centred. If we compare the universal Life with a flame, the human soul is a spark of that flame, not really separated from it. If we use the comparison of a diamond, the soul is a facet of that diamond. If we employ the symbolism of sound, the soul is one note in the mighty chord that sounds throughout the whole of creation. It is beginningless and endless, but apart from the universal Life it is nothing.

Its ray, the personal man, descends into incarnation for the sake of gaining experience, and the horoscope shows in part the powers and characteristics of that ray on its descent, the kind of experience it has come into this world to gain, and the work that lies before it to be done.

The " Divine Fragment " itself, apart from its ray, may be represented as a small blank circle in the centre of every horoscope, or the equally void centre of the circle of the zodiac.   From this centre we may imagine strands, or threads, running out in various directions within the circle of the horoscope, and becoming attached to the points within that circle to which they are attracted.

All that has been and all that is to be, is described within that circle, such as the Sun, Moon and stars, the zodiac and its manifold divisions. To that which is represented by the blank circle, all that exists apart from *That*, or the *Self*, is the Not-Self.   Probably this sounds very metaphysical, but the idea should be grasped (if we wish to penetrate into the mysteries of Esoteric Astrology) that the Self is eternally pure, immortal and divine.   In essence it is one with God, and until this essence has identified itself with a form in which first self-consciousness, and afterwards super-consciousness, is reached it does not know itself as apart from and yet *one with* its source.

THE ORIGIN OF THE INDIVIDUAL

An Indian astrologer has expressed the above idea in the following words :

" If we study the origin of the individual we find something which helps to clear the ground for us.   The individual, or, as it is sometimes called, the individualised Self, as it starts into existence, is a white spark of the Divine Light enclosed in a colourless film of matter.   It is a spark emanating from the Divine Flame and having all the qualities of the parent involved in it.   The seed is cast into the soil of the phenomenal planes, that it may grow into the likeness of its sire.   As regards the Spark of Light, *per se*, it is the same Divine Light everywhere—it is always of the substance of what is called, in the Gita, the Daivi Prakriti.

"From the standpoint, however, of this Light, there is no differentiation or evolution; we cannot posit any beginnings in time to it, for It ever is.   We must therefore seek for the root of evolution elsewhere.

" Though in essence it is colourless at the beginning, yet in its *actual* manifestation some change takes place.   The Divine spark can only reach the matrix of matter through some intermediate agencies, Rays of the Light, who are called the Sons of Mind.   The Divine Light, in manifesting the Universe from the state of *pralaya*, acts on the vehicle of matter not directly, but rather through what we may term definite 'rays.' These rays, or the pencils of Light, catch up the image of the Logos of a system and mirror it in the various *upadhis*.[1] The characters of these rays are different and so too their functions. Thus the rays energising and vivifying the matter of cosmos into several planes of matter of varying densities are sometimes spoken of in Theosophical literature as the First Life-Wave. So, too, the Devas who superintended the building of the forms and the fashioning of the tabernacle of man come out of the second Life-Wave. When the tabernacle is ready, then there is again a downpouring from the Logos called the Third Life-Wave. It is the birth of the Individual."

THE SEED IN THE CENTRE

If we can avoid materialising the idea, we may give the name of Monad to the *blank* circle in the centre of the horoscope; the horoscope will then represent the Not-Self, or the world of forms, the threads of communication from the centre will then be the relation between the Self and the Not-Self or the spirit and matter, and this relationship we may interpret as mind, intelligence or instinct.

We may also as our Indian astrologer suggests, think of the Self as a seed cast into the manifested world of form to grow into the likeness of its sire.

From an astrological standpoint we are mainly concerned with this growth, or unfoldment, of the divine qualities inherent in the seed.

The Monads, or spirits, received from the Divine Intelligences those human principles of which the soul is composed, and through the soul or ego are linked to the animal forms or physical bodies in order that they may manifest in the physical universe.

The Seven Spiritual Intelligences are connected in some mysterious way, at present unknown to us, with the "spheres of influence" whose physical centres are the planets the nature of which we seek to understand in our astrological studies. They are the Rays to which we belong in groups, and until we are super-conscious they are our guardian angels in whom we truly live and move and have our human being.

At the head of each group there stand the Masters or divine Men who have attained fully to the super-conscious state, and until we reach that state ourselves we are protected and limited by our Causal body, or

---

[1] Vehicles or " sheaths."

body of Intelligence, and must remain on the Ray to which we primarily belong.   This Causal body is the only vehicle that is permanent throughout the whole cycle of the human pilgrimage ; it continues life after life and contains all the seeds, good and bad, of each earthly existence, and upon the entry into each new physical life these seeds awaken out of latency and give forth their vibratory powers, aroused into activity by the stimulation of the Ego.

We may now return again to the blank circle in the centre of the horoscope.   Relatively colourless in itself at first, and unconscious upon any plane below the spiritual, this blank circle is primarily coloured by the planetary spirits with whose sphere of influence for the time it is associated.   This coloured circle may now be thought of as the causal or spiritual body of the Ego, and of every horoscope it will always be the centre, receiving from the horoscope more and more colouring and more power to vibrate in new directions until it becomes a glorious and radiant body, in which the real man grows stronger and stronger in preparation for the time when the circumference of this circle shall break and set him free.

The Outward and the Homeward

It may safely be assumed that every ego coming into manifestation came from the loving protection of Divine Beings, into a world of separateness to gain its own peculiar Self-consciousness.   The study of each horoscope shows the maze through which each soul is seeking either to become more separate, or to find its return to the centre of love and wisdom.

Justice is the goal for the forthgoing, and love is the attraction of the returning soul.

While separateness holds us and selfishness attracts us we are bound by the limitations of our horoscopes, but when unity and service become attractive we learn that the secret which shall set us free from all further bondage lies in the saying of the great Teacher who said that love was the *fulfilling* of the law.   When the study of Astrology is used for the better understanding of human nature we learn the Paths along which all souls are treading to this goal, and the more we know of human nature and the threads which bind it to separation the better are we able to help others.

THE THREE PHASES OF UNIT CONSCIOUSNESS

Wherever there is manifestation there is always duality, and this can be stated in various terms, force and matter, soul and body, consciousness within and the universe without; and if we study these two lines of evolution we find they proceed along similar paths and display coördinated characteristics.

Force, life, soul, or consciousness—for these are only different names for varying aspects of the same reality,—always manifests in three modes, no matter what the world upon which attention is turned. Consciousness must necessarily be active and outgoing, for if it were not it could never affect the world, do anything, accomplish any changes, or manifest itself outwardly at all; it would be for ever wrapped in slumber and inert. It must also be capable of becoming relatively passive and receptive, for if it were not the outer world would never affect it in terms of any one of the five senses; so that here again it would be inward turned only, and therefore unconscious. Lastly, it can never be wholly active or wholly passive; there must be some mode in which the two are held in relation with each other and pass over into each other; and this third aspect will necessarily be neutral and dualistic, wavering between the two extremes without becoming identified exclusively with either.

These three are only varying aspects of one and the same unit of consciousness or 'self,' and this unity is as much a necessity as are the three aspects. Without it we should have one self all activity, another one absolute passivity, and a third that was neither. But no such entities as these are ever seen in our universe; the same self that is active at one time will be passive at another, and will also display equipoise and equilibrium. Every unit, whether of consciousness or of matter, cannot avoid manifesting itself in three modes and presenting three aspects to the world, and these are only three outward presentations of an underlying unity.

In terms of man's ordinary personal consciousness, these three are (i) action, (ii) desire or feeling, and (iii) cognition or thought; and their unity is in the self. The self that acts also desires and thinks; for self is a unity upon which these constantly changing modes of consciousness are strung like beads on a string.

In terms of the zodiacal signs the three are the so-called qualities or gunas that divide the zodiac into the three quadruplicities, the cardinal or movable, the fixed, and the common or mutable.

Their unity lies in the matter or the consciousness that underlies the three and that displays these three characteristics.

For instance, Libra is a cardinal or movable sign, Aquarius is a fixed sign, and Gemini is a common or mutable sign ; but all alike are airy signs, and in that fact they find their unity.   The same air that is movable in Libra is fixed in Aquarius and common in Gemini.   The same self that goes out to the world in frequent activity through Libra, remains fixed and unchanged within its own centre in Aquarius, and holds the two extremes in a fluctuating relationship in Gemini.   They are therefore rightly symbolised by an equilateral triangle, the three angles of which form only one triangle.   Sometimes the triangle is drawn within a circle ; and then the three points cut the circle into three equal arcs, which present three different faces to the world, and the circle itself is the unity of the three.

THE FOUR BODIES

When we turn to the bodies in which man functions and the worlds or planes with which those bodies are in touch and from the matter of which they are formed, we have a picture very similar to the last, but nevertheless presenting certain marked differences.   Taking the average man, who is an Individuality manifesting as a Personality clothed in a Body, we find that he has four bodies built of different types of matter drawn from different planes.

Body	Plane	Matter	Self
CAUSAL	Higher Mental	Air	Individuality
MENTAL	Lower Mental	Fire	Personality
ASTRAL	Astral	Water	,,
PHYSICAL	Physical	Earth	,,

The difference between air and fire, to which reference has been made in previous chapters, should be borne in mind here.   That which is called air belongs in reality to a plane above and beyond the Mental; but because the average personal man with whom we are now dealing does not lift his consciousness on to that high level, fire, air, water and earth are all four regarded as being restricted within the limits of the three worlds, the physical plane, the astral plane, and the mental plane; the latter being divided into two.   Air then means the kind of so-called formless matter that is found on the Higher Mental plane.   Of this the

Causal body is built, and in it the permanent Individuality functions, enduring through hundreds of incarnations: it corresponds to abstract thought and to self as unity.

Fire means that kind of matter which is found on the Lower Mental plane. The Mental body is built of it, formed afresh at every new incarnation, and in it the practical concrete thought of the Personality functions. Fire really belongs to the whole of the mental plane and air to the plane beyond the Mental, but when our view is restricted to the three worlds only, they are said to have the correspondences here given.

Water means that kind of matter which is found on the Astral plane. Man's astral body is built of it, being formed afresh at every incarnation, and in it all emotions, passions, desires, and feelings function, good and bad, high and low. Whenever the Personal man likes or dislikes anything, the matter of this body is thrown into vibration, just as is the matter of his Mental body whenever he thinks about some object.

Earth means physical matter of the physical plane, of which man's outer body is built, that vesture which is born at birth and dies at death. Action, or will in action, is the state of consciousness characteristic of this body.

THE LADDER OF CONSCIOUSNESS

If we start from the lowest of these states of matter and imagine the self-evolving consciousness in higher and higher modes as it passes upward through them all, mere motion, which in man becomes definite action, is that which begins in the state called Earth. It corresponds to the mineral kingdom; because, while inorganic or mineral matter can be acted upon, and can react, it shows neither feeling nor thought. Its highest level is reached in plants, which correspond typically to the subtle matter or ethers of the physical plane.

When the stage of evolution called Water is reached, consciousness of pleasure and pain, likes and dislikes, is added to the mere action or reaction of earth. The self has now evolved to the level of the astral plane and functions in the animal kingdom. When the two stages are mingled, and the action of the earthy physical is carried up into the pleasure-pain of the watery astral, we have desire and its opposite aversion; for these are formed when consciousness functions in terms of pleasure or pain and then goes out towards or shrinks back from the object. The going out towards an object or shrinking back from it is the ingredient of action which has been added to and intermingled with the mere passive pleasure-pain or feeling.

When the stage called Fire is reached, a self-conscious human self with the power of thinking is evolved, and thought is added to feeling and action. The fiery Aries is the sign of this humanised self, realising its separateness from others and knowing itself as " I."

When the stage called Air is attained, the super-man beyond the mental is evolved; but, as previously remarked, ordinary humanity only shows this as thought in its various stages, the abstract thought of the higher mental plane which it is one day destined to transcend. It is synthesising and unifying when fully developed, as distinguished from the separative action of fire. The separate self of Aries and the ascendant becomes blended with another self in Libra and the seventh house ; and the same synthetic process can be seen in the brotherhood of Gemini and the third house, and the friendship or universal brotherhood of Aquarius and the eleventh house.

The Cross within the Circle

There are here four definite stages, earth, water, fire, air ; and it is to be noted that there is here a similarity to the previous classification of the triangle in the circle, and yet a distinct difference from it. The similarity lies in the fact that these four stages consist of a lower or outer three, earth, water, fire, which are fully manifested in the personality of the average man, are formed afresh with the birth of each new personality and die and disintegrate after each death ; and of a higher synthetic unit, air, from which the three come forth and to which they return. In fact, if this were all, these four bodies might also be represented by the same symbol of a triangle in a circle, the triangle to stand for the lower three and the circle for the higher synthetic one.

This symbol, however, is not used. Matter and the bodies built of it are symbolised by the cross within the circle; and the question arises why and how this distinction is made. The answer is that although the four bodies are divided into a triad and a unit, yet all four of these are definitely manifested, each on its own plane, to those whose senses are opened to perceive them. They can be separated from each other, and actually are separate to the eye of the true clairvoyant, who observes first one and then another, compares their coarseness or fineness, and estimates the degree of control the Ego has over them. But four objects that can be separated from each other demand four different points within the circle, if symbolised ; and when these points are united a cross results.

THE TRIANGLE WITHIN THE CIRCLE

With consciousness or life or spirit, considered apart from body, it is different. Here also there is a manifested three, cognition, desire and action, and a synthetic one, the underlying self which manifests the three and without which they could not exist. But there is this important distinction. The self, the synthetic unit, cannot be separated from its triple manifestation nor they from it. Wherever there is a self in active manifestation, it always displays cognition, desire and action. A self stripped of these three and their combinations and correspondences is nothing at all, is non-existent. If a self manifests at all it must do so through these three ; and furthermore, the three may be perceived, but the one, the self, cannot. There is no such thing in manifestation as an abstract naked self that displays neither thought nor feeling nor action nor any of their correspondences on higher or lower planes of existence. In this case, therefore, the three are expressed by a triangle within the circle, and the unitary self is the circle considered as the background of the triangle ; the self cannot constitute a fourth point within the circle separate from the other three.

THE TRIAD AND THE QUATERNARY

These two classifications are both found within the zodiac. The division of the circle by the Triangle gives us the three quadruplicities, each corresponding to one of the three modes of consciousness and one of the three paths along which all souls are evolving. It belongs to the life side of things and is associated with the Sun, for the Sun's house, Leo, if measured from the beginning of the zodiac, marks off one of the three segments into which the circle is divided by the triangle.

The division of the circle by the Cross yields the four triplicities, each corresponding to one of the four bodies and one of the four states of matter. It belongs to the form side of things and is associated with the Moon, for the Moon's house, Cancer, if measured from the beginning of the zodiac, marks off one of the four quadrants into which the circle is divided by the cross.

These two interpenetrate each other everywhere and at all points, and they form the first septenary classification of the zodiac; but it is a septenary which can also be regarded as either a ternary, a quaternary, or a duodenary, according to the point of view.

They are capable of many combinations and sub-divisions, some of which have already been described.

	WILL	WISDOM	ACTIVITY	
The Individual Self *AIR*	♒	♊	♎	Spiritual
The Personal Self *FIRE*	♌	♐	♈	Intellect
The Personal Self *WATER*	♏	♓	♋	Emotion
The Physical Self *EARTH*	♉	♍	♑	Action
Three Quadruplicities	Fixed	Mutable	Cardinal	
Three Gunas	Inertia or Stability	Harmony or Rhythm	Activity or Mobility	
Three Paths (suggested)	Sacrifice	Knowledge	Devotion	

An examination of the accompanying Table will show that it summarises all that has been said above, and that it gives the key to other lines of thought as well. It should be read in connection with the Table given in an earlier Chapter.

CHAPTER XXI

FURTHER DIVISIONS OF THE ZODIAC[1]

THUS number *seven*, as a compound of 3 and 4, is the factor element in every ancient religion, because it is *the factor element in Nature* . . . the universe is a septenate, in *its* totality composed of septenary groups—simply because the capacity of perception *exists in seven different aspects corresponding to the seven conditions of matter*, or the seven properties, or states of matter.

Secret Doctrine.

IN the last Chapter, starting with the simple circle, it was shown how its divisions into three parts and four parts, corresponding to the universal threefold manifestation of life or consciousness and the fourfold appearance of form in the bodies of man, are interwoven at all points ; so that wherever the one is we can discover the other also. And any given part of the circle can be classified either in terms of the ternary or of the quaternary.

The idea that any unit part of a larger whole is an image in little of the whole of which it is a part is thoroughly familiar to most people, and is expressed in such sayings as, ' the microcosm is a mirror of the macrocosm,' ' as above so below.' This idea is applied in various ways in Astrology, but in its application to the present subject it leads us to see the whole zodiac mirrored in each sign. The teaching that the seven cosmic planes each contain seven sub-planes will help us to understand how each of the twelve signs is itself sub-divided into twelve parts which reflect the whole within them. As has previously been stated, this is more prominently put forward in the Hindu books than in the writings of European Astrologers, but it affords a basis for methods not only of sub-dividing but also of combining signs, and one of these methods—that of the decanates—has already been shown to possess practical utility.

---

[1] That portion of CHAPTER IV dealing with zodiacal sub-divisions may usefully be read in connection with the present Chapter ; the remarks on wave lengths, on p. 39, being particularly applicable to the considerations here to be entered upon.

The Circle of the Day

All are familiar with the idea that the days of the week are named after the planet that rules the first sub-division of the day, but not all are aware of the fact that this can be applied in more ways than one, and that the principles underlying it are applicable to the classification and sub-division of the signs of the zodiac. The older European astrologers have all given a twenty-four hours classification of the day, but the one given by Mme. H. P. Blavatsky and founded on occult fact divides each day into four quarters as follows:

	Monday	Tuesday	Wednesday	Thursday	Friday	Saturday	Sunday
1	☽	♂	☿	♃	♀	♄	☉
2	☿	♃	♀	♄	☉	☽	♂
3	♀	♄	☉	☽	♂	☿	♃
4	☉	☽	♂	☿	♃	♀	♄

Monday is so called because its first quarter, beginning shortly before sunrise, is ruled by the Moon, which apparently exercises a kind of general rulership over the whole day. Its second quarter, which is strongest at noon, is ruled by Mercury; its third, strongest at the moment of sunset, by Venus; and its fourth, midnight, by the Sun. And so on with the other days in order.

This quite obviously corresponds to the division of the zodiac into four triplicities, fire, earth, air, water; and both can be symbolised in the same way, by the cross inscribed within the circle. The thoughtful reader will not be surprised to learn that exactly the same result can be achieved—so far as the names of the days are concerned that is—by dividing each day into three parts; and that these parts correspond to the division of the zodiac into the three quadruplicities described in the previous Chapter.

It will be noticed that in the fourfold classification we have employed the seven ‘sacred’ rulers in the order of their rapidity of motion as seen from the earth, and that we begin with the swiftest, the Moon. In the three-fold classification, we begin with Saturn, the slowest, as follows:

Saturday	Sunday	Monday	Tuesday	Wednesday	Thursday	Friday
♄	☉	☽	♂	☿	♃	♀
♃	♀	♄	☉	☽	♂	☿
♂	☿	♃	♀	♄	☉	☽

The division of the day into three equal parts was used in ancient Egypt.

This subject is introduced here, firstly, because the threefold and fourfold divisions of the circle of the day are precisely analogous to the zodiacal quadruplicities and triplicities ; and, secondly, because similar principles govern the sub-division of each sign.

The Circle of the Sign

Following up the idea previously referred to, that the whole zodiac is mirrored in each sign, it will be seen that this entails the division of every sign into twelve equal parts of two and a half degrees each. These parts correspond to the signs, are named after them, and ruled by them. The first part of any sign is ruled by the sign itself ; the second part by the next sign ; and the rest in order.

Having made a twelvefold sub-division of each sign in this way, the grouping according to the triangle and the cross can be applied ; and the results are not only interesting as intellectual curiosities but one of them at least has been found to be of considerable practical value, and it is probable that this will be the case with the others also when experience increases.

If each sign with its twelve sub-divisions is arranged like a small circle and the equilateral triangle is inscribed within it, then, starting from the beginning of the sign, we shall have the following results. The point of the triangle at the beginning of the sign will indicate that sub-division which is named after the sign itself ; and just as the planetary ruler of the first portion of the day continues its rule until the next portion is reached, so the first twelfth part of the sign will, in this classification, have a general rulership over the whole of the first third, or decanate, of the sign.

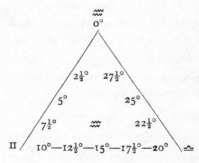

The second point of the triangle will indicate the fifth of the twelve parts into which the sign is divided ; this will be the same as the fifth sign, counted from the sign itself. For instance, if the sign is Aquarius, the fifth of the twelve parts will be of the nature of Gemini, the next sign of the same triplicity, and will extend a general rulership over the whole of the second decanate of Aquarius.

The third point of the triangle will measure to the ninth of the twelve parts, which will be of the nature of Libra and will extend its signification over the third decanate of Aquarius.

Here we have the basis of that classification of the decanates in which the first is of the nature of the sign itself ; the second of the nature of the next sign of the same triplicity ; and the third of the nature of the third sign of the same triplicity.

THE DECANATES

Having arrived at the decanates, the very suggestive classification of influences they afford should be noticed before applying the other method of the cross in the sign.

The triangle divides first the whole zodiac and then each sign into three parts. Those who have read Mrs. Besant's *Study in Consciousness* will remember that in Chapter III she illustates how "a triad naturally produces a septenate by its own internal relations, since its three factors can group themselves in seven ways and no more." [1] When the whole circle is divided into three parts, the first third is led off by Aries, a cardinal movable sign; the second third by Leo, a fixed sign ; and the last by Sagittarius, a common mutable sign. And these three, dominated by the three gunas, interact to produce a septenate.

Where a triplicity is divided into three signs, and each sign into three decanates, these triads also interact to produce septenates. This is not a mere purposeless subdivision and differentiation ; for each decanate, being of the nature of one or other of the signs of the same triplicity, while it subdivides also at the same time interweaves the whole together in one, as the accompanying table shows.

---

[1] This may be illustrated by taking the letters *a, b, c,* to represent the three factors composing the triad, and different sizes of type to indicate the relative preponderance of any one of the three. Seven groupings are possible, thus A B c, A c b, B A c, B c a, C A b, C B a, and finally A B c in which all are equally balanced or harmonised.

Air	Fire	Water	Earth
♒︎—♊︎—♎︎	♌︎—♐︎—♈︎	♏︎—♓︎—♋︎	♉︎—♍︎—♑︎
♒︎—♊︎	♌︎—♐︎	♏︎—♓︎	♉︎—♍︎
♒︎—♎︎	♌︎—♈︎	♏︎—♋︎	♉︎—♑︎
♊︎—♎︎	♐︎—♈︎	♓︎—♋︎	♍︎—♑︎
♊︎—♒︎	♐︎—♌︎	♓︎—♏︎	♍︎—♉︎
♎︎—♒︎	♈︎—♌︎	♋︎—♏︎	♑︎—♉︎
♎︎—♊︎	♈︎—♐︎	♋︎—♓︎	♑︎—♍︎

The first and highest combination in any triplicity is formed of the first decanates of each of the three signs of that triplicity taken together as equal in strength ; for the first decanate is of the same nature as the sign itself.   The six combinations that follow in each triplicity are according to the second and third decanates of each sign.

The whole shows that each triplicity forms a SEPTENATE.

DECANATES, SEPTENATES, AND PLANES

If the triplicities are related to the planes of the universe according to the tables given in the previous Chapter, there are here obvious correspondences with the septenary division of each plane.   The septenary air, when brought down on to the Higher Mental plane, corresponds to the seven subdivisions of the First Elemental kingdom.   The septenary fire, brought down on to the Lower Mental plane, corresponds to the seven subdivisions of the Second Elemental kingdom.   The septenary water gives the seven sub-planes of the astral, the Third Elemental kingdom ; and the earthy septenary brings us down on to the physical plane.

Persons born under any of these combinations or with many planets in any of them are related to the corresponding type of consciousness and of elemental essence.

PLANETS AND TRIPLICITIES

The earthy and watery groups are inverted reflections of the airy and fiery, and are ruled by the same planets ; and this is true not only of the signs as a whole but also of the decanates.   Saturn, Mercury, and Venus rule the airy signs and also their first decanates ; and the same planets in the opposite order rule the three earthy signs.   The six airy decanates are ruled by the same planets that govern the six earthy decanates.

Saturn belongs to the earthy and airy group.   The influence of

Uranus over Aquarius is not manifest until the Individuality is very far advanced in evolution ; until then Saturn is still the presiding planet, for the difference between these two lies in the degree of will power denoted by them.   Saturn represents the limited concrete will, or that which is not wholly abstracted from desire ; while Uranus denotes the will that is free and unfettered by limitations.   The former holds the Causal body and binds the man to his separate and limited Individuality ; while the latter sets him free from it to raise the consciousness on to far higher planes.   The Sun as life and Saturn as will are only substitutes until the airy influence is sufficiently strong 'for Uranus to be the ruler ; and when that planet's influence is fully expressed, the Causal body no longer limits and confines the individual, for he has arrived at full manhood.

Mercury, ruling the airy Gemini and the earthy Virgo, is a double planet and apart from any other consideration is the most dualistic of all. Just as Saturn is the bridge between the individual and the personal in terms of will, Mercury is the same in terms of memory and intelligence, a connecting link between the lowest and the highest, for it has dignity in the second decanate of Aquarius, the Causal body, and the third of Capricorn, the physical.   Its counterpart in the fiery and watery triplicities is Jupiter, the planet of expansion and permeation.   These two have relation to the Wisdom aspect of consciousness, Jupiter being on the formal or objective side, and Mercury on the vital or subjective side.

Venus, ruling the airy Libra and the earthy Taurus, denotes the creative side of consciousness, and is paired in the fiery and watery worlds with Mars, the planet of generation and objective activity.

The groups of fire and water are similarly related, except that the Sun in the fiery triplicity has the Moon for its representative in the watery.   Just as the Sun represents the Individuality until Uranus becomes the ruler, so it is suspected, although it is not absolutely known, that Neptune replaces the Moon as the ruler of the perfected Personality. The Moon's influence runs through all the lower three triplicities, for it is exalted in the earthy Taurus, it has its house in the watery Cancer, and its counterpart the Sun belongs to the fiery Leo.

TRIANGLE AND CROSS

These septenates result from inscribing the triangle in the circle of the zodiac as well as in the smaller circle of each sign.   They yield the three quadruplicities, at the head of which are the three airy human signs Aquarius, Gemini, and Libra.   Taurus, Scorpio, and Leo are fixed signs that form a strong unshaken centre capable of resisting all the blows of fate and of building up an enduring self which is expressed in its highest degree in the Will of Aquarius.   Capricorn, Cancer, and Aries are busy centres of outgoing energy that are transmuted into a higher mode in the Activity of Libra, the sign which individualises, which separates, but which also unites.   Virgo, Pisces, and Sagittarius are expressive of the harmony of opposites, which reaches its highest stage in Gemini, Wisdom, the sign of the Grand Man of Swedenborg and of the Kabalisitic Adam Kadmon.

The use of the cross inscribed in the circle will be seen in the next Chapter.

CHAPTER XXII

The Fourfold Division of Signs

IT is a cross in a circle and Crux Ansata, truly; but it is a cross on which all human passions have to be crucified before the Yogî passes through the 'strait gate,' the narrow circle that widens into an infinite one, as soon as the Inner Man has passed the threshold. *Secret Doctrine.*

THE results that follow from inscribing the triangle in the circles of the zodiac, of the day, and of the sign have been described; and also the application of the cross or fourfold division to the zodiac and to the day. There only remains to divide each sign into four parts, and this is illustrated in the following table :—

AIR

♏	♓	♋
♒+♌	♊+♐	♎+♈
♉	♍	♑

FIRE

♉	♍	♑
♌+♒	♐+♊	♈+♎
♏	♓	♋

WATER

♌	♐	♈
♏+♉	♓+♍	♋+♑
♒	♊	♎

EARTH

♒	♊	♎
♉+♏	♍+♓	♑+♋
♌	♐	♈

Reference to the previous Chapter will show that when each sign is divided into twelve parts the first part is of the nature of the sign itself, the fifth part of the nature of the next sign of the same triplicity, and the ninth part of the nature of the third sign of the same triplicity; and that this gives the clue to the rulership of the decanates.

The same rule applies to the division of the sign into four quarters.

The first quarter, as before, will be of the nature of the sign itself. The second quarter will begin with the fourth of the twelve parts into which each of the signs is sub-divided, which is of the nature of the next sign of the same quadruplicity, and which exercises a general rulership over the whole quarter. If the sign is Aquarius, this second quarter will be of the sub-influence of Taurus.

The third quarter will begin with the sub-influence of the third sign of the same quadruplicity, which in the case of Aquarius is Leo, and which will characterise the whole quarter.

The fourth quarter, following the same plan, is of the nature of Scorpio, the last sign of the same quadruplicity, beginning with Aquarius.

The accompanying table shows the quarters arranged after the plan of the four angles of the horoscope. The sign itself occupies that arm of the cross which marks the ascendant. The second quarter is placed at the angle of the fourth house; the third quarter at the angle of the seventh house; and the fourth quarter at the angle of the tenth house. The quarters of a sign and the quarters of the zodiac beginning with the sign thus agree in nature.

THE PRINCIPLES INVOLVED

The principles of sub-dividing the day, the month (or sign), and the year (or the whole zodiac) are the same, whether the division be into three or four parts ; and these various divisions are not contradictory, because they belong to different classifications. To say that Aries is a movable sign is not to contradict the fact that it is also a fiery sign, for these two characterisations are interpreted in different ways. The former results from the application of the threefold classification, whereby the signs are related to the three gunas, the three paths, and the three aspects of consciousness, knowing, desiring and doing ; and the latter follows from the fourfold classification which relates to the four elements, the four bodies, and other groups of four. The former belongs more to Life and the latter to Form.

On examining the table it will be seen that the three airy signs occupy the highest plane, as they did in previous tables; and that when each is divided into quarters, all twelve signs of the zodiac are brought up on to the airy plane, where they exist as sub-divisions or polarities of the matter belonging to that plane, and of the body formed of that matter. Similarly, although the next plane is that of fire, and although Aries, Leo and Sagittarius specially relate to it, all the twelve signs are present there as watery, earthy, and airy sub-divisions of fire; and the same principles apply to the planes of water and of earth.

This conclusion might have been deduced from the principle previously referred to, that the microcosm is a mirror of the macrocosm. If the four quadrants of the zodiac correspond to the four planes, each quadrant and each plane must mirror the whole.

In the THREEFOLD classification of signs, with decanates arranged in septenary groups all are of the same element; the septenates of earth are themselves also earthy. But all the three quadruplicities are represented within the seven.

In the FOURFOLD classification of any sign, the sub-divisions are all of the same quadruplicity but all four elements are present.

Aquarius as a fixed sign is in touch with the common quadruplicity through its second decanate, and with the movable through its third.

Aquarius, as an airy sign, is in touch with earth and the physical plane through its second quarter, with fire and the mental plane through its third quarter, and with water and the astral plane through its fourth quarter.

APPLICATION TO THE HOROSCOPE

In its application to the horoscope the following facts are deduced.

Planets in the first quarter of a sign apply directly to the native, his powers and characteristics. They express his own personal faculties, considering him as a separate self, self-contained and complete.

Planets in the second quarter of a sign relate to home, domestic, and parental influence, the sphere of the family. They express his relation with parents and children, and with other people only indirectly. The circle of self is enlarged, but it is still relatively a private and secluded one.

Planets in the third quarter of a sign express his relation to the world at large on terms of more or less equality. Marriage, partnership, friendship, enmity, general popularity, are only variations in the application of this relation. The circle of self is so enlarged here as to include a great deal of the not-self.

Planets in the fourth quarter of a sign express his relation to the world in terms of superiority, power, mastery, fame, achievement, publicity, prominence.

The nature of the combination of planet and sign determines whether these are pleasant or unpleasant, fortunate or the reverse.

Four Great Symbols

In the preliminary lessons in the study of Esoteric Astrology which ran through Vol. IX. (New Series) of *Modern Astrology*, some ideas were expressed concerning a Spiritual or Central Sun, and its connection with the Rays and Monads.   There are four symbols in Esoteric and Exoteric Astrology with which we should be familiar.   The Central Sun is symbolised by the Pole Star, and this we may take as corresponding to the Monad or Divine Fragment.   The Sun at the centre of our solar system then corresponds to the light and spirit of the Individual or Causal body ; the Moon to the shadowy light of astral-mental consciousness ; and the Earth to the physical body.

These four symbolical representations have a more definite correspondence in the four triplicities, air, fire, water, and earth.

Generally speaking there is always an interaction going on between two of these grades, the one higher or individual and the other lower or personal.   At the present stage of evolution the Individual is represented by the causal body, and the Personality by the three lower expressions of consciousness.   When, in the course of evolution, man has transcended the causal body, his consciousness is no longer limited to conditions affected by the earth's zodiac, for he can then create his own vehicles of consciousness at will.   From this it will be seen that we have human beings evolving subject to four definite grades of matter, each of the four passing through all stages of the finer and grosser particles belonging to that grade.

Gateways through the Signs

The sub-division of signs into three and four parts, as previously described, gives a sevenfold aspect to each sign ; but of these seven only five can be said to lead outside the sign itself.   The first decanate and the first quarter are both of the same nature as the sign itself.   Through the second and third decanates and the second, third, and fourth quarters the sign is kept in touch with other aspects of consciousness and other bodies and planes of being.   For instance, Leo is a sign of fixed fire, and it relates to the mental plane through its fiery nature; and to the aspect of will, which is desire in the unevolved man, through its fixed quality. Its second and third decanates bring it into touch with Jupiter and the wisdom ray and with Mars and the activity ray. Its second quarter brings in the influence of the astral or watery body; its third quarter that of the airy element; and its fourth quarter brings it down on to the physical plane.

It may be thought at first sight that these sub-divisions of signs are too complex for practical workers, and that it is sufficient to consider the sign as a whole. This is true for most purposes, and in any case the fact that a sign can be divided in no way contradicts the truth that Leo behaves as one whole, ruled by the Sun; just as the fact that a man is one individual does not disprove the idea that he functions in three modes of consciousness and through four bodies.

Types and Sub-Types

The necessity for these and other complexities will be seen if we go back to the idea, expressed in previous Chapters, that there are seven types of souls evolving on this earth under the guardianship of the Seven Great Beings who are the spiritual vitalisers and rulers of the seven chains or groups of planets. Every human soul is directly related to one of these great Beings individually, and is acquiring predominantly the characteristics, the powers and faculties, that belong to that one of the seven.

Every soul however is also acquiring, although in a less marked degree, the characteristics that belong to the other six types; and is doing so by incarnating in bodies that are built successively according to the natures of all the seven rulers in turn. For instance, an Individuality whose main line of evolution is that which is represented by Saturn will not always be born in a Saturn Personality; this will be at one birth Jupiter, at another Mars, and so on throughout the seven; so that although Saturn will represent the strongest and best side of the nature of the individual soul, the powers of all the other six rulers are being acquired, with varying degrees of success.

It follows from this that the classification of individuals on a septenary scale does not exhaust the subject. It is not sufficient to say— this man is under Saturn, that under Jupiter, another under Venus, and so forth. If the seven types were all and there were no other differences, individuals belonging to the same planetary ray should be exactly alike. Two Saturnians should be facsimiles of each other; two ruled by the Sun should be indistinguishable. We know that this is certainly not the case with the physical personality, and the reports of those who function on higher planes lead to the conclusion that it is not true of the Individuality either.

When we have classified an individual as belonging to one of the seven predominantly, there still remains the question of the degree of success that has attended his efforts to acquire the powers of the other six types. If his strongest and best faculties are those of Saturn, which comes second in order with him? There are six others, and any one of them may, theoretically, occupy the second place. So that even if there are only seven types at the start, the classification will be complicated by the fact that each of the seven can vary in six different directions; making forty-two secondary types.

This does not finish the subject, for there are still five other lines of evolution, sub-lines within the main one followed by the soul; and here again their characteristics may be acquired in any order. Any given secondary type can therefore vary in five different directions; which provides 42×5 or 210 types at the third stage.

Not to prolong the argument, it will be evident that this third stage implies the possibility of a fourth varying in four directions, 210×4, or 840 at the fourth stage; a fifth varying in three directions, 840×3, or 2520 at the fifth stage; and a sixth varying in two directions, 2520×2, or 5040 altogether.[1]

This follows from the existence of seven fundamental types, each containing the other six as sub-types within itself.

There is no need to suggest further complications, such as those due to the zodiac, which would raise the number to infinity; for the fact remains that no two individuals are ever exactly alike. The differences between them are due to the varying kinds of experience through which

---

[1] This number is perhaps significant. On p. 35 it has been stated that the Hindu astrologer considers the most minute division of a sign, which is a certain fraction of a second, to be "a seed cast into the cosmic soil or ether." Assuming this fraction to be one hundredth of a second of arc (o''·o1), then a complete "set," as it might be termed, of such 'seeds' would be 50''·40. This is exactly the amount of the annual precession, by which the zodiac of the signs recedes upon the zodiac of the constellations.

they have passed in bygone incarnations on this and other globes. Experience of the world calls forth, or educates, faculty within the soul ; and because the paths trodden by the pilgrims are never precisely alike for any two, the experience gained and the faculties called forth must vary proportionately.   The saint differs from the sinner in being an older soul with greater experience and loftier powers.   The genius has unfolded his faculties to a greater extent than has the commonplace person.   Even if all souls were of the same age, the complication (as we have seen) would be great ; but as there are great variations in age and consequently in degree of evolution, the complexity is enormous.   And yet all are included within the seven types symbolised by the planets, following the three paths of power, love, and wisdom.

It will by this time have become apparent that in Esoteric Astrology familiar expressions take on new meanings, and our next Chapter will deal with the most important of these.

CHAPTER XXIII

Esoteric Meaning of Astrological Terms in Ordinary Use

' His Breath gave Life to the Seven ' (in the *Stanzas of Dzyan*) refers as much to the Sun, who gives life to the Planets, as to the " High One," the SPIRITUAL SUN, who gives life to the whole Kosmos. The astronomical and astrological keys opening the gate leading to the mysteries of Theogony can be found only in the later glossaries, which accompany the Stanzas.

Secret Doctrine.

THE following glossary of the ordinary astrological terms, adapted to the requirements of Esoteric Astrology, will be found useful for reference.   Illustrations are given in many cases so that the explanations may be more readily followed.

Afflictions or *afflicting* are terms applied to aspects between the heavenly bodies when the total result is unfortunate.   This arises partly from the nature of the aspect, partly from the signs in which the aspects fall, and partly from the nature of the planets that are said to cause the afflictions.   Saturn and Mars afflict because they represent extremes ; Saturn by its inherently cold influence restricting and limiting the even flow of vitality and consciousness, and Mars through its rapid expansion and heat causing ill-regulated or excessive action both in the body and soul.

The square aspect between planets is an affliction because the signs that form the square are uncongenial when considered as separate from the whole circle.   For instance Fire and Water are incompatible, being really opposites or inversions, like positive and negative electricity, and similarly with regard to the volatile air and the solid earth.

Again, Saturn afflicts the Sun more or less at all times because the influence of the Sun is expansive and Saturn contractive ; Mars afflicts the Moon more or less at all times because the Moon is cold and moist whilst Mars is hot and dry.   The interpretation of afflictions requires care, for it may happen that an affliction may be beneficial in some horoscopes where counteracting influences are necessary.   We will take some of the example horoscopes to illustrate both the advantages and disadvantages of afflictions in certain cases.

The square aspect of Mercury and Uranus in the horoscope of Cecil Rhodes affected his health, and obliged him to travel to a more congenial climate—Africa, ruled by Cancer, and this gave him the opportunity he required and thus brought out his latent genius for Empire building.

Many afflictions are blessings in disguise, breaking old links and forming fresh ones, destroying that which is old and outworn and bringing the native into touch with fresh and more beneficial experiences.

The Square aspect of Mars and Uranus in Lord Randolph Churchill's horoscope brought progress and change and, if he had lived, would have resulted in many reforms and the introduction of new ideas into Parliament, but as it was he sowed seed for future generations to reap.

These examples could be multiplied indefinitely, for something similar occurs in the lives of most people, but the above are sufficient to show that afflictions should never be interpreted as wholly evil; the ancient astrologers considered all aspects useful. The attitude of the concrete mind is what really makes them evil.

Angular Positions. The Angular Positions of the planets are very important for the expression or full manifestation of their influence. All who come to the front or take up public work and live an active life have many planets angular. These positions can, however, bring unpleasant notoriety as well as popularity and fame. The afflictions and the benefic influences from angles are always the most important factors in a horoscope. They bring out of latency into potency all that they denote.

Application. In all judgments of a nativity it is important to distinguish aspects that are in process of formation and that are within orbs from those that have been completed and that are now separating. *Application* denotes that which is forming, *separation* that which is dissolving. The ☽ ☍ ♄ in Napoleon's nativity was a dissolving influence from the tenth and fourth houses. It accentuated all the estrangements and separations he passed through and finally isolated him, at the close of his life, from all he held dear. The Sun was also separating from a square aspect with Jupiter, and this denoted the overthrow of his pride by his final failure to achieve the height of his ambition. Note the applications in the horoscope of Cecil Rhodes. The Moon *applied* to ♂ ♅ ☉

and ♆, and his life was one of upbuilding and not dissolving.   See also Bismarck's Moon.

Ascending.   All planets ascending or rising in the horoscope are important but those nearest the cusp of the ascendant have chief influence.   The ponderous planets are of more importance than the minor ones.

Uranus, Saturn, and Mars are respectively stronger in their influence when rising than Neptune, Jupiter, or Venus, while the luminaries and Mercury depend upon aspects and signs to give them real strength. Uranus rising gives independence, strength of will, and some tendency to eccentricity or uncommon expression.   Saturn gives resistance, perseverance, patience, and stability.   Mars gives strength, force, and assertiveness. Neptune tends to give mediumistic, dreamy and idealistic experiences. Jupiter widens, expands and tends to bring the life to a good maturity. Venus gives love of pleasure, affection and an easy life.   Mercury tends toward versatility and adaptability.   The Sun to ambition, pride, and love of mastery, but bestows much generosity.   The Moon gives love of change, novelty, and moods.   The rising planet will in some cases become the ruling planet, and is always important as a secondary ruler or agent by which the consciousness and the life may be changed.

Take for instance the horoscope of a man showing a tendency toward exaggeration : by Saturn rising, he may be changed into a lover of truth and prudence.

Aspects.   When everything connected with sign and position has been judged, a careful attention to the aspects formed between the heavenly bodies is most desirable.   Aspects change the influence of a planet more than house or sign ; for instance the separateness and isolating tendencies of Saturn may be greatly modified by a favourable aspect to Mars or Jupiter ; and the good position of Jupiter by sign and house will be greatly modified by an unfavourable aspect to Mars or Saturn.

The influence of Saturn can also be made more adverse when unfavourable aspects accentuate selfishness and coldness.   Jupiter under adverse aspects may also denote hypocrisy and duplicity instead of wide-mindedness and expansion.

When judging aspects, those of the luminaries and Mercury should be first considered, for they are the conductors, receivers, and distributors of planetary influence. The Moon's aspects tend to affect physical conditions. The Sun influences the moral or individual character and Mercury the rational and humanising conditions.

Major aspects should never be over-looked and minor aspects never magnified into undue importance. The positions of conjunction and opposition are of primary importance, then the trines and squares, followed by the sextile and the minor aspects. The sesquiquadrate is often an important aspect but is not always understood as it is sometimes a very contradictory influence.

Benefics. Jupiter and Venus are generally the benefic planets but there are times when they can be the reverse ; for instance, Jupiter may give excess and an over-abundance of what are commonly and erroneously termed " good things." Venus may cause ruin through pleasure or gay company. The term belongs to horary more than to natal astrology.

Besieged. This is another horary term but it may be applied to natal astrology with modifications of sign, position, and aspect. A ' benefic ' between ' malefic ' planets would modify that which the benefic signified. By progress of the map, however, the opportunity to pass out of this experience would be afforded.

Combustion. This is another horary term. When a planet is very close to the Sun it is not so powerful as when further removed. It affects Mercury *more* and Mars *less* then any other planet.

Culminating. All planets culminating or near the cusp of the M.C. are powerful, and have much influence, especially if also essentially dignified, that is in their house or exaltation.

When not essentially dignified, their mere presence near the upper meridian is said to render them accidentally dignified. A planet in the tenth house higher than all the rest is said to be elevated.

There is sometimes a tendency to doubt which is the stronger, a planet rising close to the cusp of the ascendant, or one culminating. Napoleon had Jupiter rising in Scorpio, but not on the horizon ; Saturn was culminating in Cancer. Saturn was therefore accidentally but not essentially dignified. It was in the tenth house, to which it belongs, but in the sign of its detriment ; Jupiter, however, had no dignity in Scorpio. Jupiter rising gave Napoleon opportunity, and he was strong enough to seize it ; his ruling planet elevated denoted his wish to do so, and Saturn culminating gave him the power. The rising of Jupiter strengthened Mars and Saturn by good aspects. His rise and fall are both shown by these positions.

The culmination of Venus in Prince Bismarck's horoscope was of immense value to him as a statesman; fortune was thereby enabled to favour him.

Cusp. There is often difficulty in deciding as to which house a planet belongs; say a planet is 8° away from the cusp of the ninth house, should it be taken to influence the ninth or the eighth ?

While allowing a margin of 5° to the influence of the cusp of each house, no hard and fast rule should be adopted. Jupiter 8° away from the ninth if in the sign Sagittarius will have a ninth house influence, but if in Scorpio it would be in the eighth. The margin should be elastic enough to allow for the student's judgment. When near the angles, a far wider range of margin may be given ; but when *aspects* to the cusps of houses are judged a narrower margin should be allowed. A good standing rule is to treat the cusps of houses in the same manner as conjunctions.

A planet in the centre of a house is sometimes stronger than when upon the cusp ; but the nearer the cusp of the house, the stronger is the influence in a general way. It will often happen that a planet *alone* about 8° above the cusp of the ascendant will greatly influence the ascendant; this is sometimes the case with one below the seventh house also.

Decanates. The decanates of the signs are more important than many students appear to realise; there is, however, a tendency to bring confusion with the judgment, when a sign is divided into three separate parts, unless the student possesses an excellent memory. The same difficulty is sometimes felt by beginners when the circle of the zodiac is found to be divided into signs, triplicities, and quadruplicities. Each sign contains the whole triplicity in itself to which it belongs. The first decanate of 10° is always of the same nature as the sign itself. The second decanate, from 10° to 20° is of the nature of the next sign of the same triplicity, which modifies the sign by bringing a *sub*-influence into operation ; and the third sign of the triplicity is brought in as a modification of the sign by sub-influence in the third decanate. This arrangement brings the whole of the combined influence of Cardinal, Fixed, and Mutable into one sign.

We will illustrate the value of the decanates from our example horoscopes. Napoleon had his ruling planet in the first decanate of Cancer. Mercury and Neptune were also in the first decanates of the signs they occupied. Jupiter was in the second decanate of Scorpio, that of ♏-♓, and Saturn was also in a similar sub-influence, ♋-♓. Therefore, through Saturn and Jupiter the whole of the watery triangle was in evidence.

The ☉ was in the third decanate of ♌ = ♌-♈. Mars was in the second decanate of ♍ = ♍-♑; and the ☽ in the third decanate of ♑ = ♑-♍. Uranus was also in the ♍ decanate of ♉.

The distribution of the planets throughout the decanates reveals three primary cardinal influences, four primary fixed, and two primary mutable; with the sub-influences reversed, six sub and primary mutable influences, four primary fixed, and five primary and sub-cardinal influences. Further analysis shows four primary earth influences, three primary water, and two primary fire. No air influences. The sub-divisions show seven earthy, five watery, three fiery and no airy. A further analysis of this nativity would show that the angles were accentuated; Venus ruler of horoscope in a cardinal sign; Sun in seventh house decanate; Moon in fourth, Capricorn. Saturn in tenth in Cancer. Mars in Capricorn decanate of Virgo, tenth house influence, etc.

A contrast of a striking character is supplied by the horoscope of "Viscount Hinton," who has six primary mutable influences, three cardinal, and *no fixed*.

The primary and sub-mutable influences are seven; the cardinal three, all primary; and the fixed four, are *sub*-influences.

Declination. The Parallels of declination are often neglected by some students, who do not realise their value. The Parallels should be carefully noted in all nativities for they have a potent influence very often coinciding with influences that were overlooked. Although the Parallels when taken alone act similarly to conjunctions, yet when the two planets are also in aspect they are to be considered as of the same nature as the *aspect*. The Sun and Jupiter may be in Parallel while applying to or separating from a square aspect, this would make the Parallel of the same nature as the square. If we consider the parallel in the same manner as a conjunction, having always the same effect, we shall very often attribute the wrong influence to it. In the case of Napoleon's nativity a Parallel of Moon and Saturn would act in the same manner as the opposition, accentuating it and not diminishing its influence.

Descendant. The seventh house or western angle is always important when it contains one or more planets. This angle while showing the formation of unions, is not wholly concerned with marriage. It sometimes denotes the ability of the native to express, and make manifest the influences affecting that house, such as the ability to come before the public, to do public work, and give the self to service or sacrifice. It always represents that which is farthest removed from the native, such as his ideals, etc. Its good meaning, in the case of benefics and well-aspected planets may be said to be the power of co-operating with others, thinking, feeling, and working with them, the realisation of Buddhi and brotherhood. Its evil interpretation under bad aspects is the reverse of this, separateness, enmity, failure to combine, through weakness, hatred, or too intense a personality.

Detriment. A term used when a planet is in the opposite sign to that over which it is lord or ruler, such as Mars in Libra, Saturn in Cancer. The ordinary view, when the zodiac is considered quite apart from the houses, is that a planet is strong and fortunate when in its own house or exaltation, that it shows forth its full strength and the best side of its nature, and that directions to it have full effect, especially the good aspects. On the other hand, when in its detriment, a planet is weaker and less fortunate, is apt to show the less desirable side of its nature, good directions to it have comparatively little effect, and bad ones do much harm.

This applies to position in the zodiac only, and is subject to modification, because a planet may be weak by sign but strong by mundane position. Mars in Taurus, rising, for instance, lessens the assertiveness of the planet and allows some of its finer qualities to be expressed ; whereas Mars in Aries, while giving a strong and self-reliant character, is apt to give too much self-assertiveness and impulsiveness which, if uncontrolled, may be the cause of many troubles, evoking in others criticism, rivalry, or open hostility. Mars in Libra will give intuition, quickness of perception, and artistic ability in a cultivated or naturally refined person, but in one untrained or naturally undeveloped it will be detrimental and will mean an influence that cannot properly be manifested.

Saturn in Capricorn is slow, plodding, industrious, self-controlled, firm, and strong-willed, and the best side of the planet is capable of the fullest manifestation. Saturn in Cancer, while less strongly and fully expressed, may do good through slowing down the unduly emotional tendencies; but if this restriction and limitation is turned in the direction of grief and depression, or if the feelings are morbid and peevish, it is a very detrimental influence and may act most injuriously upon both physical health and worldly fortunes.

Saturn in Cancer culminating is strong by mundane position but weak by zodiacal position. In this case, karma or fate will give opportunities for the realisation of ambition, prominence, worldly success, or wealth; and if the rest of the horoscope supports it, these may actually be attained; but the weak zodiacal position brings liability to failure, or a success that is greatly diminished through weak health or some flaw of character coming from the evil side of Saturn, such as depression, selfishness, isolation, reserve, lack of candour, and so on.

Generally speaking, planets in detriment are unfortunate for weak characters, but are not wholly so for strong and advanced ones.

Dignities. These are of two kinds, essential and accidental. Essential dignity is position in the zodiac by house or exaltation. Accidental dignity is position in the mundane houses, by which strength or prominence is gained. Any planet is accidentally dignified if close to the cusps of the first, tenth, or seventh houses, and this gives prominence; the planet is thrust forward into notice, so to speak, but there is another kind of accidental dignity in which the planet may not be prominent but is in a house congenial to its own nature, such as Mercury in the third house, the Moon in the fourth, the Sun in the fifth, Jupiter in the ninth, and so on.

Directions. The horoscope of birth, while representing the personality, its possibilities and limitations, is by no means fixed; and directions are employed to show how far the limitations may be modified and the possibilities increased. Those writers who look upon the horoscope as so much fixed fate take the same view of directions; but it is better to regard these as affording opportunities for change and growth. Good directions give an opening for developing the better qualities of those planets that are concerned in forming the direction ; it is easier to do this at such a time, and effort put forth then will bear better fruit than usual. Just, benevolent, humanitarian, and religious qualities can be developed under a good direction to Jupiter ; fore-thought, prudence, and self-control under one to Saturn ; courage, enterprise, self-reliance, and self-sacrifice under Mars ; strength and activity of intellect under Mercury ; and so on. And not only will character be improved and developed but the events in the outward world that accompany the directions, the good luck as it is often called, will be intensified in their action and a better harvest will be reaped.

Bad directions offer opportunities for restraining such unfavourable qualities as are generally associated with the various planets when afflicted. The attempt to do this will develop strength of will and make the man more master of himself than if he submitted without a struggle. It is true that by the Karma we have created for ourselves in the past some of the things that happen to us are foredoomed and unavoidable ; but this is not the case with all events, probably not with the great majority ; and by ruling ourselves we rule our stars.

Apart from questions of strength and weakness, good and evil, people seem to differ in their response to planetary influence. Very devotional persons seem to respond readily, very emotional people also, and they seem therefore more subject to planetary influences of all kinds than those who have not such a responsive nature.

The most sensitive natures appear to be those who are under the influences of the cardinal signs and in the majority of cases the least responsive are those under the mutable signs.

Quite apart from the very sensitive nature of those who are born under the influence of the cardinal signs, there are several sensitive conditions shown in a nativity. There are again nativities in which very little response is shown, and yet it would seem that the progress of the native depends more upon this ability to respond to planetary influences ; the successful understanding of a nativity would seem to depend upon knowing this one fact before any other.

All persons born with planets in angles are fated, or destined, to respond to those influences, shirk them how they will ; and they generally have the most eventful, changeful and active lives. Next to this comes the succedent houses, and finally the cadent houses. All the planets in angles would show extreme activity, all the planets in cadent houses, extreme latency ; the succedents come between.

Some persons are very responsive to the transits of planets through the nativity, while others seem to be less so.   There does not appear to be any hard and fast rule by which definite and precise predictions can be made in all cases.   The result of much experience in this direction shows that from the horoscope of a thief or very covetous person, any temptation to steal or covet may be excited by the natal influences being stimulated by adverse directions.   A person whose horoscope denotes a highly sense-loving nature will succumb to sensuous inclinations when in an atmosphere that allows the natal conditions to operate, and when under adverse directions is more particularly weak in this direction than at other times.

Dragon's Head and Tail.   The Dragon's Head is the Moon's ascending node, or that point at which the Moon crosses the ecliptic—that is, has no latitude—on its northward path ; the Dragon's Tail, or the Moon's descending node, is the opposite point at which the Moon crosses the ecliptic on its southern journey.   These were considered of importance by the ancients and are in use by Hindu astrologers to this day ; the Head being regarded as benefic and having dignity in Gemini, and the Tail as malefic and having dignity in Sagittarius.   Most modern writers ignore them as having little or no value.   The only practical value they seem to have is that they point out whereabouts eclipses have been falling during the period before birth ; and it is quite possible that this subject is worthy of further investigation.   An eclipse, especially if visible, makes a strong impress upon that point of the zodiac where it falls, and this impress is apparently retained for a time ; so that it may constitute a point of some importance in a horoscope, which will be overlooked because the luminaries will meanwhile have moved away.   Eclipses, however, are not always exactly on the Head or Tail but only in their neighbourhood.

Elections.   These are the choosing of the best times for beginning important undertakings, such as travelling, buying or selling, signing documents, laying foundation stones, and so on.   If used in combination with the horoscope and directions they are of permanent value.   Claudius Ptolemy wrote :

" It is advantageous to make choice of days and hours at a time well constituted to the nativity.   Should the time be adverse, the choice will in no respect avail, however favourable an issue it may chance to promise."

Elevation. Any planet higher in the houses than another is said to be elevated over the other; but the term is generally applied to planets that are above the earth. That one which is nearest to the cusp of the tenth house is the most elevated in the horoscope. When two planets are in aspect, one is usually higher than the other, and if one is above the earth and the other below, the elevated one gains in strength and prominence by its elevation. If the aspect is a square or opposition, the lower of the two bodies will be weakened, and the things it signifies will suffer much more than those ruled by the other. In Napoleon's case Saturn was elevated over the Moon. The temperament is often affected by elevated planets. If Mars alone is in the M.C. and no planets rising, the Martial temperament will be the most pronounced, and the same remark applies to all the other planets.

Exaltation. The influence of a planet is generally accentuated when in the sign of its exaltation, and when this happens in untrained persons it may cause trouble through conceit, egotism, or over confidence, while the trained will use the influence in a transmuted and purified sense.

Mars in Capricorn will temper the force of Mars as rude iron may be tempered into fine steel. This analogy may be applied to all the exaltations. The lead of Saturn may be liquified in Libra, the vaporous and volatile emotions of the Moon may be fixed in Taurus, and the love of Venus made universal in Pisces; and so on.

Applied to Natal Astrology they have a different meaning than when confined to Horary Astrology.

Fall, see Detriment.

Feminine Signs. The even signs ♉,♋,♍,♏,♑,♓, are feminine or negative signs. They are particularly connected with the form side of expression as distinct from the life or more forceful and positive side, expressed by the masculine signs.

Napoleon had no less than seven planets in the even or form signs. He sought to rule the earth, and was always a material expression of himself. Bismarck on the other hand had six planets in positive or odd signs. He sought to build up an empire; Napoleon was always destroying.

They are, therefore, representative of the constructive and destructive forces in nature.

Fixed Stars. Modern Astrology has not yet attempted to deal with the fixed stars on a very extensive scale, or note their influence in nativities. A list of the fixed stars is given in the second edition of the little manual *Horary Astrology;* the student should place them in the example horoscopes and note their effect.

In the horoscope of Lady Burton the Moon was conjunction Capella. In Gladstone's map Mercury and the Sun were conjunction Vega. Bismarck had the Sun conjunction Caput Andromedæ, and Robespierre had Saturn conjunction Fomalhaut.

Geocentric and Heliocentric Astrology. In ancient times when most people believed that the Sun and all the heavenly bodies revolved round the earth, no one ever questioned the value of geocentric astrology. Now that we know that the Sun is the real centre of our system, however, it is not surprising that some writers should maintain that Astrology should be heliocentric and that the old geocentric system should be abandoned. We do not agree with this idea, for the following reasons.

We dwell upon this earth, and Astrology is the science of the effects produced by the influences of Sun, Moon, and planets as they are showered upon this earth. In order to judge of these effects we have to measure the angles and distances of the planets as seen from this earth, not as seen from the Sun, upon which we do not dwell. We are working out our destiny upon the earth, and the influences that are poured directly upon this earth are what concern us, not those that are poured upon the Sun.

A heliocentric science will probably be perfected some day, but nothing hitherto advanced will compare with the ordinary Astrology in results.

Horary Astrology. While admitting the value of Horary Astrology, modern astrologers have striven to separate Horary from Genethliacal Astrology, and so far with very satisfactory results. It was through the excessive use of Horary Astrology that the whole science fell into disrepute. It was easy, when the birth time was unknown, to erect a Horary figure and make it a substitute for the birth map. Thousands of these Horary figures were given during the nineteenth century as birth maps, and regarded as reliable, to the detriment of genuine Astrology. A Horary figure is useful to answer serious questions when the birth time is unknown, or when the mind is very anxious concerning any important event ; and so long as it is not confounded with natal astrology it can be exceedingly useful. It tends, however, to weaken the Will and initiative of the user who relies upon the figure, for he thereby becomes more or less a fatalist.

If used as a supplement to Directions or the horoscope it may be helpful to know if investments are safe or speculation wise. It will answer all questions upon which the mind of the enquirer is seriously seeking an answer, and the rules for its application are very simple.

Erecting a figure for the moment when a thought first comes into the mind concerning any subject, the ascendant denotes the enquirer, and the house or ruler of any particular house, regarding the question, gives the answer.

The first house then represents the querent, and the lord or ruler of that house or planets in the first should describe him.

If money is enquired about, the second house, its ruler and Jupiter or Venus should be considered.

If relatives, journeys and correspondence are the subject of the enquiry, the third house is consulted with its ruler, also planets therein and the Moon.

This is repeated throughout, each house being taken to answer the question. The whole of the art is explained in the small manual *Horary Astrology*. If abused, Horary Astrology becomes dangerous, but if wisely used it is a useful and often a reliable means of divination.

Houses. Each of the twelve houses in a nativity has an importance of its own, and is quite distinct in its special influence. These twelve houses are the concrete centres of forces, which, in the advanced person, react upon and so modify the more subjective centres of the signs and planets. The first house represents the head and face of the native, the second the throat, and so on. In this sense the houses represent hereditary conditions, and that which is fixed as fate for the current life. Persons who live in their purely physical conditions, that is habitually think that they are the physical body alone, and those who are generally classed as materialists will respond to the conditions of the twelve houses apart from the signs or planets occupying them.

Hyleg. It is important to know what length of life is shown in the
horoscope, but the ordinary rules will not apply in all cases, and judgment of a special kind is needed where the horoscope shows a tendency
to study the laws of hygiene and to live a temperate life. Astrology does
not teach fatalism, but the working of natural law. Some horoscopes
show long life, others a short duration of life, while the majority may be
said to have a limit up to which they may live. There are no special
rules for showing the limit of life in individual cases, and it is a matter of
judgment as to whether the native will pass through a critical aspect or
not; but when a train of evil directions is in force lasting over a very
long period, death may be expected when the vitality drops below the
power to recuperate. Many horoscopes show a delicate state of health in
infancy but robust conditions at middle life; and others the reverse. It
is the astrologer's duty to advise careful and temperate living, a proper
attention to the laws of hygiene, a conservation of energy, and right
methods of living, but *never* to predict death. The approximate time of
death may be stated with regard to the limit of life, but never the actual
date. The fact that what we call death, is but a withdrawal of the life
from the physical body into a finer body and to another plane should
show us that we cannot be sure in many cases as to the actual date of
death any more than we can predict the time a person will go to sleep
on any particular night. We may discover the time when there will be a
liability to serious accidents, to disease, or lowered vitality, but we cannot
gauge the actual power behind the personality to turn aside the influence
into another channel. In the undeveloped horoscopes we may see fatality
more or less clearly, but the difficulty increases when the life becomes
more thoroughly self-conscious.

An illustration of this may help students of Astrology to understand
the working of a higher law.

An astrologer many years ago publicly predicted the death of Mrs.
Annie Besant in her 60th year. Mrs. Besant has passed that critical
period, and on asking her opinion about the prediction, instead of ignoring
the prediction she showed that love of truth which she possesses by remark-
ing that "she would have passed out at the time predicted had it not
been for the help of her Master," who foresaw the usefulness of her life
and took upon himself the responsibility of preserving it. Every student
of Astrology should endeavour to realise that there is a law of love which
does not interfere with natural laws, but transmutes the lower into the

higher law; but only those who know the law and work with it have the power to change the lower into the higher.   If death could in *all cases* be predicted with absolute certainty, then it would be useless to hope that effort could be stronger than destiny.   There are always circles within circles, and all evolution is an expansion from smaller to larger circles.

Intercepted Signs.   Many students find it difficult to judge the influence of intercepted signs.   In a general sense they absorb the whole of the house in which they occur, and at the same time bring into the house a joint influence from the other signs affecting that house.   Planets in the intercepted signs have more importance than usual in their action upon the affairs of the house in which they are situated.

Lords of Houses.   Planets in Houses are usually stronger than the rulers or Lords of houses and in a general sense should be given preference.

Luminaries.   The Sun and Moon should always be considered as distributors and collectors of influence, and not as actual factors or causes of influence.

Mundane Aspects.   Students should never overlook the value of mundane aspects.   While not considered as powerful as zodiacal aspects they are nevertheless important, and usually affect the body or purely physical conditions.   Take the example of Robespierre.   If we could see the motives in this case we should know why the mundane aspects overcame the zodiacal.   Did he make bad use of his opportunity, or was he fated at birth to suffer a violent death at the hands of his enemies?

Oriental.   This word is used in two senses, first as applied to those bodies that are in the eastern half of the map, especially when in the ascendant, and secondly as applied to a planet that rises immediately before the Sun, when it is said to be "oriental of the Sun," a position of importance and strength.   Mercury and Uranus in Lord Rosebery's horoscope are oriental in both senses.   The opposite position is termed occidental.

The ascendant relates directly to the native, the Self; and planets in or near the ascendant bear upon character and upon actions that arise out of character.   The descendant, on the other hand, relates to persons and things in the outer world, with their bearing upon the native; the line of the meridian combines the two. We may therefore say that planets in the eastern half of the map, and especially those in the ascendant, tend to create fresh karma, and represent destiny that is the natural outcome of character and which is avoidable if character can be controlled. Planets in the western half of the map represent rather the fulfilling or working out of a previously made destiny, the re-action of the environment upon the native, which is less avoidable or modifiable than the former.

Part of Fortune. This symbol may possibly have significance in connection with horary astrology, but it is generally discredited in nativities. It is as many degrees from the rising degree as the Moon is from the Sun, counting from the Sun in the direction of the signs. Some of the older astrologers have suggested many other " Parts." Gadbury says that the Part of Fortune reversed gives the Part of the Spirit, counting from the Moon to the Sun in the order of the signs and then marking the Part the same distance from the rising degree. Counting from the Sun to Saturn is said to measure the Part of the love of brethren; and counting from Saturn to the Sun, the Part of the father. So far as the Sun is concerned, the Parts are nearly the same as calculating a horoscope for sunrise; but the reckoning often deals with other bodies. The Part of Marriage is said to be the same distance from the ascendant as the cusp of the seventh house is from Venus, starting the count from Venus. All these parts are supposed to be fortunate or the reverse according to the aspects they receive; but they are generally ignored now-a-days.

Quadruplicity or Quality. These terms are very important because they give a direct clue to the meaning of the horoscope as a whole and so form a basis for synthesis; they have stood the test of many years' practical work and are to be relied upon. Originally the word quality was used, because they are only an adaptation of the Hindu gunas ; Rajas, the active movable quality ; Tamas, the fixed stable quality ; and Sattva, the balancing, harmonising, rhythmical quality. More recently, the word Quadruplicity has been used, as it bears an obvious analogy with Triplicity. Each Triplicity contains three signs arranged in accordance with the so-called elements or states of matter ; three airy, ♒,♊,♎ ; three fiery, ♌,♐,♈ ; three watery, ♏,♓,♋ ; and three earthy, ♉,♍,♑ ; and they divide the circle into four parts, the cross in the circle. Each Quadruplicity contains four signs arranged in accordance with the gunas or modes of motion in matter; four active, movable, or rajasic, ♈ ♋ ♎ ♑; four fixed, unchanging, or tamasic, ♉ ♌ ♏ ♒; and four rhythmical or sattvic, ♊ ♍ ♐ ♓, intermediate in nature between the other two. They divide the circle into three parts, the triangle in the circle.

Each zodiacal sign, therefore has two characteristics, one according to Triplicity and the other according to Quadruplicity, as when we say that Aries is movable (or cardinal) fire. If we could understand to the full all that these terms implied we should know the whole nature of Aries, within and without; and similarly of the other signs. They are explained at length in the volume *The Art of Synthesis*.

Reception. When two planets are each in the house of the other, they are said to be in mutual reception, and this gives strength and good fortune and lessens the seriousness of any bad aspect between them. In Napoleon's horoscope, Saturn in Cancer and the Moon in Capricorn are in mutual reception. In the horoscope of Kaiser William II. of Germany, Saturn in Leo and the Sun in Aquarius are in mutual reception. Some would extend this to include reception by exaltation, as with the Sun in Libra and Saturn in Aries; and others would attach a similar importance to planets aspecting one another from their own houses, as Mars in Aries square Moon in Cancer, which may give much strength although of a martial and impulsive kind. A planet in house or exaltation always shows that its characteristics are strong and well developed in the person.

Retrograde. This was once considered a sign of weakness and misfortune, but it is doubtful whether there is any truth in the idea. Astrologers are much divided about it. The retrograde conjunctions of Venus and Mercury with the Sun seem to be very strong, but whether they carry with them any significance of bad luck it is not easy to determine; it has not been proved that they do.

Revolution. A map drawn for the time when the Sun returns to the exact degree, minute and second of longitude that it held at birth is called a solar revolution or birthday map. It generally illustrates the fate and fortune for the coming year of life. An alternative method used by some is to find out the hour and minute when the R.A. of the M.C. is the same as it was at birth on that day when the Sun is nearest to the longitude it held at birth (which will generally be the birthday or within a day of it), and then to calculate a map for this time; the cusps of the houses of such a map will be the same as at birth. The first method is equivalent to using the Sun's position as the exact time-measurer for the birthday anniversary; the second method is equivalent to maintaining that the Sun's position only indicates the day, and that the hour and minute are determined by the return of the cusp of the ascendant to the position it occupied at birth. Whichever method is adopted—and often there is not much difference between them—the planetary positions must be considered in their bearing upon the horoscope of birth, especially benefic and malefic transits. The birthday information given in the almanacs is practically useless because it is not related to the birth map. The whole subject deserves more careful examination than it has yet received, and the question of the progressed birthday at the rate of a day for a year needs investigation.

Synthesis. The ability to synthesise a nativity is the crown of the student's knowledge on natal astrology for it leads, by the intuition required to do this effectually, to those abstract methods of pure synthesis which will finally reveal the true purpose of every horoscope.

Students should practise the art of synthesis by giving a short synthesis at the end of every delineation on the following lines :

NAPOLEON.	Elements:—	Fire	2	Cardinal 3
		Earth	4	Fixed 4
		Air	—	Common 2
		Water	3	
				Fixed—Earth

Planets well placed and distributed.

Main features :—Libra rises, second decanate. Venus ruling planet in Cancer, near the M.C., placed in the ninth house; ♀ ✶ ♆ ✶ ♅ ✶ ♂ △ ♃, seven planets above the earth. Jupiter rising next in Scorpio.

Personality :—Tenacious, yet amiable and very perceptive, great magnetic attraction, quietly critical, a keen judge of human nature, and an abnormal ambition.

Summary of horoscope :—Determined and persistent. Love of power, excellent organising ability, some genius ♂ △ ♅, combined with practical and consistent methods.

CHAPTER XXIV

The Growth of the Ego

A person may have won his immortal life, and remain the same *inner self* he was on earth, throughout eternity; but this does not imply necessarily that he must either remain the Mr. Smith or Mr. Brown he was on earth, or lose his individuality. Therefore, the astral soul and terrestrial body of man may, in the dark Hereafter, be absorbed into the cosmical ocean of sublimated elements, and cease to feel his *ego*, if this *ego* did not deserve to soar higher; and the divine spirit still remain an unchanged entity, though this terrestrial experience of his emanations may be totally obliterated at the instant of separation from the unworthy vehicle.   *Isis Unveiled.*

ALL who have devoted any thought to the study of Esoteric Astrology will have realised what a vast subject it is, requiring the keenest intellect and the highest concentration to understand fully. Those who have sensed the inner meaning of the whole will have the best ideas regarding the true value of the science. A nativity will be meaningless to some and will convey no idea of the purpose of the life it represents, while to others it will be full of suggestion and rich in ideas as to the possibilities that lie latent within it.

In some the spark of divinity will appear too deeply buried to show any manifestation of its future possibilities; in others the manifestation will be full and nearing completion.

In the spark of divinity behind the manifestation lie all the possibilities of the mighty flame into which it will burst, for each spark contains all the potentialities of the Parent Flame, and each is destined to re-become the Flame.

Symbolically, the spark is the point in the Circle, and it is seen in its latency in the symbol ⊙ of the Sun in each horoscope, to be finally changed into the symbol of Uranus, wherein the Circle (or what is more probably correct, the Triangle) is supreme over the Half Circle and the Cross ♀. Alone, it manifests Will, and the centre between Spirit and existence. When joined with the symbol of ☿ Mercury, a fuller experience is implied, discrimination between the real and the unreal has been gained, and the pure or abstract reason is active. Mercury is the centre between Wisdom and Knowledge, the unifying principle. When linked with the symbol of Venus ♀, the principle of Creation is denoted. Venus is the centre of life and form—the human soul.

Diagrammatically we may place our symbols thus : ☉ at the head and alone ; ♅, ☿, ♀ below forming a triangle. These three symbols are the abstract representatives of the immortal consciousness—the spirit, spiritual soul and human soul. They stand at the head of the three great Cardinal, Mutable and Fixed Crosses. Of these three symbols one only, namely ♀, is exalted in any sign of the zodiac, and this exaltation of Venus in Pisces represents the end of the cycle of necessity, the universal solvent, love triumphant, the law fulfilled.

Uranus is the abstract quality or quintessence of the Fixed Cross ; Mercury is the abstract of the Mutable Cross ; and Venus the abstract of the Cardinal Cross. They are principles, and as such are never truly interpreted through the signs of the zodiac.

THE LESSON OF THE THREE CROSSES

To fulfil the mission of the Cardinal Cross, the cross of activity and creation, is to lift it from the ground of matter so to speak, and come under the free mind, which has power to create through the divine imagination, or the image-making faculty.

To fulfil the mission of the Mutable Cross is to exchange knowledge for wisdom, and to lift it from the unreal basis on which it has stood in the world of illusion. To come under the true Mercury, the influence of the adept of wisdom, discrimination must be exercised to the full, until intuition takes the place of reason.

To fulfil the mission of the Fixed Cross is to exchange desire and attraction for will and non-attachment. To be free of all ties and limitations is to become the houseless wanderer, who finds home in all homes and brotherhood in all humanity.

To fuse the whole of these three into one, to move the point from the centre to the circumference so as to know and feel all as one, is to become the Master of destiny, the Master of wisdom and compassion.

The chela or pupil of Venus becomes the adept of Mercury, through the Master Uranian, and finally the Master himself.

As the point comes out from the centre in the beginning into the planes below the divine, the Self gains self-consciousness through the triplicities of signs governing the causal, mental, astral, and physical planes. Each of these triplicities has to be made the perfect tetraktys within the consciousness of the Ego, who is at the head of each triangle in turn. Unconsciously he is drawn downwards to awaken in the physical, and to fulfil the mission of the earthy signs—obedience ♉; response ♍; self-motived activity ♑. When these links have been made by self-conscious efforts through the limitations of Saturn in environment and circumstance, the expansion of consciousness begins, and Jupiter, the expansive planet of the aura, gives benefits and rewards on all planes; for while Jupiter is the greater fortune on the physical plane, the powers he bestows can be carried upward within the soul to higher levels.

The mission of the watery triangle is to awaken self-conscious emotion and the first germs of intuition, through instinct ♋ ; attachments ♏ ; and emotional sympathies ♓. At the head of this triangle is Mars, the planet of personal devotion. Its symbol ♂, shows that spirit is ever striving to conquer matter, and its consciousness is the energy of desire, working in the astral body.

The mission of the fiery triangle is to awaken the mental self-consciousness, to gain knowledge through Aries in the intuition of the mind; through Leo, the faith of the heart; and introspection through Sagittarius, the crown of Jupiter's expansion of the mind, just as this planet is through Pisces the expansion of the emotions on the astral plane.

The mission of the airy triangle, the highest of the four, is to synthesise, abstract, and make impersonal all that has been governed in the triangles of fire, earth, and water. At the head of this triangle is Venus, the planet of " skill in action," creative power, and ideality.

THE NARROW WAY AND THE STRAIT GATE

Separating the three higher planets from the four controlling the lower or personal manifestation, is the great planet Saturn, lord of the earthy sign Capricorn and the airy sign Aquarius. This is the individualising planet, ruler of the narrow way and the strait gate; refining, restricting, and purifying, often through pain and sorrow but also through endurance and self-control. None may pass Saturn who have not purity, love, and truth as their true ideals.

The Signs of the Zodiac are always connected with the forms and the vehicles, while the Planets are always connected with the consciousness apart from the forms. When the two are in harmony all goes well and progress is rapid; but when they are not in harmony all seems to go contrary and tends to clash, conflict, confusion, and discord.

For instance, Capricorn may give responsibility, power and honour through avocation, love of duty through a sense of responsibility, etc. But Saturn, its lord, is the vibration that especially signifies responsibility, and therefore, to escape the form and its limitations it is necessary to accentuate the responsibilities self-consciously, to seek honour for honour's sake, service for the sake of service, and to work in the world because it is a duty. By so doing we come under the direct influence of Saturn.

It is the same with each cross and each angle. The unions of Libra must be exchanged for the unity of Venus, and the abstract ideal of unity realised. The impulse of Aries must be changed for the true energy of Mars, and the sensational influence of Cancer changed for the instincts of the Moon.

It is a question of the identification of the self with either the form side, in its concrete and limited mode of expression, or with the life side, in its abstract and free manifestation.

THE MEANING OF CASTE

The wise astrologers of ancient India knew the value and right use of caste, which still prevails, although now carried too far in its innumerable subdivisions.

The castes are related to the four triangles; the Shudra, or labouring caste, under the earthy triangle ; the Vaishya, or merchant caste, under the watery triangle; the Kshattriya, or governing and fighting caste, under the fiery triangle, and the Brahman, or teaching and priestly caste, under the airy triangle.

Entrance into any one of these castes was a matter of birth, not of favour, patronage, or ambition ; and when a soul has naturally outgrown any caste by learning all the lessons it has to teach, he is born into the next, until the highest caste is reached, from which he begins to take up his cross.

RESPONSE, AND NON-RESPONSE

Now although the intuitive student will be able to judge the growth of the Ego from these triangles he must be prepared for certain exceptions to the rule ; because although Astrology is clearly symbolical it is also very much more. The three crosses mentioned above, before they are lifted from the plane of dense matter are firmly rooted in the ground of ignorance or non-response to the subtler vibrations of the planets that govern them.

The fixed cross may represent the Guna Tamas, or the quality of inertia in which obedience and steadfastness are to be the first lessons. The complication involved in the correct arrangement of the three crosses and four triangles is apt to be very puzzling to those who cannot clarify the ideas by a process of abstract thinking ; but it should be remembered that the Fixed Cross, which reflects the will vibration of consciousness, is also inertia and darkness as well as stability and firmness, there being two sides to every form, the light and dark. It is the same with all the signs and their divisions. The cardinal signs can be over-active, too ambitious, separative and over-reaching, as well as skilful in action, responsive, and creative. The mutable signs also are mute, indifferent, and vaporous as well as connective, harmonious and humane.

Herein lies the difficulty in becoming *an astrologer*. As students we may analyse, dissect, and put all things into their right places, but to balance correctly, to synthesise the whole aright, and know at a glance the young from the old is a gift which in some amounts to genius. Students, however, can see enough to show them that if forms can expand and be outworn by an ego, there must be something vital in the theory of re-incarnation and also some grounds for the belief in Karma or self-created fate and destiny.

THE WAY OF PROGRESS

We are all destined to pass through a long pilgrimage to obtain the self-consciousness necessary to realise our divine destiny. A study of genethliacal astrology will not only help us to realise why we have to pass through certain conditions but also why we progress apparently so slowly towards the far off ideal end. Truly there are millions of vibrations playing upon us during every minute of each day, but we respond intelligently and self-consciously to so few ! The vehicles, instead of being useful servants of the ego behind, hold the life in bondage to their own limitations, and thus many souls revolve round and round in the circle of necessity as a squirrel in a cage, instead of ascending the spiral of new modes of matter to express new phases of consciousness.

"How shall we do it?" the earnest student will ask. That, is the final question of this book. We first seek to understand our own horoscopes and ourselves; and if we have understood one or the other aright we shall cease to do evil and learn the good we may do, by the possibilities within ourselves. We shall be more responsive to the higher vibrations in our nativity and less responsive to the lower. We shall see how far we can blend our influences with the influences of others until we come under the one great influence of the Master who stands as representative of our own particular line of evolution, and then we shall have truly become the Wise Man who has ruled his stars and no longer the fool blindly obeying them.

CHAPTER XXV: CONCLUSION

The Curse and the Blessing of Astrology

By reducing all Karma to harmony, transcending all attachment through Wisdom, firm in the One Self, actions, O Dhananjaya, do not bind.

Bhagavad Gita.

THE curse of Astrology has been its separateness; its teachings have been understood by the concrete mind only, and those who have succeeded in discovering its priceless value have used this knowledge for self-advancement. The results of this self-centred use of Astrology are to be observed in the general use of terms of the separative order, such as "my Moon," "my Sun," etc., etc.

During the descent into matter on the path of separation, each individual identifies himself with certain planetary influences, and this identification becomes so pronounced as to make the influence special to the individual. It is with difficulty that he learns to realise that others beside himself may be under the same influence, and even when he knows this to be the case he continues to separate himself from them by maintaining that no other horoscope is exactly like his own, just as no two faces are alike.

The whole curse of Astrology lies in mistaking the form, over which planetary vibration has the greatest influence, for the life. The young Ego is limited by the houses of the horoscope into which he is born. His environment and circumstances limit him at every turn, he cannot break through the bonds of fate, being neither wise enough nor strong enough, and therefore succumbs to its influence. The Ego who has made some progress is still limited by the signs of the zodiac, and the bodily faculties which they govern. His sensations and instincts bind and fetter him through his likes and dislikes, the repulsions and attractions of his senses; he cannot rise above them, and so considers the influence of Mars as unavoidable and fatalistic. He judges only by the inclinations of his senses, and allows them to rule him. The advanced Ego is limited by the planetary influences playing through the zodiac, and is bound by the limitations of his mind. He is superior to the man whose senses blind him through bias and prejudice, and yet he narrows his mind to this personal outlook and is necessarily restricted by the limitations of his own experience, his customs, habits and egotism. If he gains a knowledge of Astrology and becomes fascinated by the wonders of his horoscope he holds it as a fetish ; it is *his* horoscope, and at once he separates himself from all the rest of humanity by hugging to himself the joys of the good aspects and planetary positions, and pitying himself for the bad ones.

There are thousands studying Astrology at the present day who fail to realise the meaning of the astrologer's watchword, "THE WISE MAN RULES HIS STARS, THE FOOL OBEYS THEM."

Every student of Astrology is in touch with priceless wisdom and yet for the most part he knows it not.

THE CURSE

The enlightened Hindu astrologer knows that there is a curse upon Astrology, and that it can only be removed and made a blessing by him who overcomes the limitations of separateness. A knowledge of Esoteric Astrology will remove that curse for him who understands.

Looked at from below with the eyes of the concrete mind, the planets revolve in their orbits as separate bodies, unconnected with each other or with the Sun, Moon, and stars. The Signs of the Zodiac are separate signs each having a distinct and separate meaning. The earth is also taken as a separate and isolated body whirling in space, and by its motion causing day and night. To the concrete mind everything is separate and distinct. To the higher and enlightened mind everything is dependent upon every other thing and only complete in forming a part of the whole. The planets to the esoteric astrologer are spheres of influence moving within spheres of influence, including the whole in harmony and unity ; they are separate only in their rates of vibration and in the varying phases they present of the one underlying all-comprehensive Life in which they live and move and have their being.

The zodiac is fundamentally a homogeneous whole, complete in the harmony of its circle, and separate only in the sub-influences of its divisions or signs.

The earth is a part of a far wider sphere of evolution, which itself is only a part of the whole solar system and inseparably one with it.

THE BLESSING

The blessing of Astrology comes from its teaching of unity. In every horoscope the *same* planets are symbols of one great influence common to all of them. Every man born under the influence of Mars possesses a ray of exactly the same influence as every other man who belongs to that planet through the type of his horoscope ; and this is also the case with those who are born under any other planet. There is but one supreme and Divine influence, and all others, no matter how far they may appear to be removed are within the sphere of this one supreme influence. Each human being in existence shares with every other human being the Circle of the Zodiac, and each in turn passes round that circle assimilating so far as he can at every phase of his existence a portion of the zodiacal influence until at length he has unified and conquered the whole circle.

The difficulty in seeing this unity underlying the whole of the astrological teaching arises out of the student's inability to adjust the various parts to the whole ; and yet the difficulty is partially cleared away by the allotment of the planets to the signs of the zodiac.

THE TWO SCALES OF THE BALANCE

The seven planets, and half the signs of the zodiac, are concerned with the spiritual side of man's evolution; while the other half of the signs together with the twelve houses of the horoscope are concerned with the material side of his evolution. It is the adjustment of these two sides that is necessary in order to understand the unity of the whole.

The signs belonging to the earthy and watery triplicities are receptive of concrete experience, and answer to impacts received from the material world, so as to call forth from the physical and astral bodies of men a consciousness that is instinctual and self-preservative, which forms the separated personal consciousness. This we illustrate by drawing the straight perpendicular line that represents the upper and lower meridian of the horoscope, or of the interlaced triangles of the earthy and watery triplicities.

The other half of the zodiac, comprising the airy and fiery triplicities, is subjective and abstract, answering to impressions received from the mental world and affecting the individual in a higher region than that of the personal tendencies. This is illustrated by the horizontal line of the horizon crossing the perpendicular from east to west. From the concrete point of view there is inharmony and discord in the limbs of this cross upon which the individual and personal consciousness is bound ; for while fire and air are in harmony, and water and earth seek to blend, there is no apparent harmony between fire and water, or earth and air. The separated personality sees nothing but war and antagonism between the elements of nature, and while he realises his own separateness as an individual, he does not completely individualise these contradictory forces in himself ; for he finds a struggle going on continuously in his own nature between the mind and the senses, the body and the soul.

Into this war of the senses, fought out on the battlefield of the zodiac, come the influences of the planets, making greater disturbance and inharmony, and leading the man to view himself as a compound being instead of as a unit of consciousness with varying forms of expression.

THE MAN IN THE STREET

In the ordinary analytical interpretation of a horoscope, we find the subject of the delineation is often quite unable to see himself in a summary which presents a composite synthesis of the whole.

In the majority of cases the rising sign, the ruling planet, the Sun, and the Moon, present a fair picture of the nature of the man, and are a sufficient synthesis, with perhaps a few of the vibrations of Mars added. Very few are those who respond to the best side of the influence of Saturn in their nativities ; for its painful, sorrowful and selfish influence, bringing disappointments and hindrances is all that is usually felt.

THE GENIUS

Compare the horoscope of an ordinary man of the world and that of a great genius, whether his strength lies in wisdom, in love, or in action. The same vibrations are playing upon each ; and although the positions of the planets, the signs, and the aspects may be quite different, nevertheless the influences of each are identical in essence. The highest to which the ordinary man can reach is a complete analysis of the various forces playing around him. The lowest the Master touches is the synthesis of the whole of those forces into himself. " The Wise Man rules his Stars." He rules them truly by transmuting and harmonising their vibrations within himself, and by constantly shaking out the coarser grades of matter in order that his consciousness may work through the finer.

THE MASTER

No Master of Wisdom is limited by the twelve houses of his horoscope ; he can transcend them all.   He is not bound by the signs of the zodiac and the types of matter they rule ; neither is he limited by the influences of the planets.   A Master is ONE with the whole.   He sees all as manifestations of the one life.   In a world of apparent separation he knows that each separate unit is an integral part of the whole.

THE WISE MAN

The wise man rules his stars by co-operating with them in the world, by knowing them as beneficent forces for the fulfilment of destiny, and by sharing their influence with others.

The blessing of Astrology comes through this knowledge of unity and the belief that we are sons of God entitled to a divine inheritance.

The curse of Astrology is the limitation we set upon ourselves by seeing our horoscope as separate from the world's horoscope ; as a result of which we miss the blessing that flows to those who see the One Self in all things.

"*Just as the tortoise draws its limbs within itself, so also, when the Yogi indraws himself and his senses from the sense-objects, then his wisdom becomes stable.*"—*Bhagavad Gita.*

The Books say well, my Brothers ! each man's life
  The outcome of his former living is ;
The bygone wrongs bring forth sorrows and woes,
  The bygone right breeds bliss.

That which ye sow ye reap.   See yonder fields !
  The sesamum was sesamum, the corn
Was corn.   The Silence and the Darkness knew !
  So is a man's fate born.

He cometh, reaper of the things he sowed,
  Sesamum, corn, so much cast in past birth ;
And so much weed and poison-stuff, which mar
  Him and the aching earth.

If he shall labour rightly, rooting these,
  And planting wholesome seedlings where they grew,
Fruitful and fair and clean the ground shall be,
  And rich the harvest due.

If he who liveth, learning whence woe springs,
  Endureth patiently, striving to pay
His utmost debt for ancient evils done
  In Love and Truth alway; . . . .

He—dying—leaveth as the sum of him
  A life-count closed, whose ills are dead and quit,
Whose good is quick and mighty, far and near,
  So that fruits follow it.

THE LIGHT OF ASIA.

THE ALAN LEO ASTROLOGER'S LIBRARY

The most renowned, complete course in Astrology ever to appear! The Alan Leo Astrologer's Library has become the undisputed source for self-instruction in Astrology.

ASTROLOGY FOR ALL $12.95

A concise, easy to understand introduction to astrology, which presents the major astrological principles in a simple and fascinating manner, developed especially for the reader without prior knowledge. This, Leo's most general text, is specifically designed for the beginning student and therefore includes background material, an analysis of the characteristics of each of the signs, a description of the sun and moon through the signs, and of the significance of the planets in each of the signs. The body of the work concerns the influence of the two major luminaries, the sun and moon, on character and offers a complete delineation of the twelve zodiacal types and the 144 sub-types born each year.

CASTING THE HOROSCOPE $12.95

Fundamental to astrology is the horoscope, a map of the heavens for the time and place of an individual's birth, from which astrological interpretation begins. In this book, Leo teaches everything one needs to know to cast a natal horoscope, including calculation of the ascendant, the use of the table of houses, how to read an ephemeris, the conversion of birth time to sidereal time and adjustments of planetary motions. For the more advanced student, there is information on rectification, directions, methods of house division, lessons in astronomy and sample tables. The coverage is comprehensive and includes areas not detailed in other works.

HOW TO JUDGE A NATIVITY $12.95

HOW TO JUDGE A NATIVITY is a storehouse of general information concerning planetary and zodiacal influences. It deals with the nativity almost entirely on a purely practical level, explaining how to assess the occupations and activities of life in great detail, from health, wealth and the home to philosophy and travel. All the necessary rules and references are presented with a view to helping the student learn to give a reliable reading of any nativity. Comprehensive analysis of the individual houses as they relate to chart interpretation is included, as well as planetary positions and aspects.

THE ART OF SYNTHESIS $12.95

In this work, Alan Leo stresses the esoteric and intuitional aspects of astrology, along with the philosophical and psychological. He provides a richly detailed study of the relation between planets and consciousness, based upon first-hand experience. Particularly interesting are the planetary correlations to the types of temperment, e.g. martial, saturnine, jovial, etc., accompanied by illustrations of the types. The triplicities are analysed comprehensively. Twelve sample horoscopes of famous individuals, including Rudolph Steiner, Robespierre and John Ruskin are discussed as examples of how to synthesize the many elements which come into play in a single, natal chart. A handy astro-theosophical dictionary is provided for the reader's convenience. Where HOW TO JUDGE A NATIVITY emphasizes the scientific-technical aspect of astrological interpretation, THE ART OF SYNTHESIS demonstrates the intuitional dimension. Intuition is soul penetration; it sees through the veil that divides the subjective from the objective universe and brings knowledge that the mind alone cannot obtain from the objective world. THE ART OF SYNTHESIS brings this intuitive penetration to astrology.

THE PROGRESSED HOROSCOPE $12.95

THE PROGRESSED HOROSCOPE is the most comprehensive guide to the system of predicting the future. The methods for drawing up annual forecasts and divining upcoming influences are completely outlined. Included are a detailed and full delineation of every possible progressed aspect; solar, mutual and lunar. Their influences on character and destiny are fully described, enabling the student to form a firm foundation on which to base his judgment of any progressed horoscope he may wish to interpret. There is a lengthy chapter dealing with Transits in their exoteric and esoteric aspects. The last section, "The Art and Practice of Directing" is a complete handbook on "Primary Directions". The YES! Guide calls this " . . . the most detailed examination of progression available. Includes a great deal of background information on the why of progressions, in addition to detailed instructions on calculating the progressed ascendant, solar and lunar positions and aspects, solar revolutions and transits and primary directions."

THE KEY TO YOUR OWN NATIVITY $12.95

A complete and comprehensive analysis of all the elements of the horoscope, giving full descriptions of every position in the nativity. With the assistance of this book, any person can learn to interpret a natal chart. Shows where to find indications in the horoscope related to topics such as, finance, travel, environment, enterprise, sickness, marriage, legacies, philosophy, profession, friends, occultism. Here is the master astrologer's easy to follow method for delineation and interpretation. A must for the beginner and an essential reference for the advanced astrologer.

ESOTERIC ASTROLOGY $12.95

This work deals with Natal Astrology in a manner never before attempted by any writer on Astrology. Divided into three parts, the first part explains the theoretical aspect of Esoteric Astrology; the second demonstrates the practical side of Esoteric Astrology with many examples and complete explanations and the third part deals with the subdivisions of the Zodiac.

For the first time in the history of Astrology, an entirely new method of reading horoscopes is given. The *individual* and *personal* Stars of all persons are explained by a series of *Star Maps*, showing how the age of the soul may be astrologically discovered. It shows how the Horoscope may be changed into a Star Map.

Along with chart interpretation in terms of reincarnation, the methods for the working out of Karma are covered in detail.

THE COMPLETE DICTIONARY OF ASTROLOGY $12.95

A handy reference text of all the terms and concepts you will need to understand astrology in its technical and philosophical dimensions. Useful for quick reference to the signs, planets, houses, ascendants, aspects, decanates, planetary herbs, etc. An extensive section on Hindu astrology. An analysis of horary astrology. Simple explanations of technical terms. Esoteric interpretation of the different elements of astrology. Indispensable to the study of the other Leo textbooks and a useful companion to any study of astrology.

These and other titles in the Alan Leo Astrologer's Library are available at many fine bookstores or, to order direct, send a check or money order for the total amount, plus $2.00 shipping and handling for the first book and 75¢ for each additional book to:

Inner Traditions International
P.O. Box 1534
Hagerstown, MD 21741

To order with a credit card, call toll-free:

1-800-638-3030

For a complete catalog of books from Inner Traditions International, write to:

Inner Traditions International
One Park Street
Rochester, VT 05767